The author, Joyce Di Lorenzo, has struggled to overcome the emotionally numbing insecurities of her past life. Then, God sent her a savior. Vince was a sailor, passionate about the art and sport of sailing. One day, he invited her to join him on a sailing vacation in the British Virgin Islands. The experience changed her life and she emerged as a new person. She fell in love with Vince and the 3,000-year-old sport of sailing that formed his character. Spiritually flourished, the author discovered her heart's yearning for adventure. Now husband and wife, they travel to world-class sailing destinations chasing dreams in a sailboat.

Also, by Joyce Di Lorenzo: *Landing on a Star in Umbria*

For Vince,

"If you live to be a hundred,
I want to live to be a hundred minus one day
so I never have to live without you."

—Alan A Milne

Joyce Di Lorenzo

CHASING DREAMS IN A SAILBOAT

AUSTIN MACAULEY PUBLISHERS™

LONDON * CAMBRIDGE * NEW YORK * SHARJAH

Ordering Information
Quantity sales: Special discounts are available on quantity purchases by corporations, associations, and others. For details, contact the publisher at the address below.

Publisher's Cataloging-in-Publication data
Di Lorenzo, Joyce
Chasing Dreams in a Sailboat

ISBN 9798889107798 (Paperback)
ISBN 9798889107804 (ePub e-book)

Library of Congress Control Number: 2023917661

www.austinmacauley.com/us

First Published 2024
Austin Macauley Publishers LLC
40 Wall Street, 33rd Floor, Suite 3302
New York, NY 10005
USA

mail-usa@austinmacauley.com
+1 (646) 5125767

20240401

Table of Contents

Preface

I was thirty-six years old, crestfallen and heartbroken, the first time I stepped on the deck of a sailboat. Struggling to overcome the emotionally numbing insecurities of my past life, entrenched in a fatherless childhood, a failed marriage, and the painful break-up of a 12-year-long romance that I had hoped would end in marriage had taken a toll on my self-confidence. Not knowing where to turn, I stayed to myself or clung to my family for comfort as I hid from life around me, making little to no effort to pry myself loose from the overwhelming sadness that filled my soul.

Then, God sent me a savior; a strong, strikingly handsome, compassionate man with a beautiful name. As a recent divorcé, Vince seemed to understand my heart's state of mind. Gently, he peeled away the layers of doubt and fear, until I developed trust in our friendship. We began dating casually, and before I realized what had happened, Vince's tender persuasion and loving encouragement, helped me regain a sense of self-worth. I learned how to laugh again and how to get lost in a daydream. Gradually, my heart took flight, I let go of the past and looked forward to moving on.

Vince was a sailor, passionate about the art and sport of sailing. One day, he invited me to join him on a sailing vacation in the British Virgin Islands. Apprehensive, though cautiously intrigued, his sweet invitation was tempting and I listened with curious interest as Vince described picturesque, sheltered harbors, deep blue waters, and sun-soaked beaches with such joy, that although I had never been on a sailboat, joining him on this romantic adventure sounded heavenly.

I pondered the possibility for weeks, and eventually the idea of traveling to a foreign part of the world with a man who loved me and promised to 'take care of everything', won me over. It was just what my spirit needed. So, I threw caution to the wind, took a deep breath, and accepted his invitation.

On first class airline tickets, we flew from California to Puerto Rico, where we boarded a nine-passenger commuter plane bound for Beef Island; the gateway to all the British Virgin Island destinations. With Vince focused on building my enthusiasm for the dream vacation he planned, he spoke non-stop about the islands' unspoiled marine life and natural beauty throughout the long journey.

From the Beef Island airport, a car service brought us to Tortola; the largest island in the chain and home to the Tortola Yacht Club, where a chartered boat awaited our arrival.

From many past charters here, Vince was known at the yacht club and the staff welcomed him as if he was a long-lost family member but when the attendant at the provisioning store acknowledged his return with a hearty embrace, I realized emphatically that in this part of the world, Vince was in his element, his glory. In contrast, I was on extremely unfamiliar ground and an annoying sense of oppression began to creep into my psyche.

That was many years ago…

With Vince's steadfast, unconditional love by my side, I emerged from my life's low point with new-found confidence, gradually blossoming into a confident personality, open to new possibilities, and an eagerness to share Vince's passion for a beautiful, exhilarating sport that was a part of his character.

Chasing Dreams in a Sailboat is not about sailing, rather, it is an anthology of stories about the interesting people we met in foreign destinations, vibrant people with different perspectives, backgrounds, and life experiences, who have shaped us into more open-minded individuals. It is a collection of memoirs about the cultural experiences we have encountered.

Moreover, it is a first-hand narrative of our adventures in Vince's beloved British Virgin Islands, the shockingly beautiful Society Islands of French Polynesia, the ancient villages along the ink-blue Tyrrhenian Sea's most dazzling stretch of the Italian coastline known as the Amalfi Coast, and the magnificent Dalaman sailing region in southern Turkey, appropriately nicknamed the 'Turkish Riviera'.

In each destination, we strived to mingle with the locals and embraced unexpected opportunities so that for a passing moment in time, we could become a part of the diverse civilization we visited.

The British Virgin Islands
Arrival

Road Town
'Poetry'

On a typical balmy afternoon in April 1987, our small plane touched down at the Beef Island Airport on Tortola; the largest, most populated island in the British Virgin Island chain. Vince loved sailing these waters and did so at every opportunity. However, it was my first trip to this British overseas territory in the Caribbean; lovingly referred to by locals and frequent visitors as the "BVI".

"Look! *That* sign is always a *good* sign," Vince said, as he pointed to a man holding a whiteboard with his name on it. Pleased that we arrived on schedule and a ground transportation agent was at the terminal to meet us, Vince walked directly toward him. Cordial introductions were made, greetings exchanged, and within moments, we were escorted to Road Town; the capital city of the British Virgin Islands and the location of the Tortola Yacht Club in Nanny Cay, where Vince chartered a sailboat for ten days.

Our ride in an open-chassis bus, on a two-lane bumpy road with chickens and piglets running loose and natives walking barefoot on the hot pavement, was somewhat startling, however, I felt as if we just arrived at the friendliest place on earth. The scenic beauty of the island was jaw-dropping, with shimmering cobalt blue and emerald green bays, and brilliantly colored flamboyant trees, bougainvillea, and plate-sized hibiscus that grew wild everywhere I looked.

Bareboating, hiring a boat without a skipper or crew, is one of the main attractions in the BVI. Located between the Caribbean Sea and the Atlantic Ocean, there are more than fifty islands, coral reefs, and diving wrecks to explore. With Fahrenheit temperatures in the 80s and 90s year-round, gentle ocean breezes, crystal clear water, and white sandy beaches, it is a sailor's paradise.

Located in a quaint harbor on the South side of Tortola, nestled in a sheltered basin in Road Town is the Tortola Yacht Club; a sleepy, laid-back operation with an attentive staff. Our bus pulled up to the main entrance, where a concierge stood, ready to greet us. Delighted to see Vince, the concierge welcomed him with an embrace and a robust pat on the back, as if Vince was a long-lost family member.

In the lobby, the front-desk clerk greeted him in the same manner, and with a snap of the clerk's fingers, an eager-to-assist staff member boasting an enormous smile, suddenly appeared to carry our luggage; consisting of two backpacks and a boat-bag filled with fruits and vegetables.

Once a week, fresh produce from the US Virgin Islands arrives by boat at Tortola's main harbor and the entire load is sold out quickly to locals and the boating community. To avoid consuming canned vegetables for the duration of our charter, Vince recommended bringing a well-rounded selection of fresh produce from California.

At first, I thought this was a silly idea, however, when I peeked in the only provision store located at the entrance to the marina, I saw no more than a few overripe bananas, some onions, and a couple of sad-looking potatoes for sale. Consequently, I was pleased that we followed Vince's advice.

While Vince handled the check-in process at the front desk, I perused through a selection of travel brochures when a staff member presented us with a *painkiller*; a tropical mixed drink made from pineapple juice, orange juice, cream of coconut, and the BVI's trademarked Pusser's dark rum.

"Welcome back to the BVI, Captain," the staff member said to Vince, as he served the signature cocktails in charming, eye-catching, enameled tin mugs decorated with Great Britain's Navy logo.

"Thank you," replied Vince. "I've waited a whole year for one of these." Then, turning to me with a raised mug, he uttered, "Hon, you'll love this, these are addicting, we will drink a lot of these on this trip." Vince was certainly right, this drink was delicious, coconutty, and decadent!

Soon, another staff member, accompanied by a colleague with an enormous smile, escorted us to our boat. The docks were meticulously maintained, moreover, the fleet of world-class luxury yachts, anxiously waiting to be taken to sea, was quite impressive.

"There she is," said the staff member to Vince, as he stopped at the stern of our assigned yacht, inviting us to come on board with a sweeping hand motion and a bow of his lanky upper body. "This is *Poetry'*, welcome aboard, Captain and Lady!"

Built in 1985, the sleek and sporty Endeavor 42, with a center cockpit, festooned with a welcome card addressed to the captain and crew, a bottle of champagne on ice, and two toasting flutes was ready to set sail.

"Excellent!" Vince remarked, with a look of approval and a sparkle in his eyes. He stepped on board like a natural and without mentioning the champagne, did a quick scan below deck, "Hmmmm, there might be enough room here for the two of us," he said jokingly.

Gesturing for me to come on board, Vince offered his hand. However, it was my first time stepping aboard a sailboat and I was a bit reluctant. Nevertheless, I held my breath, laid my hand in his, and took my initial big step on deck. Oh my gosh, I was immediately taken aback by the rocking of the boat. For a split second, I hesitated to proceed and reached for a shroud to keep myself steady. Once both feet were firmly planted on the deck, I quickly stood unassisted and tried to appear confident.

Suddenly, Vince noticed the bottle of champagne chilling in the ice bucket. Compliments of the Tortola Yacht Club, Captain. Cheers!" the staff member said with an informal, two-finger salute as he stepped on shore and walked away.

"Thanks! Nice touch!" Vince shouted out in response and without further ado, presented me with the card, popped the cork, and filled our glasses.

Well, what do you think so far?" he asked, handing me a glass filled with the festive bubbles.

I did not know what to say. I was overwhelmed by the whole scene; the big beautiful yacht, the marina, the champagne on ice, the islands, and most of all…Vince! I didn't respond, I didn't know how, furthermore, I couldn't believe that I was about to embark on a vacation-style far different from anything I had ever experienced before.

"To *Poetry* and you…my Love and First Mate," Vince said, as we clinked glasses and kissed. "I am looking forward to sailing with you," he added sweetly.

I acted sheepish, but inside, my heart was bursting with joy!

There was much to do before leaving the harbor in the morning. While Vince attended the required safety checks and orientation meetings, I assessed our accommodations below deck. As I looked around, I truly felt like a fish out of water and it took some time to acclimate to my new marine surroundings.

I pondered how to transform *Poetry*'s posh, bright, and airy interior into our living quarters for the next twelve days. To let a breeze flow throughout the cabin, I figured out how to open the locks on the side hatches, which were covered by curtains that slid open. I kept them that way with the hook-and-loop strips attached. The galley, outfitted with everything necessary to prepare and serve meals appeared to be ready for use, although I did not know how to operate the gimbaled gas stove.

With Vince managing matters on shore, I was left to my own devices and began to gain my bearings. I unpacked our luggage and transferred the produce from our bags to sliding metal baskets, which I discovered underneath the sink. Suddenly, *Poetry* shook under the heavy footsteps of two sweaty dockworkers. Unannounced, the men came on board to deliver a large supply of pre-ordered beverages. An ample stock of bottled water, tonic, club soda, fruit juices, colas, a few bottles of rum, gin, beer, and a selection of red and white wines was loaded into the cockpit. My Goodness, I thought, someone on this boat planned to party!

The beverage containers occupied a large amount of space and I wondered where to stash everything. I was able to fit several wine bottles upright, in a cabinet in the main salon and just as I began removing the plastic wrappers from the 12-pack, large bottles of water, Vince returned from his meeting.

"Good, our libations arrived. Is everything here?" he asked, handing me two sheets of paper, representing a copy of the beverage order. As he came down the companionway, he noticed my attempt at stowing the large inventory of cans and bottles.

"Oh no, Hon, not like that," he remarked, pointing to the open cabinet where I stored the wine. "If you place the bottles on their sides, they won't roll around while we're sailing." He laid the bottles down, one on top of the other, and stuffed a rolled-up bath towel in the space remaining in the cabinet. What a brilliant idea, I wished I would have thought of it! If I realized that the boat heeled under sail, I may have had the forethought to store the bottles differently.

While I continued organizing and stowing the rest of the beverage supply, Vince removed the seat cushions from the benches surrounding the dining table in the salon. The hinged top opened to reveal a built-in storage rack specifically designed for bottles.

"Let's keep the liquor in here," Vince suggested, "and we can keep a few sodas, water, and beer in the cooler on deck where we can easily reach them under sail. We'll refill the cooler as needed. We can stash the rest in the galley lockers. Oh, and keep the plastic wrappers around the large packs of bottled water until we are ready to use them. It'll keep them from rolling around. Anything you can't find room for, we can toss in one of the extra forward cabins."

It was obvious that Vince had done this before!

Three staterooms *(bedrooms or cabins)* and two heads (*bathrooms*) were ample space for two people to live aboard comfortably. I chose the aft stateroom with an attached head to be our ensuite quarters for the duration. The two smaller staterooms located at the bow, with a shared head between them, seemed difficult to maneuver in and out of, especially during those untimely trips to the bathroom, in the middle of the night.

The yacht club provided plenty of towels and linens, however, there was no standing headroom to make the bed, consequently, I crawled on my hands and knees to cover the mattress with a flat bedsheet as best I could, followed by the top sheet and blanket, placing the pillows at one end of the berth *(bed)*. Pleased with the result, I stepped away to survey my work. When Vince saw what I accomplished, he shook his head in disapproval.

"Oh no, Hon," he said again, "the nights are hot and humid here. The blanket should go underneath the bottom sheet as an anti-perspiration, thermal control layer. Trust me, we will sleep better if you remake the bed, and Hon, our pillows should be at the other end of the bed so we can catch the breeze that comes through that hatch at night," he added, pointing to a hatch located overhead.

Honestly? I had so much to learn!

By late afternoon, Vince returned from the yacht club briefing, and all the required documents were properly submitted to the marina. We were officially cleared to set sail in the morning. Provisioning the boat with food was the last chore remaining. Our only option for grocery shopping was the market with the over-ripe bananas and a meager selection of potatoes and onions. Upon entering the store, a big, jolly, native man approached us with a lively step, both hands fully extended.

"Welcome back, sir. It is a pleasure to see you again."

"Hi Ali, it's great to be back," Vince replied as the two men shared a hearty handshake and a man-hug. "This is my first mate, take good care of her, will you?" Then, directing the conversation to me, he said, "Hon, this is Ali, he owns this establishment, just tell him what you need."

Welcome to the BVI," Ali said with a smile, as he offered me an empty woven basket, "we have everything you need for your charter. Please make yourself at home."

As I selected food items and staples for our trip, Ali accompanied me through the store, carrying another empty basket. Patiently, he filled up the baskets with the items I selected, brought them to the counter, and placed them near the cash register. What a delightful way to shop!

Although Vince let me wander through the store with Ali alone, he was astutely aware that I struggled. I had no experience shopping for a trip like this. Should I be looking for basic chow or culinary elegance? Nevertheless, I chose items that looked tasty, familiar, or interesting.

Much to my appreciation, Vince suggested buying the basics for breakfast; coffee, English muffins, butter, and orange marmalade.

"Buy what you think we'll need for only a few days," he added, "there will be another opportunity to stock up in Cane Garden Bay. Plan for easy breakfasts and lunches. In the evenings, we can grill fish or meat on board and occasionally we will eat at a local restaurant onshore."

That bit of information was extremely helpful. Armed with my new knowledge, I was able to proceed with my shopping, readily filling up several baskets. In addition to the items Vince suggested, I bought frozen chicken thighs, pork chops, fish, pre-formed beef patties, bread, rice, a dozen eggs, cooking oil, island spices, salt, pepper, onions, a few of the sad-looking potatoes, and something called Caribbean Chili Habanero Hot Sauce.

I also stocked up on housekeeping essentials; such as paper towels, plenty of toilet paper, dish soap, plastic bags, aluminum foil, matches, and cleaning supplies. Lastly, I selected several cans of mixed nuts, dried fruit, chips, a variety of hard cheeses, and a jar of olives; must-haves for a ritual Vince insisted on being part of our daily schedule; Happy Hour on deck at sunset.

Feeling confident that I selected wisely and that we had enough food for our first week at sea, I joined Ali at the cash register. Efficiently, he scanned each item before placing it in a box. When the box was full, he loaded it onto a pushcart. I was astonished at the amount of food we purchased as if we planned to feed an army!

"I'll have this delivered to *Poetry* right away, Captain," Ali said, nodding his head in Vince's direction. "I'll do it immediately."

While we waited on board for the provisions to arrive, Vince demonstrated the use of the gimbaled stove, the shower-head, the shower pump, and the hand pump on the marine toilet. He showed me how to lock down the hatches and properly latch the cabinet drawers and doors.

More importantly, he covered a few safety tips, showed me where the lifejackets were stowed, and explained the use of the ship-to-shore radio, including how to call for help in case of an emergency. Intimidated by my lack of knowledge about this world of sailing and overwhelmed by the enormous amount of instructions and information I received, I hoped that my feeling of inadequacy was not outwardly apparent.

Soon, our bounty from the grocery store arrived. This time I was more efficient, able to stow everything properly, and before long, it was finally time to unwind and de-stress.

Too tired to explore our dining options away from the marina, we decided to eat an early dinner at the yacht club's restaurant exclusive for boating clientele. Feeling a bit like an elitist sitting among such patronage, I felt snobbishly out of place.

The menu listed an array of unfamiliar, local specialties, therefore it took some time for me to decide what to order. Ultimately, I chose a spicy conch fritter appetizer with sweet peppers and onions; a West Indies favorite. It was crazy delicious! The locally caught grilled fish entrée Vince and I shared was equally divine. After dinner, instead of lingering at our table with aperitifs, we returned to *Poetry* to loosen our clothes and unwind.

Before going to bed, we enjoyed one more drink on the foredeck. On the horizon, a glorious sunset prevailed. Different from the lush tropical Hawaiian Islands I often visited in prior years, the BVI was more natural, wild, more rural, and at night, the beauty of these islands easily transformed into a stunning paradise. The lack of glaring lights from high-rise hotels let the stars shine brighter. Brilliant as diamonds against the dark sky, each star twinkled as if competing to be the most dazzling.

Jet-lagged and dog-tired, at last, we ducked into our cabin and drifted off to sleep rather quickly. Unfortunately, I did not stay asleep. Every unfamiliar sound frightened me and kept me awake, wondering if our boat was drifting. Occasionally, the bilge pump sounded as if it was running, the wind blowing through the rigging caused me concern and on a neighboring yacht, a lively group of people in a celebratory mood kept me from sleeping soundly through the night.

I began to feel anxious about leaving the harbor in the morning.

Caribbean Island Hopping
Norman Island

The Bight

Vince slept peacefully until dawn, waking well-rested and cheerful. Like a child on Christmas morning, he was outwardly excited, looking forward to leaving the harbor.

"Good morning," he said. "Are you ready to sail?"

While we enjoyed a leisurely light breakfast on board, Vince explained what leaving the harbor entailed as we headed to The Bight; our first overnight anchorage in a sheltered bay on the north shore of Norman Island. Intensely, I listened and prayed that I would be a capable first mate.

For ease of access ashore, boats in the Caribbean are moored in Mediterranean Tie (*Med-tie*) fashion; meaning that the stern, instead of the bow, is tied to the quay with port *(left)*, starboard *(right)*, and spring *(middle)* dock lines. When it was time to leave the harbor, a dock worker released our lines, while Vince took his skipper's position at the helm and steered the boat out of the slip. His expertise was immensely evident; Vince was born to be a sailor.

Towing a dinghy behind, we were finally going out to sea. As we approached the end of the marina, Vince asked me to take the helm, freeing him to bring in the fenders and coil the lines which had hastily been thrown on deck. Eager, at first, to learn and share in the sailing aspect, I stepped behind the wheel and began to steer the boat like a car in the direction Vince indicated. "It's like driving a bus from the backseat," I teased, "this is a piece of cake!"

When we passed the red and green channel markers leading the way out to sea, the water became rough and I began to feel nervous and afraid. With fear in my eyes and my heart pounding wildly, I looked at Vince and hoped that he would say something to comfort me, however, he seemed unconcerned and stayed on the foredeck, coiling and organizing lines. Then, without warning, all hell broke loose! The bow began to dip and rise through the larger waves; I became terrified, panicked, and screamed at Vince, ordering him to relieve me from the helm.

My outburst took us both by surprise. While I dove into our cabin for safety and refuge from all the clattering and commotion on deck, Vince sped to the cockpit and grabbed the free-spinning helm. Fright and anxiety left me trembling, it was difficult to breathe, and I wanted to jump ship but didn't know how to swim. To make matters worse, Vince still did not come to console me, he left me cowering in the cabin alone. Furious at his lack of caring, I didn't realize that he could not leave the helm unmanned to tend to my outlandish behavior.

When I was finally able to breathe again, I gained my composure and realized that I had another emotion to cope with; my terrible shame for acting so childish. Deeply humiliated by my over re-action, I didn't quite know how to emerge from our cabin to show my face on deck. I felt remorseful and ashamed.

At last, with the boat under control, it was safe for Vince to come to my side. Patiently, lovingly, he explained that the boat's action through the waves was normal and that nothing beyond his control was going to happen. Utterly embarrassed, I found comfort in his arms and came to my senses. Eventually, Vince lured me back on deck and promised not to raise the sails for the short passage to Norman Island.

On such a beautiful day, it felt exhilarating to be on deck, in the open air. In the distance, the marina was behind us and our destination was directly at our bow, approximately eight to ten nautical miles away. Settling down in a comfortable spot inside the cockpit, clear of anything that required adjusting, I focused on being in the sunny Caribbean with a handsome man who loved me.

As we approached the entrance to Bight Bay, Vince became my tour guide, providing interesting information about the area. Among several other islands in the region, Norman Island inspired Robert Louis Stevenson to write his acclaimed novel 'Treasure Island', an adventure novel loosely based on the pirate treasure buried here in August 1750 by the crew of a Spanish galleon. Secretly, I imagined what it would be like to find the ultimate souvenir; a gold doubloon from the infamous 300-year-old shipwreck.

Soon, we motored past Treasure Point. Vince described this spot as an outstanding place to snorkel inside shallow caves with crystal clear water and vibrant sea life. Curious about several boats tied up to mooring buoys near a unique series of spiked stone formations, I inquired about them.

"That's The Indians," Vince replied. It's another great area to snorkel. It's like an aquarium down there. He made everything sound so exciting. The BVI Cruising Guide mentions a myriad of tropical fish and crustaceans that swim there, between giant sea fans and brilliant coral. Just then, a group of snorkelers raised their heads and waved to alert us of their presence.

Poetry was equipped with snorkel gear. However, I didn't think I dared to breathe through an air tube while keeping my face underwater. Not knowing how to swim and having snorkeled only once, in knee-deep water at Hawaii's Hanauma Bay a lifetime ago, I was inexperienced and afraid to give it a try.

Inside the harbor, Vince searched for an ideal place to anchor near the shoreline and away from the ocean swells. When he found a suitable area, he slowed the engine down to an idle, shifted to neutral, hustled to the bow, released the anchor, and lowered it to hover above the waterline, before gently dropping it precisely in a sandy spot at the bottom of the sea. Fascinated by the process, I stayed firmly planted in my seat inside the cockpit, as I watched Vince hurry back to control the helm and shift the boat in reverse until the anchor grabbed a firm hold of the ocean floor, indicating that *Poetry* was secure. Somewhat breathless, he finally turned the engine off, and to my delight, announced, "We are here!"

Astonished by Vince's ability to anchor the boat without assistance, I gave him a well-deserved hug and complimented him on his sailing skills, "Good job, Skipper," I said and patted him on his tush, "I am impressed!"

The first stop on our itinerary was The Bight. I took a moment to stand on deck, gazing directly at the picture-perfect, crescent-shaped beach with a relatively shrubby, hilly landscape, enhanced by the brilliant blue, iridescent water and the white sandy beach that formed this sheltered bay on Norman Island.

"I'm going to take a look at the anchor, to make sure it's holding," Vince said, seated on the transom *(a flat surface forming the stern of the boat)* with his snorkel gear in hand. As he climbed down the swim ladder and slid into the water, he asked me to stand on the bow to watch over him. Accordingly, I followed Vince to the front of the boat, where I could see the chain down to the anchor at the bottom of the ocean.

While Vince snorkeled back and forth over the anchor and tugged firmly on the chain, I watched diligently for a hand signal or instructions indicating that adjustments were needed. Thank God the signal didn't come. Instead, Vince bounced up like a cork, kept his head above water, and held up both thumbs, signaling that we were anchored correctly and free to relax. Thrilled that no further action was required, I let out a sigh of relief, "Phew!"

When Vince returned to the swim ladder, I was already there to meet him.

"We're good," he said, though he remained in the water with his snorkel mask raised on top of his head.

Great, I thought to myself and wondered what we would do next....

"Hey Hon, morning is the best time to snorkel, the water is marvelous and there is a school of bright yellow fish right under the hull," Vince almost pleaded with me to join him. "Why don't you put on your snorkel mask? We'll go together."

"No, thank you, I'm not ready yet, you go ahead, I'll stay on board for now."

"Ohhkaay…" Vince sounded disappointed, drawing out the word as if he questioned my answer, but before I turned away, I heard a splash from his fins and several deep blows through his snorkel tube. He was already on the other side of the boat, following a school of colorful fish. For a minute, I contemplated climbing down the ladder, one step at a time, until I was immersed up to my shoulders. If I held onto the bottom rung, maybe I could stay there and at least experience the sensation of being in the ocean. However, my fear stopped me from proceeding.

Hoping that Vince would not snorkel too far out of sight, I grew impatient on deck. What if something happened to him? What would I do? Nervously, I kept a watchful eye on his yellow swim shirt and the tip of his blue air tube, praying that he would not stay in the water too long. I despised feeling so apprehensive. While Vince explored nature's underwater wonders, in my heart I wished I was with him, however, the longer he snorkeled, the more I missed my familiar environment and longed to go home.

An hour or so later, Vince finally came closer to the boat. I felt relieved to have him near, although he appeared distracted, treading water in one spot, intensely focused on something underneath the boat. Quite curious, I waited for him to tell me what had caught his attention. Finally, he pushed his mask upon his forehead and removed the tube from his mouth to speak. "There's a barracuda under the boat, he's this big!" Vince cried out, spanning his arms to indicate the size of the fish. "Stand on the beam *(the widest part of the boat)* on the port side, you can probably see it."

Running my left hand along the lifeline to guide me, I dashed to the designated point on deck and peered over the side of the boat. No, Vince certainly did not exaggerate, this fish was enormous! Ferocious in appearance, it stayed motionless, suspended in the water as if it was stalking him. Swimming a safe distance around the barracuda, Vince climbed up the ladder and removed his snorkel gear. "Did you see it?" he said, nearly shouting, "That is one ferocious-looking fish. Each of his protruding bottom teeth looked like a little knife!"

I was pleased that Vince's first snorkel adventure on the trip was an exciting success. He was elated and thoroughly fascinated by the predatory monster beneath our boat. Somewhat envious, I prayed for the courage to share the next underwater adventure with him.

Absorbed in the unspoiled natural beauty of Bight Bay, we spent the remainder of the morning relaxing on board. Several times, Vince offered to take me ashore in the dinghy, but that would require me to transfer my body from a big boat to a small boat with a rubber bottom; for Christ's sake! Although the wave action was not particularly rough, I did not foresee that as being a successful move for me.

When the sun hung high in the sky, it was time to prepare lunch, the first true test of how well-equipped the galley was. I felt content cleaning and slicing cucumbers, radishes, carrots, and celery for my vegetable medley appetizer with a zesty salsa dip, followed by a deli-style tuna salad sandwich made with diced onions, pickles, celery, and black olives, topped with Swiss cheese and lettuce. All the kitchen tools I needed appeared to be on board, although the knives were dull and flimsy.

During lunch, our conversation was largely about overcoming my fear of water sports. Vince suggested using one of the cockpit seat cushions as a floatation device. If I wrapped my arms around it, I could drift close to the boat. Although I appreciated the thought, I was not ready to undertake such a daring endeavor.

Poor Vince, I sensed his dismay and wished wholeheartedly that fear didn't stifle me so. I was grateful that he didn't push me, rather, Vince allowed me to discover my comfort level at my own pace. I hoped he would remain patient while I tried my best to come around.

By late afternoon, five other yachts were anchored in our vicinity. Armed with a bottle of wine, two glasses, a can of salted mixed nuts, and a can of dehydrated, stackable potato chips, we moved to the foredeck. Vince leaned his back against the mast, so I could lean mine against his chest and sink into his arms to watch the sunset.

As the sun lowered into the sea, the mood in the bay became more tranquil, it was the best part of the day. Gradually, every fellow yachtsman also gathered on deck to watch God's changing color palette. Nursing our wine, we remained there for hours, until the sun dipped below our field of vision and the sky transitioned from shades of gold and rosy-pink to lavender. The sunsets in the Caribbean are among the best in the world and this one was no exception.

I looked forward to preparing dinner. It was a task I could easily manage and it pleased me to show off my cooking and homemaking skills. Earlier in the day, I removed a package of beautifully lean pork chops from the freezer to marinate them in lime juice, olive oil, salt, pepper, garlic, shallots, red pepper flakes, and a few dashes of the Caribbean Chili Habanero Hot Sauce. They smelled savory and delicious when I opened the Ziplock bag to transfer the chops to a plate.

When the rail-mounted kettle grill on the stern reached an adequate temperature, Vince lifted the lid and placed the chops on the hot cooking surface. I loved to hear them sizzle when they touched the heat. While Vince tended to the chops, I made a tasty coconut-rice salad with fresh tomatoes, finely diced sweet red onion, green olives, and fresh pineapple. I hoped to redeem myself for this morning's outburst by creating an extra special meal and setting a romantic table, complete with tiny votive candles.

When dinner was ready and the wine poured, Vince raised his glass. "I'd like to propose a toast," he said adoringly, "thank you, Hon, for joining me on this adventure, here's to our first day in the BVI." We clinked glasses and gave each other a kiss. It was a lovely toast and a special occasion.

I was about to serve the salad when, without warning, Vince jumped from his seat behind the expanded table in the cockpit and headed below deck.

"Sorry, just a minute…I forgot something," he said before disappearing. Wondering what he was up to, I faintly heard the flip of a switch on the navigation station. "Look up at the top of the mast," Vince directed, as he pointed his finger in the air.

I tilted my head back and gazed directly upward, not exactly knowing where to look. Then, suddenly, I saw it; a brilliant, bright light at the top of our mast.

"Oh my gosh, Honey, it's beautiful! What is that?" I gushed.

"It's your star," Vince said sweetly, "it's your own star at the top of the mast."

I was deeply moved, unable to speak. My eyes became misty as I stretched out to hug him. No one had ever given me a star.

Dinner was a delicious success; the pork chops were juicy and tender and the pineapple chunks in the coconut rice salad added a refreshing touch of sweetness. We savored our wine in the moonlight, under a starlit sky, and by the light of my very own star.

Tortola
Soper's Hole

Few aromas allude to the beginning of a wonderful day, like bacon and eggs frying in a skillet. This is especially true when that aroma is enhanced by the smell of fresh coffee brewing in an old-fashioned aluminum percolator on a galley stove.

Busily preparing breakfast, my heart beamed with happiness as I looked out through the companionway hatch. It was a beautiful morning, the water was smooth as glass, and although the sun had only been up for a few hours, the temperature outside was already quite warm. I pinched myself to make sure I wasn't dreaming. Was I really in the West Indies, aboard a luxury yacht with a handsome sailor?

"Mornin' Love, the coffee smells great. Is there anything I can do to help?" Vince called out from the bow.

"Not a thing, breakfast is almost ready."

I am quite handy, some say, almost an expert, in the kitchen. On this trip, I didn't want to relinquish the one thing I knew I excelled in, moreover, I wanted our first breakfast at anchor to be a bit celebratory.

Facing the stern, I set an attractive table with the blue Melamine dishes, mismatched silverware, and stemless glasses on board. A red, diner-style plastic basket lined with a white napkin looked adorable loaded with the English muffins I browned in a skillet with unsalted butter. I paired my light and fluffy scrambled eggs, diced green onions, ham, and cheese with a fresh fruit compote and I made a mimosa from the remainder of the Yacht Club's complimentary champagne.

Years ago, I learned that dangling the narrow end of a stainless steel utensil in the neck of a champagne bottle and sealing it with plastic wrap before storing it in the refrigerator, retains the effervescence in the leftover beverage. It worked like a charm, the mimosas were bubbly, cold, and a lovely way to start the day!

"Breakfast looks tasty," complimented Vince as he seated himself at the table and sipped his mimosa. Before long, a few black-faced seagulls joined us in mid-air. At first, they were playful, hovering behind the boat, hoping that we would share our breakfast with them.

After Vince finished most of his meal, he threw a morsel of food into the air. Before it hit the water, a greedy gull caught it in his beak and headed out to sea. Instantly, a flock of his friends came out of nowhere waiting for the next offering. Soon, an onslaught of gulls flew around our stern, squawking, squealing, demanding food. Fortunately, when we moved below deck to clean up, the birds left and shifted their focus to another boat.

By mid-morning, everything on board was shipshape and it was time to weigh anchor *(a nautical term meaning to raise the anchor)*. We were headed to Pusser's Landing at Soper's Hole, a protected bay that once hid Captain Morgan; one of the most notorious *Pirates of the Caribbean*, from the authorities.

We planned to have lunch at Pusser's Pub and Restaurant; a popular eating establishment that served wood-distilled rum-and-cokes, painkillers, and some of the most outstanding local cuisine on Tortola. "They make the best cheeseburgers in paradise," Vince promised.

Although visiting another harbor seemed exciting, that familiar nervous tinge began to gnaw at me. I wondered if Vince was going to raise the sails? Was it too windy today? Was I required to assist? I felt a shiver and wished I was invisible.

Thank God, my worries subsided when Vince announced that we would motor *(travel under engine power)* to our next destination. "We won't bother with the sails today," he announced, "the distance is too short." I let out a huge sigh of relief. Now, unencumbered by worry, I looked forward to exploring a new waterfront.

While Vince was a bustle of activity preparing to leave The Bight, I remained in the cockpit, out of harm's way, until he started the engine, shifted the boat into neutral, and called for my assistance to take the helm.

"I'll take over as soon as I can. The water is completely calm, it's like steering a car," he said, while he hustled to the bow and opened the anchor well.

As he began to hoist, the chain made a racket, clanking and grinding as it lifted the anchor off the ocean floor. All the commotion was nerve-wracking, but I stayed silent, grit my teeth, and held my position at the helm. Then I heard a final clunk.

"We're free!" Vince shouted as he hurried back to relieve me. A split second later, he pushed the handle forward, increased power, steered a wide circle around the other boats in the harbor, and aimed for the sea.

When The Bight was barely behind us, Vince engaged the autopilot (a self-steering device that steers the boat to a pre-set course on the compass); freeing him to fidget with 'stuff'. Even though we were not sailing, Vince enjoyed tightening and tidying things, while I enjoyed watching him engage in those seaman-like chores.

As we approached Soper's Hole on the west end of Tortola, Vince directed my attention to the elegant, tropical-style homes that graced the cliffs marking the entrance to the harbor; impressive glass villas with outstanding views of the Sir Francis Drake Channel.

Upon first impression, Soper's Hole appeared more urban and industrial than The Bight. To my slight disappointment, there was no beach for taking long walks hand-in-hand or shallow areas for wading in the water. I noticed a ferry dock and a bustling boat repair marina, although, the Pusser's Company Store adjacent to a rum pub and restaurant appeared worth exploring. Before long, this iconic BVI outpost on a typical West Indies-style wharf front aroused my curiosity. Furthermore, I trusted Vince's reason for choosing this anchorage.

Once again, Vince's skill in anchoring without assistance took my breath away. Our position in the harbor was perfect; on port, we were well clear of the wake from the inter-island ferry boats that arrived and departed at various times throughout the day, and on starboard, we were comfortably protected from the wind.

Eager to mingle among the locals, I changed my clothes and grabbed my camera while Vince prepared the dinghy for our departure. I stood idly by as he untied the outboard motor, removed it from its storage place, transferred it to the rubber vessel, and attached it to the rear. It was against charter rules to travel between islands with the outboard motor attached, therefore, this was a procedure he would have to repeat at each anchorage if we wished to go ashore.

With the dinghy properly prepared, I asked, "How do I get in?"

"Stand on the transom and step into the middle, one foot at a time," Vince instructed, holding tight to the dinghy line with one hand while offering me firm support with the other. Though awkward, I followed his order and sat down immediately on the inflated air tube to keep from losing my balance.

"Good, now move forward so I can sit behind you, next to the motor," and with one determined, solid step, Vince came on board, bringing the line with him. Positioning himself next to the motor, like a pro he cranked it over with one jerk of the starter cord, steered us to the dock, and tied us up precisely in front of the Pusser's Company Store.

I couldn't wait to go in. Without thinking, I left Vince behind to tie up the dinghy alone. "Hey, wait for me!" he shouted, poking fun at my eagerness.

The Pusser tradition began in 1540 when Henry VIII established Great Britain's Royal Navy. Onboard each ship, he appointed a Purser responsible for protecting supplies and outfitting his crew with clothing and the gear necessary for defending the ship. In time, the crew referred to the Purser as the *Pusser*, and all goods issued by him preceded the possessive noun *Pusser's*. In addition to food, every man on board was issued a daily one-gallon ration of beer.

However, after several months at sea, the beer became sour. Eventually, a mix of five West Indies rums replaced the beer, and in 1655, the special blend was appropriately named Pusser's Rum. Today, the Pusser's brand is world-renowned for its excellent quality merchandise and rich, historic rum.

The Pusser's Company Store exuded pirate charm and offered an extensive line of interesting merchandise, attractively displayed. The first thing that caught my eye, was the enameled tin mug the Tortola Yacht Club used to serve our Welcome Painkillers with the painkiller recipe printed on the back!

I was thrilled to find this wonderful memento of our trip and bought it immediately, along with a t-shirt for Vince, souvenirs for our families, and a selection of postcards that depicted the islands beautifully. I vowed to write and mail them at my first opportunity. Vince purchased a handsome ceramic flask filled with Pusser's Rum and a book with intricate sketches of island life created by a native artist.

Happy with our purchases, we left the store to investigate the local businesses on the beach. At the end of the dock, next to the prevailing white building that housed the customs control office, several colorful clapboard cottages and a scattering of typical wooden sloops beached under a palm tree, formed the waterfront toward the ferry dock. Native toddlers dressed in only diapers chased a dog chasing a chicken down a sandy path. Suddenly, Soper's Hole appeared utterly charming.

As we turned back toward the dinghy dock, a wide-eyed Vince asked, "Are you ready for the best cheeseburger in paradise?"

Smiling from ear-to-ear, I turned around, grabbed his hand, and swiftly lead us to the Pusser's Restaurant and Pub.

"And a painkiller!" I replied. "I am thirsty and famished!"

A cordial hostess with an intricate hairstyle of mini braids piled high on her head promptly greeted us at the door and escorted us to a dockside table overlooking the harbor. "Welcome to Pusser's," she said, presenting the lunch menus and two tall glasses of water filled with chipped ice and a fresh pineapple spear.

The food selection included a variety of local favorites among several mouthwatering hamburger styles. I was tempted to order every unfamiliar item on the menu! Roti; a meat and potato curry, wrapped in a flat, unleavened bread wrapper, immediately piqued my interest. Smoked to juicy tenderness, the Jerk Chicken; flavored with a marinade made from Scotch-Bonnet Peppers, cinnamon, nutmeg, turmeric, and cloves sounded delicious, but the Coconut Curry Mussels served with matchstick fried potatoes tempted me the most.

However, as a serious fan and connoisseur of an outstanding burger, I concurred with Vince and ordered a cheeseburger; cooked medium rare, with a side of home-style French-fried potatoes. Additionally, Vince ordered the must-have painkillers and a lovely thing called an Onion Blossom; one large, sweet onion, cut to resemble a chrysanthemum, lightly battered, deep-fried and served with a spicy dipping sauce. When this dish reached the table, it made a stunning impression. I had never seen anything like it.

"Wow!" I cheered, "That is gorgeous!" Breaking a crispy piece from the bottom of the onion, barely touching it to the sauce, Vince gently placed it in my mouth.

Oh my goodness, it tasted like heaven, delicious, lighter than ordinary onion rings, and more flavorful! Equally tasty were the hamburgers, generously sized, perfectly charred, juicy patties, covered by a gooey slice of melted cheese; each one was a work of culinary art and undeniably, without a doubt, the best cheeseburger in paradise! The thick fries with salted, crispy skins were an excellent complement to the burger. Oh, and that painkiller…I could feel the pounds begin to stick to my hips!

After our food settled and our drinks were gone, it was time to return to the boat. Toting my shopping bag, Vince helped me board the dinghy. Even though it was a quick commute back to *Poetry*, my shorts had become uncomfortably wet from the splashing water. Next time, I would wear quick-drying bottoms when going ashore in the dinghy.

Vince shut the motor off just before we reached the stern, letting the wind blow us the rest of the way to the boat. He grabbed the gunwale *(the edge of the boat)* to hold us in position and waited for me to make the next move. However, I was not sure how to board the boat from the dingy. Instinctively, I placed my right foot on the pontoon.

"No, Hon! *Do not* step on the tube," Vince scolded, almost shouting. The firm tone in his voice took me aback and I withdrew my foot immediately. "Love, I'm sorry," he added quickly, putting a hand on my shoulder to soothe me. "I didn't mean to yell, but the tube is slippery and unstable, all it takes is one wrong step…" Grateful for his warning, I was not offended.

We whiled away the rest of the afternoon, each of us retreating to separate spaces to relax and unwind. While Vince putzed around on deck, I made journal entries, addressed postcards, and daydreamed about the wonderful events of the day. My heart was eased and I relished in my "alone time" as I imagined Vince did too.

In preparation for Happy Hour, Vince made a pitcher full of Gin and Tonic with a robust twist of lime and a few muddled mint leaves. Feeling a bit tired and tranquil, we savored our cocktails on the foredeck to watch another glorious sunset unfold. Due to the enormous lunch we enjoyed earlier in the day, neither of us had an appetite for dinner, therefore, a salad of fresh orange sections, sliced mango, and fresh avocado, dressed with a splash of seasoned olive oil, was the perfect meal to end the day.

With the sun below the horizon, our third day in the BVI was gently drawing to a close. The stress of travel and boat planning was behind us, but we had not completely adjusted to the local time, and being in constant abundant sunshine and salty ocean air also drained our energy. We both anticipated a serious cuddle, snuggle, and a good night's sleep.

Jost Van Dyke
Foxy's

Five miles northwest of Tortola, steeped in West Indies' rustic charm, Jost van Dyke is a small island with picturesque anchorages and rugged scenery. During breakfast, Vince talked extensively about Great Harbor, the sandy, horseshoe-shaped, sheltered bay made famous by the legendary Foxy's; a beach bar and restaurant, world-renown for outstanding local cuisine, live music, and spirited beach parties. Listening to Vince describe our next destination was entertaining and made me equally eager to visit our next port of call.

After the breakfast dishes were stowed away and everything on board was securely stored, Vince hoisted the anchor, turned on the motor, and programmed the autopilot for a direct course to Jost van Dyke. Again, feeling apprehensive about too much wind, boat heeling, and a thousand other insignificant factors regarding our mode of travel, I kept my fingers crossed in the hope that Vince would not raise the sails. Fortunately, my wish was granted once more, and we made the three-hour, smooth and uneventful journey under power.

As we approached our destination and the beach came into view, Vince pointed to the eastern side of the island, the location of the renowned Foxy s; surrounded by palm trees, a tamarind tree, and the canopy of a huge, fiery orange flamboyant in full bloom.

"The dinghy-dock in front of Foxy's will be crowded tonight, they're hosting a barbecue buffet," Vince said. That sounded like a fun event! Before dinner, locals and boaters with cocktails routinely gather on the beach to watch the sunset and tonight we planned to be among the crowd.

With the mastery of a skilled sailor, Vince navigated *Poetry* into Great Harbor, straight down the middle, between the red and green buoys. He was almost breathless as he spoke with wild enthusiasm in his voice, "The reef extends several hundred feet off the inner shore here, so the snorkeling is world-class!"

Cautiously, he drove the boat forward, in search of a suitable area to anchor. When the ideal location was chosen, he slowed the engine, turning in wide circles, pondering our distance from shore. I wondered what he was looking for.

"This bay is fairly well protected, but we need plenty of swing room in case there's a wind shift tonight," Vince explained, concentrating on what he was doing. Unable to help, I watched as he stalled the boat, hurried to the bow, lowered, and positioned the anchor before dropping it precisely in the desired spot.

Again, I was dumbfounded! With the anchor on the bottom of the ocean, Vince moved the boat backward in a straight line until he felt the flanges dig into the sand. His boat handling was flawless! Finally, he turned the engine off, smiled, and blew me a kiss. Nevertheless, I dared not breathe a sigh of relief until Vince snorkeled over the anchor and flashed his thumbs-up sign, confirming that we were properly secured.

When he returned, I stood ready on the transom, offered to take his snorkel gear, stored it in the locker under the cockpit seat, and asked if there was anything I could do to prepare for our ride to shore. Understandably surprised at my sudden willingness to help, Vince looked at me with a puzzled expression on his face.

"Can you pull the dinghy up to the boat, so I can attach the outboard motor?" he asked.

"Of course," I replied firmly. Hmmm? Was I beginning to get the hang of this sailor's way of life?

When we reached the shore, Vince drove the dinghy directly up to the beach. Clumsily, almost stumbling, I stepped off into the shallow waves while trying to keep my beach bag from slipping off my shoulder as I attached my rubber flip-flops to my feet. Like a native, Vince calmly walked barefoot on the hot sandbar to bury the foldable anchor under a heavy rock in the sand.

"Are you OK?" he asked, while I shook myself off and grabbed his arm to steady myself.

"I am perfect," I replied, once I gained my bearings and looked at our surroundings. "Gosh, it's beautiful here!"

The shore, lined with the typical West Indies-style, white clapboard buildings with bright pink roofs, housed a customs control office, church, bakery, dive and t-shirt shop, several open-air eateries, and the BVI's beloved Foxy's. Hand-in-hand, we walked along the beach, peeked inquisitively into the open buildings, perused through the t-shirt shop, and gazed out at *Poetry* among the other boats at anchor in the bay. This was a jaw-dropping, stunningly beautiful, tropical oasis.

In the late 1960s, under the shade of a tamarind tree, Foxy Callwood opened Foxy's; a ramshackle beach bar that served rum drinks to beachgoers. Since then, Foxy's has grown into Foxy's Bar and Restaurant; a legend and a BVI cultural force.

Vince and I walked up to the bar, surrounded by wooden picnic tables and benches scattered about in the sand. A bright-eyed bartender with a million-dollar smile welcomed us and asked what we would like to drink.

"Gin and Tonic," Vince responded without hesitating.

The bartender acknowledged his order, turned to me, and asked, "And for you, Miss?" Knowing that I didn t want a glass of wine or another painkiller, but not sure what I longed for, I asked the bartender for a suggestion.

"No problem, Miss, I'll make the perfect drink for you."

The bartender grabbed a cocktail shaker, tossed in ice cubes, and with artistic execution, began mixing in the contents of random bottles behind the bar. When the shaker was adequately full, he added rum, a bit of cream, and the juice of a freshly squeezed orange, applied the top, and still smiling that million-dollar smile, vigorously shook the icy container with both hands. With entertaining bartender flair, he poured the fragrant potion into a tall glass, inserted a straw, and proudly presented it to me. "For you, Miss, give this a try."

Eagerly, I took a sip, it was indescribably delicious! The fresh flavors of coconut, raspberries, orange, mango, and rum danced on my tongue. It tasted amazing!

"Oh, My God, this drink is wonderful," I gushed. "Thank you! What is the name of it?"

"It's a Foxy's Special. Would you like another one, Miss?"

"Yes," I replied. "This is the best cocktail I have ever had!"

With our second drinks in hand, we wandered over to a group of picnic tables and sat on a bench facing a local entertainer. The native man in bare feet, wearing khakis, a yellow t-shirt, and a colorful knit cap stuffed full of his matted, reggae-style hair, sat on top of a table, strumming a guitar and ad-libbing amusing lyrics to impromptu off-beat tunes. Surrounded by an intimate audience who chuckled whenever a punchline was delivered, he seemed to enjoy their company.

When a few more onlookers gathered around, the entertainer became more animated, witty, and comical. Laughingly, he pointed to a tired-old, black dog laying in the sand. Looking directly at Vince, he said, "That's a real island dog. Do you know how I know that's a real island dog?"

Vince shrugged his shoulders, and replied, "No, how do you know that's a real island dog?"

The small audience began to take notice, paying closer attention. "Well…," the entertainer said, "he's black, he's lazy, and…" pausing for impact, before delivering his punchline… "he doesn't know who his daddy is! Ha, ha, ha!" The entertainer let out a hardy laugh after telling his joke, the audience laughed too and applauded wildly.

Before leaving this idyllic scene, we stopped by the bar to reserve a table for the barbecue dinner buffet tonight. Imagine our surprise when the bar hostess told us that the entertainer on the beach was Foxy himself! We looked forward to an excellent meal and a very memorable evening.

During our usual Happy Hour on board, Vince told stories about his past sailing experiences in the BVI; exciting stories, full of adventure. The story that fascinated me most, was about being holed up in an anchorage alone for an entire night, on a 37-foot chartered boat, waiting out a storm with hurricane-force winds.

Sitting on the edge of my seat, I listened with captivating interest, as Vince reminisced about being tossed back and forth due to the waves and wind. He stayed awake all night to watch for surrounding boats dangerously adrift. Oh, I couldn't imagine my fear in that situation. However, Vince spoke of it nonchalantly, as if to say, "I survived, it's in the past, and now it just makes for a good story."

Taking a shower in the small head on board was always awkward and took a bit of pre-planning. I didn t mind taking a hand-held shower, but I disliked getting everything completely wet; including the toilet, walls, and mirror. It was unavoidable. Although it is difficult to maneuver in the small space, after showering, I felt compelled to wipe the area dry with a towel and sponge. I also emptied the pool of water that accumulated on the floor by pushing a knob to activate a drainage pump.

Since our fresh water supply was limited, Vince warned against taking leisurely long showers. Consequently, I rushed through each time, without washing my hair. However, tonight we were going on a date. I wanted to look my best; freshly washed and moisturized, with soft and shiny, well-conditioned hair. I planned to wear a sexy, short sundress, strappy sandals, eye makeup, and a dab of perfume.

Dressed in evening beach attire, we arrived at Foxy's feeling hungry. It was twilight and with the sun barely below the horizon, once again, a touch of God's magic and wonder attributed to the world around us as breathtaking, fiery streaks of orange and lavender washed across the sky.

Through the steadily growing crowd of beachcombers and boaters, we elbowed our way from the dock to the bar. The bartender who created the Foxy's Special cocktail for me earlier was busily mixing and serving drinks. However, when our eyes met, he recognized us and acknowledged our presence.

"It's nice to see you again, welcome back to Foxy's. What can I get for you?" he asked immediately. "A Foxy s Special for you, Miss?"

"Of course," I replied.

"Coming right up, and for you, sir? A Gin and Tonic?"

Judging by the number of communal tables, set with the appropriate red and white checkered tablecloths, Foxy's expected quite a crowd for dinner tonight.

We found a seat overlooking the harbor and anxiously waited for the buffet to officially open. Tonight's menu included grilled mahi-mahi, barbecued chicken and ribs, pulled island pork, Caribbean seasoned rice, Foxy's famous pasta salad, corn on the cob with garlic butter sauce, a wide selection of seasonal vegetables, and several decadent desserts.

Impatiently, we watched the efficient staff carry huge pans, heaped high with piping hot traditional island dishes to the buffet tables. The aromas wafting by us from the oversized pans of mouthwatering barbecued meats left us salivating.

Finally, someone rang an old-fashioned brass dinner bell fastened to a palm tree, indicating that it was time to eat. At once, the hungry guests lined up to fill their plates. However, Vince chose to wait until the crowd thinned out. *Why?* I thought privately…for goodness sake, I'm ready for chow!

Nevertheless, agreeing to wait a respectable few minutes together, eventually, we joined the buffet line. Vince aimed for the salad bar, while I headed straight to the main courses; a piece of chicken, two luscious beef ribs, a serving of the juicy pulled pork, a slice of mahi-mahi, and a spoonful of the Caribbean seasoned rice filled my plate.

On the way back to our table, I couldn't resist strategically balancing an ear of corn, drenched in the garlic butter sauce, on top of the mound. Fortunately, I managed to carry the overflowing plate to my seat without spilling a thing.

While my food selections were rich and fattening, Vince's choices were healthy and calorie-restricted. I felt a little ashamed, but Vince reassured me that he was just getting started and would indulge in a second helping from the buffet table.

After eating and drinking to our heart's content, we stayed to listen to a talented steel-drum band playing popular Bob Marley tunes and other rhythmic, Caribbean-style music. The balmy evening was socially festive, a few guests danced while others strolled along the moonlit beach. We didn't want the evening to end, however, to avoid a fleet of rubber inflatables departing from the dock at once when the party was over, Vince suggested leaving before the music stopped.

Reluctantly, we boarded our dinghy, and through the darkness, Vince steered us safely back to *Poetry*. As I started down the companionway to head to our cabin, he turned to me and said, "Don't go yet Love, I want to show you something." He held out his hand and led me to the foredeck.

"What is it?" I asked. Vince stopped just forward of the hatch, stood behind me, and put his arms around my shoulders, my back was against his chest.

"Look up for a minute, Hon. Have you ever seen stars so bright?" he asked, drawing me closer. Indeed, the evening sky was blanketed with a million twinkling lights, begging us to marvel at their heavenliness, but the star that was the brightest was the one on top of our mast.

Tortola
Cane Garden Bay

Still bowled over by our unforgettable experience at Foxy's last night, throughout breakfast, we hardly spoke of anything else. The joy in my heart spilled out onto my journal as I feverishly documented the event. I especially noted that meeting Foxy Callwood in person was the evening's highlight, only outdone by Vince's adoring mood. I will cherish the memory of our evening on Jost van Dyke forever.

As I continued reminiscing and writing, Vince flipped through the Cruising Guide. "It's a beautiful day for sailing," he said, "are you ready to explore a new harbor?"

"Sure!" was my immediate answer, followed by the question that loomed large in my mind. "Are we raising the sails today?"

"We're going to Cane Garden Bay; an excellent anchorage, with a shallow sandy beach. If we sail, we will probably be there in a few hours. Tonight, I'll take you to Stanley's Welcome Bar for a fresh lobster dinner."

Ughhhh! The idea of sailing frightened me again and I could feel the hairs on the back of my neck begin to rise. "And if we motor…how long will it take us to get there?" I nearly stuttered as I asked the question, hoping that Vince would sense my reoccurring apprehension.

"We'll be there sooner," he replied, then paused, looked at me, and added, "OK, I see that you're not ready to sail, no problem, we'll motor to Cane Garden Bay."

Oh, Thank God, what a darling man! I appreciated Vince's patience and understanding immensely, although I don't know how long I could take advantage of his compassion. As the nervous feeling in the pit of my stomach began to subside, I eagerly anticipated our lobster dinner on the beach later this evening.

Vince re-programmed the autopilot set for the new heading, five and a half nautical miles away. When we passed the green starboard buoy indicating that we were in clear water, he pointed to several radio towers high on a lush, green mountaintop across the channel "That's where we're headed," he declared, "to that beach below the mountain with the towers. See, it is not that far." Able to see our next destination, I liked this line-of-sight sailing.

Nicknamed 'The Jewel of the BVI', for its aqua-marine blue water and the long stretch of white sandy beach lined with the ever-present palm trees, brilliant flamboyant, and indigenous bay leaf trees that grow profusely in the area, Cane Garden Bay is the most famous for the sugar cane plantation and distillery located near the beach.

The Callwood Rum Distillery has been in operation since the 1600s, producing rum in the original boiler and storing the beautiful, intoxicating beverage in original casks. Marked by a giant breadfruit tree, the rustic site was nearly hidden by wildly sown sugar cane and an overgrown bay leaf tree. The Callwood family produces rum from locally grown sugar cane and perfumes from the leaves of the bay leaf tree. Beauty and health-beneficial products are made from the fiber-rich breadfruit. Made by hand, in small batches, they sell quickly to locals and tourists.

During the relatively smooth three-hour journey, I was able to prepare a simple lunch below deck without having to hang on to the fixtures for dear life. While Auto *(now our affectionate nickname for the autopilot)* drove the boat, we consumed our open-face sandwiches and ice-cold beers, sitting comfortably in the sun-filled cockpit. We kept our eyes out for turtles and dolphins, but alas, we only saw an occasional glide of flying fish skimming gracefully across the water.

As we advanced toward our destination, Vince studied the Cruising Guide for the best lead into the bay. The guide warned of a high headland close to a rocky area on the north side. Nevertheless, he spotted a large white house in a prominent position above the cliffs, confirming our correct location and safe approach to the harbor.

Finding a sandy area with good holding ground was fairly easy here, so Vince was able to anchor quickly, without problems. After his routine snorkel over the anchor, he gave the thumbs-up signal, climbed on board, and turned off the engine. Suddenly, I realized that I was becoming comfortably familiar with the anchoring procedure and liked knowing what to expect. With the boat fixed and secure in our new location, I reposed and poured us both a glass of wine.

"Welcome to Cane Garden Bay," Vince said, as I presented him with a glass. "I can't wait to show you around."

Cane Garden Bay's kidney-shaped, tranquil harbor's natural, untamed coast was lined with several funky establishments. The most well-known of these was Stanley's Welcome Bar, marked by a classic tire-swing suspended from a wind-swept palm tree, eminently located in the middle of the beach.

"That's where we're going to dinner tonight," Vince said, pointing to the swing. "Let's go ashore, have a drink, and make a reservation."

Like yesterday, we drove the dinghy up on the beach, however, this time I was better prepared to take my first step off into the shallow water and since I didn't bring my beach bag or flip-flops, I was a bit more steady and poised as I approached the sandbar in my bare feet.

Walking in the breakers along the shore toward the center of the bay's activity, I adored seeing chickens and roosters amble through the prickly plants and the pristine, powdery white sand so bright it hurt my eyes to look at. Feral fowl living seamlessly among the locals was completely conventional in the BVI. This quaint sailor's destination saturated in Caribbean charm resonated with me and I felt at ease in this quintessential island village.

The first building on the beach strip was a humble, bright pink store and restaurant known as Rymer's. Their lunch menu offered the usual conch fritters, potato roti, and painkillers. The adjacent grocery store sold freshly baked loaves of coconut bread, guava, and pineapple pies in addition to simple homemade arts and crafts created from seashells.

There was no shortage of eateries on this coastline, among them was the iconic Stanley's Welcome Bar, with its world-famous tire-swing; the most photographed spot on the island. Equally famous was the restaurant's succulent, grilled lobster served every evening in an open-air, disheveled but island-charming dining room.

Next door, a small diner in a make-shift, wooden structure advertised local dishes such as pulled pork cooked in a rich, savory sauce, coconut curry conch stew, and spiny lobster sautéed in butter sauce. Myett's Cafe featured conch chowder, grilled island chicken, and mahi-mahi fish burgers. Everything sounded interesting and wonderfully delicious.

As we walked higher up on the sandbar, closer to where the palm trees grew, I noticed several coconuts in dry, brown husks lying on the beach; a tender, heartfelt reminder of my grandmother, who enjoyed husking coconuts sitting at an outdoor table in the backyard of our home.

With care, she poured the coconut water into an aluminum saucepan and with a wooden-handled paring knife, released the meaty white flesh from its shell. On a box-grater, she grated the fresh coconut and spread it out on a baking sheet to toast in the oven, before storing the precious end product in airtight containers for future use in various recipes.

I picked up a medium size husk, shaking it close to my ear to confirm that the nut inside contained water. "Have you ever husked a coconut?" I asked Vince. "Here, try this one," I added, tossing it to him as if it was a football.

"What do you mean, is this a coconut?" Vince asked, with a quizzical look on his face as he caught the husk. He was surprised by its lightweight. "It doesn't look like one."

"It is a coco *husk,* you have to break it open to get to the coconut," I replied, eager to show him how it was done. I looked for a hard surface among the organic rubbish along the shore. Near the top of the sandbar, I found several suitable rocks which I gathered and arranged on the sand to create a surface on which to balance the husk with its pointed end up. Curious, Vince watched as I searched for one more rock. When I located a perfect one for the job, I handed it to him.

"Here, aim for the pointed end and drop this rock on the husk until it cracks."

"Really?" Vince questioned in disbelief. Nevertheless, with a forceful whack, he heaved the heavy stone on the husk several times, each time awkwardly jumping out of the way to avoid the jagged stone from landing on his bare feet. The operation was hilarious to watch and I couldn't help laughing out loud. His third attempt was successful!

"YES!" Vince cheered as he picked up the husk to examine it. "It's cracked!"

"Great, now tear off all the brown fibers," I said while attempting to demonstrate, although I found that tearing off the stubborn dry substance took more strength than I seemingly had. Vince stood in the breakers, undeterred and eager, shredding the husk apart like a caveman, and before long, he rinsed the fibrous residue from his bare chest and arms and held up a beautiful clean coconut.

"Look, a coconut," he exclaimed, proudly showing off the result of his painstaking effort. "Now…how do I crack it?"

His question prompted another adoring vision of my grandmother, lovingly, teaching me to hold the coconut with the three pores; the dark spots on one end, toward me. "Imagine that this is a face," she would say in her sweet voice. "Look at it closely and determine which one of these is the mouth."

Of course, it was just make-believe, but my grandmother insisted that the mouth was always the softer pore and therefore, the easiest to penetrate. When I identified the mouth, she would carve a perfect hole into it with her trusty little paring knife, insert a straw, and present it to me as if it was a precious gift. It was the most wonderful drink of my childhood; fresh coconut water right from the nut!

Patiently, Vince listened as I shared my special memory with him, then, insistent and anxious as a child about to order an ice cream cone, he asked again, "OK, but how do I open this thing? Where is the white, edible part?"

"Here, hold it in one hand and gently tap on its side with this rock, all the way around, until the shell slightly splits in half," I instructed, handing him a blunt-shaped stone. "Once it's split, open it slowly, as if it was a clamshell filled with water. Be careful, after all your hard work, you don't want to lose a drop."

While Vince tapped on the coconut with the stone, two curious tourists approached and asked what we were doing. The couple confessed to watching us from a bar on the beach, mistaking us for locals. We told them that we were also just tourists, enjoying the beach and cracking a coconut.

After a few taps of the stone, the coconut easily split in half and Vince finally reaped the fruit of his labor. With the shell divided, he brought the water-filled half to his mouth to taste the sweet, nutty liquid, then pried loose a piece of the clean, white flesh and took a bite.

"This is delicious! Here, try it," he said, wide-eyed and beaming with pride as he handed me a piece of the fruit. I can t recall ever seeing him so animated and excited. Sharing my knowledge with Vince was fulfilling and a pleasure. For the first time on this adventure, I felt as if I was a contributor.

I could have happily spent the rest of the day, strolling along the beach together in search of coconuts, however, we decided to return to the boat in time for our usual Happy Hour before sunset.

While I created a few effortless appetizers, Vince made the *gin and tonics* with a shot of his fresh coconut water; a nice added flavor to the refreshing beverage. Tonight's sunset hinted at being a show-stopper and our boat's position was perfect to watch the giant orange orb slip silently into the sea, framed by Jost van Dyke to the North and St. Thomas to the South.

Cuddled up on the transom, sipping cocktails, and playing footsies in the water, this moment was hard to beat. When the sun was completely from view and only traces of pink remained in the sky, Vince reluctantly suggested getting ready to go ashore for our dinner reservation.

On the beach, the staff at Stanley's Welcome Bar was bustling, filling well-blackened, oversized grills with heaps of charcoal and lighting them with the touch of a fiery torch.

"When those grills reach the ideal cooking temperature, they'll load them up with locally caught lobster, mahi-mahi, and prawns the size of your fist," Vince said. My mouth began to water as I envisioned the Grill Master at his post, proficiently drizzling the amazingly fresh seafood with lemon and garlic butter while each piece grilled to perfection. Oh, I couldn't wait to indulge!

As the first diners to arrive at the restaurant, we selected a table with the best view of the harbor. In the distance, *Poetry* was peacefully at anchor. However, with no one on board, she looked somewhat abandoned.

Suddenly, Vince realized that he had forgotten his wallet. With little warning, he hastened back to the dinghy, hopped in, and headed back to the boat, leaving me seated at the table. I watched him travel between the other yachts, tie up to a stern cleat, and jump on board. Eagerly, I awaited his return when, suddenly, I saw our mast-star shine against the dark sky! What a surprise and what an endearing thing to do…my sweetheart remembered to turn on 'my star'!

Dinner was truly outstanding! The lobster lived up to Stanley's reputation, the caramelized corn-on-the-cob, cooked on the grill in a foil wrapper, was just the way I preferred and the unlabeled, house-made wine complemented the meal superbly. For dessert, we shared a homemade dish of ice cream made from almond milk, sprinkled with chocolate hail and cinnamon.

One more delicious than the next, the calorie-rich meals I've had on this trip were going to take a toll on my figure! Maybe I would exercise tomorrow, maybe I would walk laps on deck! Maybe…

Finding it difficult to leave the moonlight and the romantic glow of my star shimmering in the water, we were the last guests remaining in the restaurant. I was choked with emotion, longing to tell Vince how much he enriched my life and how much I wished this adventure would never end. However, as usual, I was timid, refrained from showing my feelings, and kept silent.

We slept like babies and woke up mid-morning, caressed by sunbeams streaming through the open hatch above our heads. As our sixth day in the BVI began, we felt refreshed and adjusted to the local time.

"Good morning, Love," said Vince, "I have a surprise for you."

"Good morning, I love surprises. Tell me what it is?"

"Let's stay here today. We can relax and spend the day on the boat and on the beach. Would you like to stay another day?"

I was ecstatic! Not having to weigh anchor, travel, and re-anchor again would allow us to do nothing, and that sounded appealing.

There was something marvelous about staying in Cane Garden Bay for the entire day without plans to move on or do anything specific. I took my time to fry the last two eggs and toast the last English muffins we had in our pantry. While the coffee brewed, I sliced an apple and the last pieces of Vince's fresh coconut. Maybe later, we could do some light provisioning at Rymer's Grocery Store, but for now, there was no need to rush, and so…we didn't.

After enjoying a long, unhurried breakfast, Vince took a morning dip in the crystal-clear water. He swam with a turtle near the boat while I had time to hand-wash a few clothes and hang them on the lifelines to dry. I also changed the bedding in our cabin and organized food items in the icebox. It was a day to 'nest' and I thoroughly enjoyed it.

We spent the afternoon at the beach, wandering through the shops and taking photos. For the ultimate photo opportunity, we asked a passerby to snap our picture while Vince gave me a push on the famous tire-swing. I enjoyed acting like geeky, carefree tourists! Vince found another coconut husk and discovered that if he washed it off in the breakers while rubbing it with sand, the coconut became fairly clean and smooth.

"Look at this beauty!" he exclaimed. Proudly showing it off as if it were a jewel.

"Now you're a true island boy," I teased, while he cracked and broke the coconut apart with ease.

At Rymer's Grocery Store, we located an ice cream freezer, filled-to-the-brim with ice cream bars on a stick, covered in thick dark chocolate. "It's been years since I've had an ice cream bar," Vince said. Without further thought, he grabbed two, paid for them, and offered me one. Gratified in our frozen treats, we waded out into the warm, shallow shoal where the waves broke over the reef. It was a large, sandy area; the perfect playground for frolicking in knee-deep water, splashing each other with each step.

Eventually, there was just enough time before sunset to stock up on a few provisioning items for our Happy Hour tradition. A quick re-visit to Rymers was inevitable. Happily, the market had a good selection of everything we needed.

Our evening on board was equally slow-paced. Vince grilled chicken while I prepared a pineapple-mango salsa and a basic green salad. Eating dinner later than usual was a welcome change, it made the fun-filled day a little longer.

After the meal, we lay naked on the foredeck to gaze at the stars. Vince identified the constellations and I adored listening to him intently, naming them one by one. Serenaded by soothing steel band tunes from a restaurant on the beach, we embraced and made love in the dark.

I treasured the lazy, blissfully happy hours we spent in Cane Garden Bay and the memory of showing Vince how to peel and crack a coconut will be with me forever.

Virgin Gorda
Gorda Sound/North Sound

We rose early, stumbled to the companionway together, and poked our sleepy heads through the hatch to greet the day. Last night s velvety, fairytale evening became a glorious, bright morning, and we were immediately struck by a staggering, clear blue heaven, and mountain crests cinematically illuminated by the sun.

"Ohhh, this light is incredible," I remarked. "Let me get my camera, I've got to take some pictures!" Vince retrieved my camera from the nav *(navigation)* station and handed it to me. Quickly, I moved to the bow, snapped photos in every direction, and silently thanked God for this magnificent morning. I was completely lost in the moment and the extraordinary light.

While I replaced the used roll of film in my camera with a fresh one, my state of mind was jarred when Vince announced his plans for moving on.

"Hon," he said heedfully, "we are going to Virgin Gorda today. I won't raise the sails, we'll go under power but getting there will take most of the day."

Suddenly, I felt a resurgence of tenseness in my body. Pretending to focus on preparing our breakfast, I asked, "What's in Virgin Gorda?" not letting our eyes meet when I posed the question.

"The Bitter End, I don t want you to miss it," Vince answered, "it is the most famous anchorage in the BVI, with unspoiled, hidden beaches where we can swim naked and collect shells," he continued while he showed me aerial shots of the area in the Cruising Guide.

Protected by surrounding islands and large reefs, Gorda Sound on the northern end of Virgin Gorda is one of the great harbors of the world and the location of the Bitter End Yacht Club Resort and Marina.

Indeed, it looked impressive and since Vince had been completely understanding about my fear of sailing and other trivial impediments on this trip, I felt that I owed it to him to project a positive attitude, even if it meant that we would be at sea for the entire day. Maybe we would see a school of sociable dolphins, turtles, or other sea life. I hoped that the ocean would be gentle without large swells and that the time would pass quickly. I could read a book, write in my journal and take a nap on the shady side of the boat.

When our coffee pot was empty and breakfast consumed, Vince weighed anchor before the sun became too hot. We left Cane Garden Bay, turned the corner, and headed east to the island Columbus named the 'Fat Virgin' almost 500 years ago.

Once we were underway, Vince tended to essential boat-keeping chores; coiling lines, stowing winch handles, and other equipment not needed for our passage to the Bitter End. When everything on board was shipshape, he cuddled up next to me in the cockpit, put a strong arm around my shoulders, and said, "Let's get naked!"

What a grand idea! We stripped off our clothes and, for the next few hours, lazed naked in the sun while Auto drove the boat. Oh, how I loved feeling uninhibited and being completely natural! Sometimes, we scurried to the bow where cool ocean splashes refreshed our bare bodies and made us giggle.

After nearly six days in the tropics, we sported healthy tans and ran the risk of getting sunburned. The Caribbean is closer to the equator, where the sun's rays hit the earth more directly. The reflective blue water and *Poetry*'s white deck also intensified our exposure to the sun, contributing to the danger of damaging our unprotected skin. Just when I considered seeking shelter below deck for a while, Vince raised the Bimini *(a canvas top supported by a metal frame that covers the cockpit)* which instantly provided ample shade, making it bearable to stay on deck.

With the boat moving forward at a comfortable speed, time passed rather quickly as I dozed off stretched out on a cockpit seat, with my head nestled cozily on Vince's lap. Suddenly, he nudged me and, trying not to scare them away, shouted in a stage whisper, "Look, dolphins!"

I jumped up like a shot. "Where, where?"

"There, port-side, they want to take a look at you," Vince teased.

Just in time, I saw three beautiful, silvery-white bottlenose dolphins breach in unison while making lovable clicking sounds as if they were saying, "Hello welcome to our world."

"Oh my gosh, they look like they're smiling," I remarked. "They're smiling at us."

Before I could grab my camera, the dolphins disappeared into the deep blue ocean. Still, I was thrilled that I saw them in the wild, although minutes later, it seemed as if it had been a dream.

I continued to peer out over the water for hours, scanning the surface for dorsal fins, in the hopes that the smiling dolphins would return.

At noon, I slipped into the galley to investigate our options for a lunch on-the-go. I discovered that being below deck for any length of time if the boat was moving forward made me feel nauseous, even though I took an over-the-counter motion sickness medication religiously each morning.

Swiftly as I could manage, I opened a can of tuna, diced a large tomato, some green olives, and the remainder of a red onion, tossed the ingredients into a plastic bowl, added a dash of salt and pepper, a long drizzle of bottled Italian salad dressing, and mixed everything. I divided the tuna mixture between two pre-sliced sandwich rolls and stuffed in a few leaves of the precious lettuce we brought from California. Through the companionway, I handed one of the sandwiches up to Vince before climbing on deck with a can of potato chips, a couple of napkins, and the other sandwich.

"Hmmm, that was fast and these look tasty," Vince remarked, sounding appreciative. I could not speak but nodded my head in response as I gulped big breaths of fresh air to stop the queasiness in the pit of my stomach.

The sandwiches were easy to eat out of hand and the can of potato chips stayed within reach, steadily balanced in a cup holder built into the cockpit.

Although my seasickness subsided, I was certainly ready to stop moving. "How much longer before we enter Gorda Sound?" I queried, trying not to appear too anxious.

"We're over halfway there, maybe another three hours," Vince replied. Ughhh! Another three hours seemed like an eternity!

The remainder of our passage was uneventful, our boat speed seemed ever so slow, however, I kept a stiff upper lip, counting the hours until our arrival. When we reached a cluster of three uninhabited islands off Virgin Gorda s north shore, surrounded by ink-blue water and an enormous colorful reef, Vince shouted, "Those are The Dogs, that s George Dog, that s Great Dog and the small one is West Dog. The snorkeling here is outstanding!"

The Cruising Guide provided further details about the islands, citing a historic legend of earlier sailors who named them for the characteristic sound of monk seals that came from their shores, mistakenly taking them for the sounds of barking dogs.

Finally, after six and a half hours of motoring, we approached the channel leading into Gorda Sound. Mosquito Island was on starboard and Prickly Pear Island was on port. Due to the limited amount of available mooring buoys in the harbor, several boats were on the same tack. Everyone's goal was to pick up the best mooring before sunset.

When we were well inside the channel, a high-performance, sophisticated, inflatable powerboat sped directly toward us. Immediately, Vince slowed our boat down to an idle, allowing the pilot to catch up. He approached on starboard and reached for our gunwale.

"Ahoy, mate," the friendly young man said in a thick Australian accent. "Welcome to Virgin Gorda."

"Thanks!" Vince shouted back. "Can we help you?"

"I'm from that bay over there," was the reply, as the young man pointed to the shores of a beautiful blue lagoon. "We have a new resort over there, just inside the channel on the right. The Leverick Bay Resort and Marina; we are a full-service marina, with a Laundromat and swimming pool. The restaurant serves amazing food and all types of rum drinks. I hope you'll give us a try."

Before heading off to the next boat entering the Sound, he presented us with a bottle of Pusser s Rum and tipped his red cap in a parting salute.

"What a great way to introduce the new facility," Vince commented, "this is a nice bottle of rum!"

Historically known as Gorda Sound; North Sound is the luxury epicenter of the British Virgin Islands with marinas, and upscale resorts, including the world-famous Bitter End Yacht Club, Resort and Marina; casually referred to as the 'Bitter End'. Many boaters allocate several days to exploring this destination due to the variety of things to do here and the astonishing remote beaches just a short dinghy ride away.

In the distance, the Bitter End came into view and I understood immediately that this harbor was different from the others we visited, evidenced by the multi-million dollar, mega yachts at anchor.

Suddenly, Vince became very focused as he explained that instead of dropping an anchor, he would pick up a mooring buoy. I listened intensely, but all the unfamiliar nautical terms made me nervous. It sounded like a daunting task and I was curious to see how the process would transpire.

Continuing on our gentle approach into the harbor, Vince looked for the ideal spot to spend several nights, while I admired the stunning scenery as if my head was on a swivel, making comments and asking questions. However, Vince couldn't be distracted and remained focused.

With a mooring ball chosen, he came upon it at a dead-slow speed, killed the engine, and hastened to the foredeck where he waited for the wind to push our boat toward the target. When the ball was within reach, he used a boathook to fish for the pendant line floating from the top of the ball on the surface of the water, pulled the line on board, fed it through a channel on the bow, and tied it to a cleat. It was a magnificent feat to watch and I was duly impressed!

We were tied up securely and there was no need for Vince to snorkel over the anchor to confirm our stronghold. Immediately, I preferred picking up a mooring buoy to anchoring.

"We're here!" Vince announced directly. "Welcome to Gorda Sound. I could use a drink!" Since old habits are hard to break, Vince always referred to the North Sound as Gorda Sound. Getting him a drink was the least I could do! I sped below deck, grabbed a cold beer from the icebox, popped the top, and offered it to him.

"Oh my gosh, Honey, this place is extraordinary," I exclaimed. "I love it here already!"

With our bow turned into the wind, I stood on the very tip of the bow for an uninterrupted view of the Bitter End Yacht Club and Resort. As the last island outpost before the Caribbean Sea meets the Atlantic Ocean, the lavish resort, located on more than sixty acres overlooked the breathtaking Gorda Sound.

Nestled on a hillside with manicured, tropical gardens and walking paths along a private beachfront and posh marina, lovely red-roofed cottages and villas peered out at the harbor between flamboyant, bougainvillea, flowering shrubs, lush ornamental climbing foliage, and palm trees. Established in 1973, the Bitter End is the destination of choice for yachtsmen and adventurous sailors.

"This place is unbelievable! Look at all the super-yachts, that one has a helicopter pad on deck!" I said, pointing to a sleek, white powerboat with a uniformed crew on board. Anchored on our port-side *Mustang* from George Town in the Cayman Islands; was a 45-meter, dark red sailing yacht with a classic, exquisitely detailed teak deck. Magnificent luxury yachts were all around us, some with garages to store jet skis, windsurfers, and other water-sport equipment. I had never been anywhere this rich, this opulent!

Vince chuckled at my reaction to our new location. He was pleased that I was excited to be here. "Let me show you around," he said, as he joined me on the foredeck.

Located in the Northeast corner, to the right of the Bitter End, was Biras Creek; only accessible by boat or helicopter, this highly exclusive resort was the ultimate getaway. Across the Eustatia Sound was Saba Rock; less than an acre in size. Loaded with marauder charm, this tiny island was the location of The Pirates Pub and The Dive BVI water-sports shop; owned and managed by a local marine archaeologist. Behind us, at the entrance to the Sound, was Leverick Bay; the new facility that welcomed us with a bottle of rum. This was the ultimate tropical paradise and I was ecstatic beyond belief to be here!

It was nearly an hour before sunset, time to prepare Happy Hour nibbles. Instead of mixing our usual Gin and Tonic cocktails, Vince opened a bottle of wine, filled a glass, stretched out on a seat facing the horizon, and let out a satisfying "Ahhhh...Perfect!" Exhausted from today s long journey, he deserved this time to chill out while I doted on him.

The white plastic cutting board from the galley was a good substitute for a serving board and I began to assemble an extra-special hors-d'oeuvre platter with Spanish green olives, cherry tomatoes, sliced cucumber, chunks of cheddar, blue and Swiss cheeses, and a handful of mixed nuts. A tangy egg salad made with Dijon mustard, olive oil, and diced onions served with the grainy whole-wheat crackers we bought in Cane Garden Bay completed the appetizer menu. When I arrived in the cockpit with my abundance of finger-food snacks, Vince poured his second glass of wine.

"There you are," he said, apparently happy to see me, "just in time to enjoy the show. I get a kick out of watching novice sailors pick up a mooring buoy," Vince elaborated as he took the platters from me and placed them on the table. I sat on a comfy cushion beside him and once I had a glass of wine in my hand, Vince and I settled in to watch the funny mishaps that inexperienced boaters often make.

It wasn't long before a chartered sailboat approaching on starboard became an excellent case-in-point to watch. A crew member stood ready at the bow, boathook in hand.

However, the helmsman came up on the mooring ball much too fast, causing the crew member to miss snagging the pendant line. Consequently, the helmsman circled back to the target to make several more unsuccessful attempts. Alas, it appeared as though they gave up and moved to a different location. Vince laughed out loud. He looked so handsome when he laughed.

We watched another boat with a crew member positioned on the transom snag the pendant line and pass it to a second crew member, who walked it up to the bow. Unfortunately, the boat traveled faster than the crew member could move, causing him to drop the pendant in the water along with the boathook! Amused to the hilt, Vince almost roared with laughter at the free entertainment.

"Watch this guy," he said, as a sailboat came slowly into the harbor under power, with an anchor dangling free above the waterline. Several people standing on the bow stared into the water as if they were looking for something. Unexpectedly, one of them shouted to the helmsman, "Now!" while he made an emphatic motion with his left arm to indicate dropping the anchor immediately.

In reaction to his command, Vince stood up from his seat and shouted back, "No, not NOW, you're right on top of us, you need more swing room!"

Someone on board must have heard him and advised the helmsman, who glared at us as the boat passed and moved to another location in the harbor.

We stayed on deck cuddled in each other's arms, watching the blunders of newbie sailors until the light from the sky appeared diffused and pinkish. I loved being a bit mischievous with Vince, while we delighted in the mistakes of others.

Eventually, it was time to talk about dinner options. "I've got chicken thighs marinating in white wine and peanut oil with dried herbs and garlic. If you do the grilling, I'll make a salad. Let's not go out for dinner tonight," I suggested.

Without further prompting, Vince prepared the grill, and before long, placed the chicken, skin side down, on the hot grate. As the chicken became juicy and bursting with flavor, the enticing aroma wafted through the galley. I didn t realize how hungry we were. I made a quick bean salad from a can of red beans and Cuban black beans, added diced onions, garlic, parsley, thyme, olive oil, lime juice, salt, and gave everything a quick toss. We were both looking forward to a hearty meal.

It must have been after 10 o'clock when we finished dinner and another bottle of wine. As usual, before going to bed, we lay on the foredeck like star-crossed lovers gazing at our mast-star and the other stars in the sky. Straight ahead, the Bitter End glowed in the dark and we heard the muffled, happy sounds of boaters and other tourists socializing onshore.

This was a spellbinding place. I looked forward to what tomorrow would bring.

Virgin Gorda
The Bitter End

I woke up with a sense of intense happiness and the surreal realization that I was blessed beyond belief. Refreshed and re-energized after a good night's sleep, the overwhelming emotion lured me on deck. Since Vince was still asleep, a few moments of privacy were a precious gift as I soaked up the morning light. On my tip-toes, I climbed up the companionway and, quiet as a mouse, crept out on the foredeck. There, I closed my eyes, raised my face to the sun, and rejoiced with both arms stretched out toward the sky. Oh, it felt intoxicating!

Suddenly, though, I felt self-conscience and sensed that I might look a bit conspicuous to anyone who saw my odd behavior. I took a more natural stance and looked at the neighboring yachts, relieved to see that only a few boaters on deck seemed to be enjoying the early sunlight with me. On this lovely, peaceful morning, my heart was light as air.

An hour or so later, I heard stirring below deck, "Good morning, beautiful. Is it beautiful enough for you out there?" Looking disheveled, but childlike and adorable, as he rubbed the sleep from his eyes, Vince appeared in the cockpit.

"Good morning, Captain," I replied. "Did you sleep well? Gosh, I love this place, Vince, it is unreal! I haven't even been on shore, and this is already my favorite anchorage."

"I thought you might like it here. There are many wonderful places to snorkel. We can explore after breakfast," Vince proposed as he came toward me with open arms, ready to give and receive a morning hug. At the mention of the word 'snorkel', that annoying, re-occurring feeling of apprehension disturbed my happy spirit. I preferred to spend the day on board, to be unhurried and luxuriate in our ostentatiously wealthy surroundings, making journal entries, taking naps, and observing the comings-and-goings of the incredible mega-yachts. I was cautious to respond.

"Sweetheart, you had an exhausting, long day yesterday. Enjoy your morning. I'll make coffee and a big, healthy breakfast," I said, hoping to change the topic of discussion.

Soon, the warm, nutty aroma of coffee perking filled the salon and drifted on deck. "OK, maybe we'll go this afternoon," Vince replied, as I handed him a mug full of the piping hot beverage, further encouraging him to stay on board.

To reward Vince s safe and successful navigation to Gorda Sound and his impeccable job mooring to a buoy without assistance, I searched our makeshift pantry for the ingredients of a celebratory breakfast. Luckily, there was an adequate selection of food items remaining on board to create a special meal.

For our first course, I made a fruit salad with a beautifully ripe mango, juicy orange, and the last piece of Vince s Cane Garden Bay coconut, dressed with lime juice and a teaspoon of brown sugar. With a diced onion, green pepper, a handful of shredded cheese, five eggs, and a can of chopped Spam, I whipped up a tasty omelet, puffy and golden, served right out of the pan. The addition of toasted muffins, butter, orange marmalade, and a pitcher of spicy Bloody Mary, made this meal fit for British Royalty.

"Breakfast looks delicious and I'm starved!" Vince said.

"You deserve it," I replied, while I garnished our Bloody Marys with a sprig of fresh green onion and a lemon wedge. "I'd like to make a toast," I said, raising my glass in Vince's direction. "Thank you, sweetheart. Thank you for everything; for inviting me to join you on this trip, for taking care of absolutely everything, for making me feel safe, and for introducing me to the Bitter End. It is a dream to be here with you." I sincerely meant every word I said.

"I am happy I was able to convince you. I hope I can make a sailor out of you," Vince replied, leaning in to give me a kiss.

Joined by the occasional seagull begging for scraps, we languished over our extra-special breakfast while we discussed a possible agenda for the day.

Eager to go to a secluded beach, Vince continued to talk about snorkeling; discovering giant coral sea fans, and mingling with exotic fish, but I tried to discourage any activity that required me to submerge in water deeper than my knees. In the end, we agreed to go ashore to visit the Bitter End Yacht Club where we could explore our dining options, tour the exquisite tropical gardens, and shop for souvenirs. That was *my* kind of exploring!

My heart became aflutter with excitement as I quickly ran a brush through my hair, grabbed my camera, flip-flops, and a backpack. Impatiently, I waited on the transom while Vince prepared the dinghy for our trip to shore. As I watched him transfer the weighty outboard motor from its perch on *Poetry* to its mounting position on the dinghy, I happily realized that he would not have to repeat this daunting chore for the duration of our stay here; a definite benefit of staying in one place for a few days.

Cruising to shore in our dinghy and seeing the luxury yachts up close was extraordinary. In their shadow, I felt incredibly tiny! *Mustang's* open garage housed jet skis, kayaks, and paddle boards inside her oversized hull. But perhaps, a magnificent, white, sleek super-yacht with a grand sundeck, helipad, and a helicopter ready for take-off was the most impressive. As I admired each vessel in awe, Vince mentioned that similar yachts chartered with a captain, helicopter pilot, cook, and crew could cost as much as a million dollars per week! Honestly, I found it unfathomable!

Only a handful of rubber inflatables were tied up at the dock when we arrived. Within moments, I stood on solid ground, straightened my clothes, and steps ahead of Vince, headed toward the resort's entrance.

"Wait!" he called out. "You'll miss the shark tank!"

I was in such a hurry to enter the Bitter End's beautiful guest lobby that I didn't notice the large in-ground pool located at the end of the dock, filled with sharks and other interesting marine life. Waiting for me to return, Vince stood at the foot of the tank, gazing at the odd creatures on display.

"Oh my gosh, look at them, are these sharks?"

"They are *nurse* sharks," Vince explained, "they live at the bottom of the ocean. They're completely docile."

Curious to know how they would feel to the touch, for a split second I was tempted, and almost reached inside the tank, to pet one of the submissive shark's flat back and dorsal fin, however, I imagined the skin to be slimy and resisted the urge.

Vince looked at me, smiled, grabbed my hand, and said, "Wait until you see the lobby."

The lobby was hugely impressive, a welcoming space, with dark wood beams, intricately entwined panels, tropical-style furnishings, and decor inspired by organic textures, colors, and forms. Dramatic flower arrangements of anthurium, bird of paradise, red and orange ginger, protea, and handwoven ti leaves placed on tables and countertops added to the casual, yet opulent resort atmosphere.

Snapping countless photos, I wondered what the resort's guests' rooms looked like. I perused through one of the advertising brochures, which I slipped in my back pocket to keep as a remembrance of our visit. Amenities included a sailing school, apparel and souvenir shops, a movie theater, and a wide variety of water sports, along with several bars and restaurants for casual and fine dining.

From the diverse collection of eating establishments, Vince chose The Clubhouse Steak and Seafood Grill to make a dinner reservation for this evening. I was delighted and already envisioned the glorious sunset view from our outdoor table and anticipated taking a romantic stroll on the beach after the meal.

While I still had film left in my camera, I suggested walking to Biras Creek along a paved, meandering path lined with brightly colored, fragrant flowers, and a palm tree variety I had never seen before. The Traveler's Palm grows enormous paddle-shaped, banana tree-like leaves on long stalks in a distinctive fan pattern. I was amazed by this unique, tropical tree and assumed that creative landscapers shaped the elaborate fans.

The Bitter End's Quarter Deck Marina, with accommodations for several yachts, including those over 100 feet in length, was located halfway down the path. With many boats being refueled, serviced, or washed and polished until they gleamed, the state-of-the-art marina was a bustling place.

A provisioning store called the Emporium was well stocked with produce, locally caught fresh fish, a good selection of wine, and beer in addition to almost everything else anyone could need in a boating environment.

Winston's Bakery offered a variety of freshly baked goods. The intoxicating smell of cinnamon rolls baking lured us inside, where we found it difficult to choose. Eventually, we settled on buying naturally sweetened coconut macaroons and a moist, rich, loaf of banana bread to slice up for breakfast tomorrow morning.

Biras Creek was a meticulously maintained, tropical oasis with outstanding views of Gorda Sound. Unfortunately, the exclusive gated property prohibited onlookers from entering. With no other options, we turned back toward the Bitter End.

On our way down the path, I snuck into The Reeftique; a beach-style, apparel and souvenir shop near the marina. Vince looked at me with a Cheshire Cat grin on his face and followed me into the high-end establishment.

The faint, lovely fragrance of gardenias permeated throughout the attractive shop. Oh, I wanted to buy everything I saw; a sexy straw hat with an extra-large brim, a flattering, intricately hand-painted t-shirt, a white, lacy swimsuit cover-up, and a pair of stylish sandals decorated with tiny seashells. I was in absolute Caribbean fashion heaven!

Thank God, Vince kept me in check and helped me limit my buying spree to a bright pink t-shirt, a souvenir mug, a Bitter End logo beach bag for my mother, luxurious bars of plumeria-scented bath soaps for my grandmother, and a beautiful selection of picture postcards to send home. Vince bought a white, breezy, organic cotton, hooded pull-over shirt depicting the classic Bitter End logo and an embroidered D-ring belt to complement the shirt. I was thrilled with our purchases!

Although it was technically still morning, Vince proposed having an adult beverage and nibbles at The Crawl Pub; Virgin Gorda's first and oldest bar.

"The sun is over the yardarm somewhere," he teased, "let's have a drink and a bite." I loved when he used that ol' traditional nautical saying to mean that it s acceptable to have a drink before noon.

"Sure, I can eat and drink right now."

We seated ourselves at an outside table and ordered Caribbean-style nachos and a round of painkillers. Before long, we were indulged in food, drinks, and delightful conversation. While we noshed and admired our shopping acquisitions, we also made plans for spending the afternoon at a secluded beach where Vince promised that the marine life would be phenomenal.

It had been a wonderful morning with the added benefit of adequate exercise from the long walk to Biras Creek. Back on board, we threw a few essentials in a boat bag and moments later, we climbed in the dingy, and off we went. Vince navigated between Virgin Gorda and Saba Rock to a rocky beach below Biras Hill. The water was translucent and the natural collection of rocks, coral, and marine life made this an excellent area for snorkeling.

"This looks like a great place, we can go ashore over there," Vince said, as he powered us through the breakers, cut off the outboard motor, and jumped into the water, unexpectedly landing in a chest-deep hole. The beach appeared too rocky for me, but Vince noticed my fear immediately and pulled the dinghy into calmer water, a shallow area where I could step off with ease. With me safely standing firm on the beach, he wedged the dinghy anchor between two rocks on the shore and unloaded our belongings.

"Here are your fins and mask," he said, handing me the gear. "We ll see lots of fish, and the water is shallow so you should be able to walk in from the beach." Eagerly, Vince prepared to mix with the fish, while I digressed and decided to remain on the beach. "Aren't you going in?" he asked, with a look of concern, "See? I am standing here, it's honestly not deep," Vince added, trying to coax me to jump into the water.

"No, you go ahead, have a great time," I replied, waving him on. Feeling remorse and sad that I disappointed him again, I shouted out, teasingly, "Bring me a treasure…."

Vince snorkeled away, although he remained in the vicinity. I spread a beach towel on the sand and felt distraught for being so afraid. Once in a while, Vince raised his head, looked up, and waved in my direction.

Time passed rather slowly while I waited for Vince to return. I made several attempts to keep myself occupied by building sandcastles or climbing on rocks, but frankly, I was more at ease watching for his snorkel tube and yellow t-shirt. I liked knowing where he was.

Just as the afternoon heat became almost unbearable and I soaked up more than my share of sun, Vince returned, snorkeling directly toward me, with his arms extended, as if he was holding something precious. When he reached the beach, he sat in the shallows, lifted his snorkel mask and tube onto his forehead, and said, "I have a treasure for you!"

Almost bubbling with enthusiasm, he presented me proudly with a large, pink conch shell in nearly pristine condition.

"A conch shell," I cheered, "and it's gorgeous!"

I was beyond excited when Vince placed the shell in my hands. Approximately 10-inches in length, it was the largest shell I ever held. Although I was innately surprised at how heavy it was, I handled it as if it was a delicate object. The empty shell was a thick hunk of mollusk, with a horny exterior, formed into a spiral with a whitish-yellowish fan. The interior was shiny-pale to bright pink. Its cavity smelled like seaweed and, when I held the shell up to my ear, I heard the ocean's roar.

Natives use a conch shell as a wind instrument by holding it upright and blowing through the small hole at the bottom of the spiral. This was an incredible treasure!

Vince wrapped the shell in a beach towel and carefully placed it underneath the seat in the dinghy.

"I'll rinse it off with fresh water when we get back to the boat," he said, as he grabbed a bottle of water and tossed one to me.

Sitting comfortably on a rock facing the ocean, Vince spoke in detail about the underwater conch shell graveyard that he discovered while snorkeling over a grassy area not far from the beach. Since there were signs of past campfires in the vicinity, he guessed that locals harvested, barbecued, and consumed the conchs on the spot, then tossed the empty shells into the ocean. Most of the shells were severely discolored but the newer ones were still quite lovely. The shell he found for me was exceptional, and I was happy to take it home as a remembrance of our trip.

"Did you enjoy the beach while I was gone?" Vince asked. "Did you look for seashells? There must be some beauties hidden on this beach."

On no, why didn't I think of that? The thought of looking for shells never crossed my mind. How could I be so uninspired? I never looked for seashells before.

"Let's see what we can find," Vince suggested, offering his hand to lead me to the rocky barrier on top of the sandbar. With the eyes of a hawk, he began to search for shells while I wondered, why in God's name, we were not searching near the water. Why were we looking for seashells among the rocks, plastic bottles, broken glass, and other washed-up debris? I didn't like it up on the barrier. Nevertheless, I followed him and together we scoured the beach with intensity.

Suddenly, Vince picked up a lovely yellow shell with a circular design and white ridges.

"Look! Here's a beauty," he cried out, showing off nature's pretty little gem in the palm of his hand. "It's in perfect condition. Oh, and there's another one," he said as he stooped down to pick up a large snow-white cockle. Once Vince explained that the best place to look for shells was between the rocks, where they become trapped and wave action doesn't sweep them out to sea again, I scavenged closer behind him instead of wandering through the surf.

Before long, I picked up a few seashells of my own, first an olive-green periwinkle and then a conical-shaped violet one, streaked with shades of orange and brown. A large spiny shell with delicate edges and a pink exterior quickly became my favorite. Soon, I had a handful of lovely treasures of various shapes and sizes. Then, unexpectedly, Vince picked up a sparkly, translucent object.

"Look, I found a diamond," he said, dashing toward me, holding a jewel between his thumb and forefinger.

Oh, you're right, it looks like a real diamond," Upon closer inspection, it was merely a perfectly tumbled, piece of clear-colored sea-glass, rounded off and smooth, its sharp edges and slickness were worn to a frosted appearance. It was fun making up a story together, about the piece of glass originating from a bottle of an old treasure ship that wrecked in these waters a century ago. We pretended that it rolled and tumbled into the ocean until we found it. Our silliness made us chuckle.

That little jewel was the first of many sparkly pieces of sea-glass we collected along with a heap of pretty, little shells. Brown, green, and white glass was easy to find, although finding a cobalt blue or a ruby red piece made the hunt more challenging. I enjoyed this new activity wholeheartedly, and Vince was pleased-as-punch that I finally found a favorite pastime on this trip. We collected shells for most of the afternoon, it was nice to share a common interest.

All of a sudden, I noticed that Vince's back and shoulders appeared dangerously red and puffy. Alarmed and concerned about over-exposure to the sun, I suggested packing up and returning to the boat where we could comfortably escape below deck for the remainder of the day.

On the dinghy ride back, I positioned myself on the bow, feeling carefree, immersed in the beauty of Gorda Sound when I noticed an unusual activity near the shoreline of a long stretch of beach.

"Sweetheart, look over there," I shouted, pointing in the direction of a strange sighting directly before us. "Spotted fin-tips, bending in and out of the water near that beach. Do you see them?"

Cautiously, Vince steered us closer to the area I pointed to until we succinctly saw three, mature spotted eagle rays swiftly moving through the water simultaneously. It was an amazing sight, the rays appeared to be 10-feet in length with an enormous wingspan! What a wondrous thrill to watch them pass by, gracefully floating through the blue water. It was an exciting end to our adventuresome afternoon.

Back on board the boat, Vince secured the dinghy and stored our snorkel gear, while I bolted for the main salon, intent to glance in the mirror. The reflection was shocking! My skin appeared ashy and dark, and the backs of my hands were nearly black! "Vince, I look like the locals," I shouted. "Look at my hands!"

"Monkey paws! Your hands look like monkey paws," he teased, "you're an island girl with monkey paws!" Vince made me laugh.

"Oh my god, we are going to be in such pain tonight," I muttered to myself, carefully peeling off my clothes to take a shower. Careless and stupid, we spent too many hours unprotected in the sun today.

By the time we showered and dressed, we only had a short time remaining for a Happy Hour cocktail on deck before it was time to return ashore for our dinner reservation. This day flew by much too quickly.

So, once again, we boarded our trusty dinghy and kept our fingers crossed in the hopes of finding space to tie up at the already crowded dock. The Clubhouse Steak and Seafood Grill was a popular place to dine. Fortunately, Vince pushed his way through cautiously and claimed an accessible spot toward the end of the pier. The Bitter End looked especially romantic, with hundreds of pathways and garden lights, the entire resort was aglow in a soft and silky golden light.

Upon our arrival at The Clubhouse, a hostess welcomed us, acknowledged our reservation under our boat name, then addressed Vince as *Captain*; a classy, elegant touch, I thought. We followed her to the best possible waterfront table with a sensational view of the Sound.

The attractive dining room, with its dark woods and countless hanging burgees from yacht clubs around the world, made us feel as if we were 'living the dream', hobnobbing with international yachtsmen and boating enthusiasts. The impressive bar was constructed from the remains of *Ondine*; a historic wooden racing ship and winner of many of the world's most challenging ocean races spanning the 1960s.

Ondine s mainmast was handcrafted to form the grill s unique center post, located in the middle of the restaurant. When The Clubhouse opened in 1969, hungry boaters announced their presence at the wooden pier by sounding their air horns. If the establishment was open, the proprietor responded by a megaphone, allowing the guests to enter. Today, The Clubhouse blends West Indies' tropical style with nautical flair to create an upscale atmosphere in which to enjoy a drink and a typical Caribbean meal.

Served buffet style, tonight's menu selections included a spicy bouillabaisse, broiled lobster, crab cakes, grilled wahoo salad, locally caught fresh fish, and a classic burger, ending with a thick slice of Key Lime pie for dessert. We each chose the bouillabaisse and lobster, followed by a cup of freshly roasted artisan coffee and a shared piece of the pie. Every mouthful was a scrumptious treat and I considered this the most decadent meal of our trip.

Contently stuffed to the gills, we could barely move away from the table to pay our bill. To help digest our meal, we pondered taking a stroll along the path to Biras Creek to admire the rare exhibition of flowers that bloom exclusively at night. In particular, Jasmin, the moonflower, and a variety of cacti emit a subtle sweet perfume as they show off their blossoms after dark. However, just as we were about to leave the restaurant and head to the path, a live band began to play on the Bitter End s private beach.

"Oh Honey," I pleaded, "let's stay and listen to the band, I love steel drum music. Let's stay for one more drink."

"You talked me into it," Vince replied. As one of the first couples to enter the performance area, we quickly claimed two oversized lounge chairs ideal for cuddling near the surf with a cocktail. As if on cue, a waiter appeared and asked for our drink order.

"Ahhhh, this is romantic," I sighed, stretched out on the lounge chair.

"Come join me underneath this heavenly blanket of stars," I said, taunting Vince. He bent down for a kiss, pulled up a chair, leaned back, and folded his hands behind his head. The band began to play a melancholy tune and we let our thoughts drift away with the music.

"This is excellent," Vince said, "what a wonderful way to end a wonderful day."

Later that evening, when we finally crawled into our berth, it was difficult to fall asleep. I lay awake for hours reminiscing about the day s events. I could barely recall a happier time.

After a restful night's sleep, I opened my eyes to find Vince lying next to me, staring at me as if he had been waiting for me to wake up.

"Good morning, beautiful," he said sweetly, sitting upright. "Did you sleep well?"

Initiating a hug from my captain, I yawned, stretched a bit, and wrapped my arms around his neck, "Like a rock!" I replied coyly, "I love it here and I never want to leave the Bitter End."

"Good, because there is more I want to show you here," Vince replied "Let's have breakfast on board, then later this afternoon I will take you to another secluded beach," he continued with a boyish gleam in his eyes, "one where we can take a picnic and go skinny-dipping."

Our plan for the day sounded exciting and I looked forward to exploring a different beach.

When we stepped on deck, Vince saw the harbormaster's launch boat heading our way, busily collecting garbage and overnight fees from the other yachts in the harbor. He slipped back into the salon and reappeared with his wallet and three hefty bags of garbage. I was thrilled to hand off the smelly trash for such a nominal fee!

A short while later, a group of locals in a small lightweight boat with a sputtering outboard motor, stopped by offering a selection of charming handmade arts and handicraft items for sale. Similar vessels followed, selling mangoes, pineapples, and coconuts or locally harvested mussels and clams shucked on the spot presented on paper plates with diced onions, a lemon wedge, and a plastic fork for spontaneous consumption. What a splendid way to support the local economy, and although I already planned a light breakfast for us, I happily purchased more food from this parade of floating merchants.

Not following a schedule today was blissful. After enjoying some of the delicious banana bread from Winston's Bakery, food items from the floating market, and plenty of good, hot coffee, we lallygagged on board, each in our own way.

Comfortably positioned on a beach towel draped across the foredeck, I applied a generous layer of sunblock on all exposed areas of my body and scribbled copious notes in my journal. Vince putzed around with boat equipment, studied the Cruising Guide, and eventually settled down in the cockpit with a book to read. We were engrossed in life at its best, our thoughts a million miles from work, commitments, and our normal existence back home.

Eventually, it was time to get ready for our afternoon excursion. Spellbound about skinny-dipping for the first time, I looked forward to hiding away again on a secret beach with Vince and becoming "one" with nature. I prepared a packable lunch, grabbed our beach towels and sunscreen lotion, and feeling a bit willful, deliberately left my swimsuit behind!

In the dinghy, Vince steered us north toward Prickly Pear Island and the entrance to Gorda Sound, until we were well out of the boating community's public eye. There, he slowed the motor down to a hum and hugged the shoreline until we came to a pristine strip of beach where the water was shallow and crystal clear.   What do you think of this private little spot," Vince asked, "isn't it perfect?"

"Yes, it's perfect," I responded, "but all the boats entering the Sound can see us."

"Don't worry, the reef will keep them at a good distance. Unless they're specifically looking at us with binoculars, they won't see us swimming naked."

That was good enough for me, this beach was ideal!

After tying the dingy line to a shrub and transferring our boat bags to a flat rock on the beach, Vince spread out his arms and said, "Today, *this* is our world."

He stripped off his clothes, I did the same and we entered the water without wearing a stitch of clothing, engulfed in a joyful, slightly naughty feeling of freedom. Like children we played together, naked as jaybirds splashing, shrieking, laughing, running through the waves, kicking up the white, powdery sand beneath our feet. We had a blast, we had a sheer and utter blast!

Much too soon, however, Vince put on his snorkel gear and said that he was going to frolic with the fish in deeper water. Oh, I was crestfallen. I wasn't ready to separate, but I understood his desire to go. I watched as he snorkeled toward the reef, wishing that we were still playing together in the surf. Unfortunately, like every time before, my fear and lack of self-confidence won over and I stayed on the beach.

This time, while Vince snorkeled, I searched for seashells and sea glass. Lost in my quest to find the most beautiful exotic shell, the offensive, familiar sound of an outboard motor disturbed my peace and solitude as an overloaded dinghy with six giddy adults approached our tiny secluded beach. Confident that the intruders would surely realize how much we desired privacy, I was shocked and appalled when it appeared as if they planned to invade our space!

To cover up my naked body, I scampered to find my sarong and frantically signaled for Vince to stay in the water. I hoped that he could see me as I emphatically signaled and pointed to the intruder's dinghy. With all the secluded beaches in the area, why would this inconsiderate bunch of tourists choose our tiny spit of sand as their playground?

Thank God, Vince became quickly aware of the invasion, ran up the beach while removing his snorkel gear, and randomly spread out our towels on the small space of sand to occupy as much area as possible. Angrily, he glared at the unwelcome guests, who understood Vince's intention. One by one, they stepped back into their dinghy and submissively moved on.

"What a great idea, spreading out on the beach was a good move," I said as I walked over to meet Vince, ready to give him a hug, "but I can't believe you came out of the water butt naked!"

"Ughhh," he replied, with a hand gesture to signify their irrelevance, "We'll never see those people again. Now that we have our beach back, let's have lunch!"

My hero! Vince saved the day. Thrilled to be alone again, I assembled our picnic-style lunch. To keep the pineapple chunks chilled, I packed them in a make-do lunchbox on top of some ice cubes which I kept contained in a zipped plastic bag.

Hoping that Vince would not miss the mustard and mayo that we finished off days ago, I loaded up the partially prepared ham sandwiches with Swiss cheese, thinly sliced cucumber, red onion, and lots of iceberg lettuce which I packed separately to keep the bread from getting soggy and the lettuce from wilting. A handful of chips on the side and ice-cold bottled beers to wash it all down, completed our lunch.

Under a sea grape tree, we found a bit of shade and a flat-topped rock served as an impromptu buffet table. "Cheers," I said in a salute to Vince as I presented him with a beer, "you are my hero," I added with a clink of our bottlenecks.

"Here's to no more rude interruptions for the rest of the day," Vince concurred, as he raised his bottle, took a sip of his beer, and helped himself to a sandwich.

Throughout lunch, Vince described the plethora of tropical fish he encountered while snorkeling near the reef; a school of squid fluttered in a graceful line-dance as if suspended in midair, a couple of striped black and yellow angelfish swam in unison around the rocks, and a bold blue and green parrotfish grazed on nutrient-rich seaweed and algae.

Mesmerized by their changing color, he followed a large school of blue tang; that changed from vibrant blue to brilliant black when they swam in the opposite direction. Intently I listened, as Vince spoke with whole-hearted passion, drawing me into his experience, and tempting me to join him on his next underwater adventure.

One day, I will go with him to see the stag horn coral that has been building enormous atolls in this region for over 5,000 years. One day, I will see the deep purple sea fans that wave in the currents, while fish swim among them. One day I will go with him and we will marvel at all the exotic fish together.

Remaining on our private slice of heavenly paradise until we were brown as coconuts and our skin was dried and dusted with sea salt was a dream. Eventually though, Vince proposed returning to *Poetry*. "Hon, we should head back, we are at the mercy of the sun, if it sets any lower, it will be difficult to navigate the dinghy around the coral heads."

I concurred but hated to pack up our belongings to leave our beautiful, secret beach. I filled the empty stackable potato chip container with my newly found collection of delicate seashells, layering paper napkins between them.

"Hey, I almost forgot," Vince cried out enthusiastically, as he held two large shells in the palm of his hand, "look what I found near the reef. I had to dive for these beauties. They'll clean up nicely and a drop of olive oil will bring out their colors."

"Oh, they are gorgeous!" I responded, admiring his treasures before gingerly placing them between our beach towels.

All packed up and ready to go, Vince led the dinghy away from the sandbar, lowered the motor, and pulled the starter cord. Holding on to the anchor line, I sat on the bow, shielding my face from the saltwater splashes that burned my eyes and cheeks. Before long, *Poetry* came into view and our pristine slice of heavenly paradise was in the far and faded distance behind us.

Eager to take a nice, freshwater shower, I stepped up on the transom and darted straight to our cabin. Slowly, ever so carefully, I peeled my bathing suit from my body and tossed it on the bathroom floor. When I caught a glimpse of my reflection in the mirror, I nearly laughed out loud! Seeing my somewhat painful, reddish-brown tan lines, sandy wet hair plastered to my head in unruly strands, and the grainy layer of salt which covered me from head to toe had me in stitches. How did I manage to look like such a mess when Vince looked so ruggedly handsome? He was born to be in this environment.

Ahhhh, the freshwater felt grand as it washed away the thick salt and revived my sun-drenched body in a refreshingly tepid, luxurious spray. Admittedly, I felt no guilt in taking the longest shower of our trip, washing and conditioning my hair, while stomping my bathing suit clean on the shower floor with my feet.

By the time we were refreshed, re-energized, and wearing comfortable, loose clothing, it was time for Happy Hour. While Vince prepared the usual pitcher of Gin and Tonic, I fixed a few fuss-free appetizers.

"Meet you on the foredeck," Vince called out, as he moved up the companionway, pitcher, and cocktail glasses in hand. The evening would bring another gorgeous sunset, I thought to myself, one that will transition from gold to orange and that unbelievable shade of lavender. I did not want to miss a single sunset in this part of the world.

Carrying a platter of finger-food, dressed in my ankle-length orchid and white batik sarong, with my long, dark hair blowing slightly in the breeze, I approached Vince on the foredeck. He took my breath away, wearing his new breezy, white Bitter End pull-over shirt, unbuttoned to mid-chest, untucked over khaki cargo-style shorts, he looked extremely sexy. Standing at the bow with the sun setting behind him, Vince resembled a male model posing for a Caribbean sailing magazine.

He beat me to a compliment. "Good evening, Island Princess," Vince said, as he walked over to assist me with the food. "You look beautiful."

"Good evening, handsome," I replied, "so do you."

Our last evening at the Bitter End was a bit melancholy, although the most touristy and lavish of the harbors we visited, it was my all-time favorite by a mile!

The sunset was a showstopper. Cuddled up in our favorite position against the mast, we whiled away the hours of drinking, snacking, and reflecting on the places we'd been. We laughed again at Foxy's joke about the black island dog, guessed at how many painkillers we polished off on this trip, relived Vince's barracuda encounter at The Bight, remembered our joy when we found our first piece of sea-glass and recalled the fantastic local cuisine we consumed in every harbor.

A few hours later, all traces of the glorious sunset had been replaced by the light of a pale yellow moon shimmering in the ocean's inky blackness. For a split second, the evening's magical ambiance enticed me to invite Vince for a moonlight swim. A part of me yearned to be impulsive and romantic, but I was well aware that swimming at night was unwise. One day, however, I vowed to act on a whim!

Before we fell asleep, we lay embraced in each other's arms, gazing at the stars through the open hatch, while Vince described our next destination.

"In the morning, we'll head for Cooper Island," Vince said, "it's a gem of a picturesque stopover. We'll anchor at Manchineel Bay on the leeward (*wind-protected*) side of the island. There is an excellent restaurant, a beach club, and a small shop with a nice selection of t-shirts and souvenirs," he continued, attempting to build my intrigue. "And there are cocktail tables set up in the sea. What better way to enjoy a painkiller or a local beer?" With happy anticipation, I looked forward to visiting this quintessential BVI anchorage.

Suddenly, I realized that there were only three nights of our sailing adventure remaining and a subtle sense of sadness came over me as I drifted off to sleep.

Cooper Island
Manchineel Bay

When we stood on the companionway in the morning and poked our heads through the hatch like usual, a glorious rainbow arced over the Bitter End in a stunning kaleidoscope of color.

"Oh my gosh, Vince look at the spectacular rainbow, it's a parting gift from God. He knows that we are leaving today," I whispered. I grabbed my camera from the nav station and jumped up on deck to capture this magical morning in a photograph. A bit lackadaisical, Vince followed behind.

"For a minute, I thought I heard it rain last night," he muttered as he climbed up the companionway, "oh, *that's* why we have such a beautiful morning." As we admired Mother Nature's phenomenon that occurs when light meets water, the rainbow appeared to become more brilliant.

"It's a sailor's superstition that when you see a rainbow in the morning, the storm is behind us, so it should be a beautiful day for sailing," Vince said. I did not react to Vince's comment. Instead, I grumbled in silence, and thought; there's that word again... *sailing!* Were we going to sail to Cooper Island? I crossed my fingers and hoped that we wouldn't.

Quiet and sulky, I assembled a minimal breakfast while Vince prepared *Poetry* for our departure. By the time the coffee was perked, he had slacked the dinghy line for travel, positioned the boat hook for easy release of the mooring buoy, and stowed the seat cushions below deck. My stomach was beginning to feel that familiar nervous twinge I despised, however, I continued to set the table and hoped that Vince did not notice my mounting anxiety.

"Hon, we won't bother with the sails today. It is a short trip from here to Cooper Island. We'll take it easy and let Auto get us there," Vince said, pondering as he took a sip of his coffee, "it's only seventeen nautical miles," he added. I was not sure of the difference between a nautical mile and any other mile, but I was elated that we were not going to be sailing. Only a few days of our vacation remained and I hoped that we would not sail during any of them.

By mid-morning, we were on our way to Cooper Island's Manchineel Bay. The weather was humid, it felt good to be on deck and have the wind in my hair. I observed a few sailboats traveling in our direction and hoped they would not go to the same harbor. After spending a few days at the touristy Bitter End, I preferred being in a less populated anchorage tonight.

We left Gorda Sound and motored west toward The Dogs, then south into the Sir Francis Drake Channel. We passed Spanish Town on the port as we headed toward Virgin Gorda's southern tip. The shore looked different there.

Unlike the other shorelines we visited, huge granite boulders seemed to rise out of the ground and tumble into the ocean. We were approaching The Baths; a geological natural wonder of giant boulders that form crystal-clear, sheltered pools, tunnels, and grottos in which to snorkel, swim or wade through. Although it was early morning, several boats were already anchored in the area but Vince insisted that this was a BVI tourist highlight that I simply *must* see.

Oh no, I thought, he's going to drop an anchor again, a tedious process I had not missed these last two days. However, all went smoothly and quickly, and before I realized it, Vince reminded me to wear my reef shoes as he stood ready to help me board the dinghy for our short drive to the beach.

The closer we came to shore, the more I was in awe of the boulders. Is there a word that exceeds 'colossal'? According to the Cruising Guide, the boulders were of magma origin, occurring over fifty-million years ago. Over the geological ages, the molten rock became covered with hard, crystalline layers. Weathering rounded the corners and shaped the boulders into what they are today. A few of the largest exceed 40-feet in diameter. I had never seen anything like it!

Although there were already a few rubber inflatables on the small strip of beach, Vince scoped out an open spot for us to land and tie up to a shrub on shore. I followed him to a designated path leading between the boulders. "This is unbelievable, I have never seen rocks this size anywhere!" I declared.

"Let me take your picture," Vince said, "stand in that light-filled pool between those two massive boulders over there. It's called the Cathedral Room, the most photographed spot in The Baths."

Like a cheeky tourist, I posed for the picture and asked a passerby to take one of us together. It was easy to understand why this dramatic, natural wonder was one of the BVI's supreme attractions.

We climbed through the grottos and grabbed onto the rope handrails that lined the wooden steps through the tight crevices until we reached Devil's Bay; a pristine, white sandy beach at the end of the path with a 360-degree view of the BVI. It seemed unfitting to find an impromptu t-shirt stand in this natural setting, however, I couldn't resist taking a look and bought one depicting cartoon-like, dancing, Reggae Band characters, with typical island hairstyles.

Just as we were about to head back to the dingy, I noticed that everyone on the beach seemed to be gazing in the same direction, their attention sharply focused on a classic, wooden sailing ship in the distance. Vince guessed the magnificent, two-masted ship to be 70-feet in length. Its glistening white hull appeared to be gliding on the water as a calm wind filled its billowing spinnaker, pushing the ship gently forward.

With the head sheet tied to the mast and the clew sheets tied together, the bright blue spinnaker formed a trapeze for two bronzed, blond-haired, topless bathing beauties who swung gracefully back and forth. Tourists' cameras clicked excitedly as we all tried to capture the breathtaking theatrical sight before the wind changed the shape of the giant sail.

"They may be filming a documentary," Vince commented. "Do you see a helicopter overhead? Maybe they are shooting videos for a travel magazine, or maybe they are just having a good time."

We watched until the topless beauties on the trapeze ceased to swing, the crew released the spinnaker, hauled it on deck and the crowd dispersed.

"That was a beautiful sight!" I said, "I'm glad we were here to see it."

The return hike between the boulders to the small beach seemed easier. We reached our faithful dinghy just as a large group of tourists disembarked a ferry boat from Tortola. Thank God, we left before the crowds arrived.

By early noon, we approached Cooper Island, turned left to enter the harbor, and located a suitable spot to anchor for the night. The crescent-shaped beach that formed Manchineel Bay, fringed with palm trees, was indeed picturesque. This anchorage was the smallest one we visited, however, I found it enchanting. The ramshackle t-shirt shop adjacent to a hammock strung between two palm trees immediately caught my interest and the West Indies-style restaurant seemed as if it would be a nice place to have dinner tonight.

Once *Poetry* was anchored properly for the duration of our stay, Vince described our new surroundings. "The water here is very clear. We can snorkel right from the boat to the shore. An octopus lives in the coral reef to the right of the dinghy dock and there are plenty of colorful fish; angelfish, clownfish, parrotfish, schools of blue tang, and bright yellow skipjacks. Oh, and often a family of sea turtles swim around the boats here."

It sounded wonderfully exciting, but to avoid an invitation from Vince to go snorkeling, my response lacked spirit. "Gosh, it's beautiful here, sweetheart. Would you like some lunch? We still have enough food on board for a healthy meal or two."

"That sounds good! Right now, I'd like a beer, and tonight, we'll have dinner on shore."

Vince pre-warned me that there were no onshore dining options at our last anchorage and I was acutely aware that there were only 2 ½ days of our vacation remaining. I planned our food consumption on board accordingly.

After taking a quick inventory, I tossed together a creative salad with two oranges, a cucumber, some celery, green onion, various seasonings, olive oil, and lime juice. I also prepared a couple of tasty, open-faced sandwiches from the leftover slices of slightly stale bread which I toasted in a skillet with a lick of butter to bring back the freshness. I topped each slice with cheese, tomato, salt, pepper, and a drop or two of chili oil.

We ate lunch in the cockpit and as the wind turned *Poetry*'s bow toward the shore, we had an excellent view of the beach. In contrast with the glitzy Bitter End, Cooper Island was a true tropical oasis. Without the mega-yachts or exclusive resort-style accommodations, this was the tranquil, serene, more natural style of the Caribbean I preferred.

"Will you join me for a snorkel after lunch?" Vince asked, almost hesitantly, as if he knew my answer.

"Tomorrow is our last day, Honey. Maybe I'll join you tomorrow," I replied.

Vince didn't say a word.

After savoring lunch together, Vince changed from his shorts and t-shirt into swim trunks, I handed him his snorkel gear and sent him off with a kiss before he slid into the blue yonder while I stayed on deck. Since our boat position was near the shore, if Vince snorkeled to the beach, I would still be able to see him from the bow. As a matter of fact, due to the bay's small scale, I would be able to see him where ever he snorkeled. I loved this anchorage, I felt self-assured here.

Vince stayed out longer than usual, but I was not worried, I knew he was in the vicinity. While he chased after tropical fish, I kept an occasional eye out for him, wrote in my journal, did a few housekeeping chores, took a nap, planned our Happy Hour menu, and prepared some nibbles. In my solitude, I realized that I felt more at ease here, maybe I've adapted to this sailing way of life, or maybe I felt a connection to the low-key vibe in Manchineel Bay.

When I finally heard the blows from Vince's snorkel tube, I rushed to the stern to meet him.

"Hi Honey, welcome back, I've missed you," I shouted when Vince came within earshot. "Did you bring me anything?"

"No, not this time, but the water is outstanding," Vince replied. "Did you see the turtles? There are several in the area. I swam with a couple of giant rays. I followed them around the boats, it was incredible!"

Vince climbed on board, excited and eager to share his experience. While he stowed his gear and dried himself off, I offered him a beer.

"Our Happy Hour snacks are ready for the sunset, and with only two other boats in the bay, the restaurant shouldn't be crowded tonight," I said, to assure Vince that there was no rush to go ashore. "You can relax and take a nap before we head in."

Vince took a quick shower and reappeared on deck, looking sexy as ever, dressed in shorts and his Bitter End pullover shirt. That breezy, lightweight shirt had become his favorite. As usual, when it was my turn to shower, I rinsed a few clothes on the shower floor and handed them to Vince through the open hatch. He pinned them to the lifelines at the bow so that the clothes could dry by morning.

With our snacks and drinks within easy reach, we took our regular positions at the mast to watch the sunset over Tortola. Happy to be together again, I noticed a slight pang of regret beginning to penetrate my joy. I didn't want our trip to end.

The Cooper Island Beach Club Hotel and Restaurant was a low-key, laid-back establishment without electricity or hot running water. Overnight guests stayed in charming, rustic cottages with basic furniture, a washbowl, a jug filled with clean, fresh water, a flashlight, and a shared outdoor shower stall.

To add to the rustic, yet enchanting ambiance, kerosene lamps illuminated the restaurant in the evening, and meals prepared on a charcoal grill and a camp stove were served by candlelight. The limited menu included conch fritters, Cornish pasties packed with seasoned meat and vegetables, locally caught grilled lobster and grouper, painkillers, pina coladas, and beer.

As our dinner entrée, we both chose the grouper and shared an order of delicious, spicy conch fritters with a couple of ice-cold local beers while we sat in comfy lounge chairs on the beach, waiting for our dinner to arrive. Vince pointed out the unassuming bar stands set up in the shoal. Although they were just wooden platforms on a stake dug into the sand, they provided a place to set an elbow, a drink, and a bite for a guest who stood at them in knee-high water during low tide. I found the bar stands delightfully quaint, a photo opportunity not to be missed tomorrow.

The grouper was brought to our table, hot off the grill, served with a charred half lemon, a generous scoop of potato salad, and coleslaw. I could not wait to dig in! What is it about being outdoors that makes one so hungry?

Two couples from another boat in the harbor entered the restaurant. They also appeared to be guests on a chartered bareboat. Vince acknowledged their presence with a head nod greeting, and even though a response from the newcomers was received, no conversation sparked between us. In the fellow bareboaters' defense, Vince was quick to explain that this was typical behavior. The reason they seek out these out-of-the-way, remote places in the world is to minimize socializing. I understood and respected the sentiment.

It was nearly midnight by the time we returned to *Poetry*. However, Vince offered a rum and ice nightcap before we went to bed and of course, I did not decline. Once again, with our feet in the water, we sat on the transom and sipped our drinks by the light of our mast-star, the other two mast lights in the bay, and the billions of stars in the sky.

"Oh, wait a sec," Vince said, without warning. "I want to show you something." He ducked below deck and re-emerged with a flashlight in his hands. "Let's see what's down there," he added. I did not know what he meant. He turned the flashlight on and aimed the beam directly at our feet. Suddenly, it looked like a small school of milky-white, translucent-like fish came swimming toward my toes.

"Wow!" I said, swiftly yanking my feet out of the water, "What are they? Do they bite?"

"No," Vince replied in a comforting voice, "they are harmless. They are attracted to the light. When I am snorkeling, I often see huge schools of these tiny fish. Dolphins, sailfish, and tuna feed on them. It's interesting to see what kind of fish are attracted to the light in the dark."

"Oh," I said in a calmer tone of voice, "I can't believe how clear the water is, even at night."

"Maybe a turtle or a ray will come over to say hello."

No turtle or ray came, but we enjoyed shining the light in the water, while we sipped our rum and made up silly stories about creatures that might surface from the deep. Before we turned in for the night, Vince had one more idea up his sleeve. "Come up to the bow. There's something else I want to show you," he said.

We left the flashlight in the cockpit and walked up to the bow. There, Vince hunkered down to grab a piece of the anchor line, which he shook up and down in the water. The splashes made glowing sparks in the moonlight. "Look," Vince said, "do you see those sparks? It's phosphorescence."

As I looked at the spot where the anchor line entered the water, I was treated to a continual display of electric sparks of light; the result of the bio-luminescence of organisms in the surface layers of the sea. The luminescence is emitted by irritation, such as the movement in the water caused by the vibration of the shaken anchor line. "It's a nighttime phenomenon, isn't it beautiful?" Vince asked.

"Yes, Honey, it's beautiful. It's magical," I replied.

Without any specific plans at all, I woke up looking forward to spending the entire day at Manchineel Bay. This was our last day of leisure and I planned to enjoy it fully. Tomorrow, we would move to Little Harbor for our last night at anchor. There were no amenities onshore. From Little Harbor, it was a straight shot to Nanny Cay where *Poetry* was due back at the marina by 11 AM. Ughhhh! I forced myself not to think about it now.

I used our last two oranges for breakfast, and toasted two English muffins to serve with strawberry jam and sliced cheese. We still had plenty of coffee, so I brewed a full fresh pot. To my delight, I discovered a can of orange juice and a can of vegetable-tomato juice in the bottom of the icebox. Perfect! This morning's meal was complete. I crawled into our cabin and kissed my captain awake.

"Morning, Honey," I said, "wake up, we are in paradise."

"Morning," Vince responded, a bit wearied. "Have you seen the turtles yet?"

"Yes, they are waiting for you. Breakfast is ready, I'll meet you on deck."

It was a bright, sunny morning, without a cloud in the sky. The bay was tranquil, the water crystal clear and wonderfully cooling, inviting willing bathers to go for a swim.

"What do you want to do today, Honey? Are you going for one last swim with the turtles and rays?" I asked, while we consumed our paltry breakfast.

"That depends…what are you going to do?" he answered my question with a question.

"I am going to sit on the beach, under a palm tree," I said, pointing to a comfy lounge chair on the beach, perfectly positioned under a palm tree, "and I would like to buy a Cooper Island t-shirt from the shack with the hammock," I added as an afterthought.

"OK, that can be arranged," Vince replied, "the water clarity is best in the morning, so I'm going for a snorkel at Cistern Point, on the west side of the bay. You'll be able to see me from the beach. I'll join you in the afternoon. We'll have lunch under the palm tree."

I filled a bag with my journal, suntan lotion, the Cruising Guide, and two large bottles of water. Vince dropped me off at the dinghy dock and wished me a happy morning. I became a little nervous when I realized that I was on my own until he returned. There was no way to contact him should there be a reason.

Timidly, I spread out my towel on the lounge chair, took off my flip-flops, and adjusted the back of the chair until I found a comfortable position. Feeling self-conscious and strangely out of place, I looked around, sat down, and leaned back in my chair. With no one to talk to, I fumbled with my bag, my sunglasses, my bottle of water…I did not know what to do. Where was Vince?

Eventually, my nerves settled down and I peered out at Manchineel Bay and the Sir Francis Drake Channel toward Tortola. The view was awesome! I didn't open my journal to write or looked at the Cruising Guide. For over an hour, I just gazed at God's incredible landscape until an unfamiliar sensation tugged at my heart. It was a revelation, a sudden realization that I loved being here, alone on Cooper Island. Waiting for Vince to return from his snorkel adventure, I felt completely at ease.

I sauntered over to one of the bar-stands set up in the breakers and imagined enjoying a drink while standing in the shallow water. Unexpectedly, a waiter from the Cooper Island Beach Club approached me with a menu. Since I occupied one of their lounge chairs, I ordered a glass of mineral water with a slice of orange.

I watched him return to the bar when two island fishermen in an aluminum boat with a loud outboard motor pulled up to the dock. While the waiter walked out to meet them, the men climbed out of the boat carrying the largest live lobster I had ever seen. Holding the lobster by its front antennae at arm's length, its tail reached the dock! I wondered what the men were saying and tried to photograph the moment, but the distance between us was too great. A few minutes later, the fisherman and their lobster got back into their boat and headed out to the channel.

Curious to know what happened, I struck up a conversation with the waiter when he returned with my drink.

"Thank you," I said, taking the drink from his tray. "That was the largest lobster I have ever seen. You sure grow them big here in the BVI," I continued, hoping that the waiter would elaborate.

"That was a 5-pound lobster, caught this morning, off the coast of Ginger Island. They hoped to sell it to me for the restaurant."

"Oh, but why didn't you buy it? Was it too expensive?"

"No, a lobster that big, is tough and dry," the waiter explained in more detail. "But we do buy most of our lobsters from the local fishermen. They sell the freshest fish at the best price. Enjoy your drink, Miss."

How interesting, I thought…when it comes to lobsters, I always assumed *that bigger was better*.

Just as I began to miss Vince's company, I saw his yellow t-shirt, dark arms, and the blue top of his snorkel tube approaching the beach. I couldn't wait to hear about his adventure.

I hurried to the sandbar to meet him. "Hi, Honey," I shouted, "did you bring me anything?" I asked the usual question.

Vince reached the shallows, turned his body around, sat in the sand, and pulled off his swim fins. Soon as he could steady himself, he motioned for me to come closer.

"Yes, I brought you a treasure," he said as he held out his fist and opened his hand to reveal a West Indian top; a seashell in beautiful condition. Although it is the most common shell found in the BVI, this one was exceptional with a silvery-gray mother-of-pearl interior and a greenish-black and pearl-white exterior.

"It's beautiful! Thank you, I love it. Are you staying on the beach for a while?" I asked as I pulled another beach chair next to mine.

"Yes, I am hungry. Let's order lunch."

Without further thought, we ordered a couple of cheeseburgers, waffle fries, and two tall glasses of ice-cold beers.

While we waited for our food to arrive, Vince talked about his exciting morning. Snorkeling near Cistern Point, he saw hordes of reef fish, crabs, and a barracuda. Closer to the shore, he saw a herd of tiny sea horses, but watching an octopus swim until it hid under a coral reef was the highlight. Tucked deep inside a crevice, he saw a large spiny lobster and a flat-bodied peacock flounder swimming on its side along the bottom caught him by surprise. Listening to Vince describe each exotic fish encounter was captivating and I was thrilled to know that his last snorkel adventure was such a big success.

I told him about the island fishermen with the giant lobster and my sudden revelation; the clear realization that I loved these islands and somehow felt a connection to them. Nothing made Vince happier.

We were famished by the time lunch arrived. Vince dove into his meal with both hands. The cheeseburgers were truly the best of the trip and the waffle fries were hot, crispy, and well-seasoned. I enjoyed sitting together under the palm tree, having lunch, and sharing how we spent the morning on our own.

With our second beers in hand, we walked to the Sea Grape Boutique; a native woman's rickety home in which she offered a good selection of colorful t-shirts for sale, along with a few hand-crocheted beach bags, a meager offering of locally found seashells, and some picture postcards that looked like they had been there a while. After looking at every t-shirt in my size, I selected an orange, stonewashed, sleeveless tank top, tastefully decorated with two hand-painted rowboats, marked Cooper Island, BVI. The casual style and bright color enhanced my dark Caribbean tan.

We spent the rest of the day on the beach, sitting under the palm tree, playing in the surf, and walking far out into the bay until the sandy bottom turned rocky. We didn't return to *Poetry* until it was time to shower and prepare for our Happy Hour ritual.

Manchineel Bay is an excellent place to watch the sunset. Locals and tourists scope out the best spot to watch the dramatic transformation down the Sir Francis Drake Channel. Vince stood at the mast with an open bottle of wine and two glasses, waiting for me to join him. Since our galley cupboards were now almost empty, my creative but meager, finger-food snacks were limited to carrot and cucumber sticks with salsa for dipping, mixed nuts, peanut butter-filled celery sticks, and a few slices of salami. The evening was not about the hors d'oeuvres, it was about the romantic sunset that was about to unfold.

Vince poured the wine and began to make a toast when I interrupted, and asked if I could do the honors.

"Here's to you, my love," I said, as I touched my glass to his. "Thank you for bringing me to Manchineel Bay, this anchorage is my favorite."

"Cheers, Hon. You're welcome, but I thought the Bitter End was your favorite," Vince teased.

"I prefer Cooper Island. I adore the peaceful, natural setting," I replied. "I feel a connection here."

"Well, then, maybe you'll let me bring you back here."

After watching the sunset crescendo and fade to darkness, we boarded the dinghy for our last meal on shore. Due to a Sail Caribbean tour group that arrived earlier, the restaurant was more attended this evening.

The same waiter who served our lunch greeted us and showed us to a table.

"We'll have *the usual*," Vince teased.

To our surprise, the waiter responded accordingly; "Two cheeseburgers, cooked medium rare, with waffle fries on the side and two tall, ice-cold beers. Will that be all?" I was impressed that he remembered our order.

The burgers were even better than the ones we had for lunch, another reason why I loved this anchorage; it had the best burgers and fries in paradise!

After the tour group departed, Vince and I found it difficult to leave, so we lingered on the beach with an after-dinner cocktail. I wanted to hold on to the calming sound of the tide as it reached the shore and the way the moonlight looked as it shimmered on the surface of the ocean, turning it a cobalt blue. Manchineel Bay touched my heart, and somehow, also transformed my soul.

Peter Island
Little Harbor

I left my heart in Manchineel Bay…although I changed the words when the familiar tune of *I Left My Heart In San Francisco* played in my head from the moment I opened my eyes this morning, the sentiment was the same. Eager to arrive at Little Harbor, a small anchorage with limited boat space, Vince suggested getting an early start.

Therefore, wearing only our smiles, we left Cooper Island without having breakfast. Watching Vince raise the anchor in preparation for our departure to Peter Island was melancholic, and I knew what it felt like to leave a part of me on the island. Soon, the sweeping arc of the beach I had fallen in love with grew small in the distance behind us.

Before long, Salt Island came into view on port. Once known for its three ponds where salt was harvested, Salt Island is now famous for the shipwreck that lies just off its west coast. In 1867, the 310-foot RMS Rhone sank in a storm while carrying mail and passengers from Great Britain. Now covered in bright yellow and orange coral, the sunken ship is home to a huge variety of sea creatures and a well-loved site for diving enthusiasts.

By 11 o'clock, Vince made our approach into charming Little Harbor on the north coast of Peter Island; the second island in the chain lining the southern side of the Sir Francis Drake Channel. It seemed like a serene spot for us to spend our last night on board and to prepare *Poetry* for her return to the marina in the morning.

Happy to see that we were the only boat in the region, Vince proceeded to the end of the harbor, noted for the best anchoring in a sandy bottom, with good holding. A secluded area toward the shore seemed to be ideal. Immediately upon our arrival, I spotted two turtles as they poked their little heads up, took a breath, looked around, and continued swimming without making a sound. I wished they would swim closer to the boat.

Soon as *Poetry* was moored correctly, we sprang into action. Vince focused on cleaning and organizing boat equipment, scrubbing the deck and cockpit, while I cleaned the galley, cabins, and heads, before partially packing our bags.

First, I took a careful inventory of the provisions remaining on board, dividing the lot into the number of meals we still had left to eat on board. Vince was already hard at work, while I stuffed dirty bed linens and towels into pillowcases before stowing them in one of the forward berths. It is how the Tortola Yacht Club preferred to have those items returned.

Vince scrubbed the deck and the Bimini top, rinsing them off with bucketloads of seawater. I cleaned the stove (Thank God, we never used the oven. I hate cleaning ovens!) and emptied the refrigerator and freezer so that Vince could drain them later. How could there be so much to clean, stow, and toss after living on a boat for less than two weeks?

When we were hungry, I divided a partial head of iceberg lettuce into two portions, added sliced cucumber, a drained can of whole kernel corn, a diced green pepper, and a large can of tuna fish. After seasoning the ingredients well, I tossed the mixture in a drizzle of olive oil and a squeeze of lime juice. The result was a tasty salad that I served with mixed nuts and the last of our potato chips instead of bread.

We ate lunch in the cockpit when a large sea turtle swam by on starboard. Vince tossed out a piece of lettuce, which the turtle eagerly snapped up.

"Oh no, I wish we had more lettuce! What else does a sea turtle eat?" I said, tempted to toss my entire salad to the turtle.

"Seagrass and algae," Vince teased, "do we have any?"

By early evening, *Poetry* was shipshape and our luggage was partially packed. It was time to relax and wait for Happy Hour to commence. Without warning, Vince put on his swim trunks and ordered me to go below deck. "Quick, get dressed…another sailboat is approaching the harbor entrance."

With six scuba tanks tied to the lifelines and a deck littered with wetsuits and fins, the crew on board the approaching boat appeared to be divers. Disappointed to relinquish our privacy, we watched the skipper cruise around the small harbor in search of a suitable spot in which to drop anchor.

Eventually, with their bow anchor properly deployed, they settled a safe distance from our port side. One of their men boarded a dinghy with a second anchor, which appeared to be tied to a stern cleat. He drove the dinghy downwind, dropped it in the water, returned to the boat, and got back on board.

Completely puzzled by what they were doing, I asked Vince, "What is going on? What in the world are they doing?"

"This small harbor only holds a handful of boats. To avoid being back-winded, they dropped a stern anchor," Vince explained. I had no idea what that meant, moreover, I was curious why Vince snickered and shook his head.

When the activity on our new neighbor's boat seemed quieter, Vince joined me in the galley. "Will you join me for a drink?" he asked. Although we were out of lemons and limes, we had enough gin, tonic, and ice to make a few Happy Hour cocktails. It amazed me how much I missed the squeeze of lime in my drink, nevertheless, we celebrated the end of our charter appropriately with adult beverages and a handful of roasted almonds.

When our neighbors began grilling, the aroma of meat cooking over an open fire wafted our way, tempting us to do the same. Vince grilled three leftover hamburger patties, while I loaded the buns with a slice of tomato and onion. That was the last of our perishable food, and I commended myself for planning our meals with limited waste. Fortunately, the provisioning market in Nanny Cay willingly refunds the cost of unopened water bottles and cans of food.

Our discussion during dinner was about the outstanding people we met on this trip. Everywhere we visited, it was apparent that British Virgin Islanders place great importance on mannerly behavior. We were consistently impressed by how polite, attentive, and friendly the locals and working personnel treated us.

As we did after dinner in Cane Garden and Manchineel Bay, we dawdled on the transom with our feet dangling in the water.

"Where's the flashlight?" I asked, curious to see what sea creatures might come up to kiss my toes.

"It's in the nav station, I'll get it. There is also something I want to try…" Vince replied. He did not return directly and when he did, he was equipped with a flashlight and an empty can of tuna fish tied to a yard of string.

"What's the can for?" I inquired.

"It's empty, but I thought the tuna smell might attract some fish," Vince said as he lowered the can into the water and aimed the beam of light directly at it. My immediate reaction was to pull my feet out of the water again. However, Vince assured me that no creature would bite me. With our eyes fixed on the can, we kept it in the water for a while, but no fish appeared.

Finally, we lost interest, pulled the can out of the water, and tended to the dinner dishes which we left on the cockpit table. I threw a scrap of yellow onion over the side of the boat into the water. Suddenly, we heard a splash.

"What was that?" I asked as Vince jumped up on the rail with the beam of his flashlight directed at the splash.

"I think it's a fish. What did you throw in the water?"

"A piece of a yellow onion," I replied.

"Can you throw another one?"

"OK, keep the light on it…ready?" I asked as I tossed the onion.

Vince held the light on and directed it at the onion. A creature darted out from underneath the boat, gobbled it up, and swam back.

"It's a shark," I screamed.

"It's a remora!" Vince corrected me calmly. "It's a suckerfish, they use a sucker-like dorsal fin to attach themselves to the bottom of the boat, or a host fish like a whale or a dolphin. They eat parasites, algae, plankton, scraps of food, and apparently…yellow onions."

I had never heard of a suckerfish before and was startled by its size. This one was more than a foot long, although Vince informed me that they often grow to be 2-feet long and can weigh up to twenty pounds!

Before we turned in for the evening, I invited Vince to lie down on the foredeck for the last time. We lay very close, next to each other, held hands, and gazed up at our mast-star, the North Star, the Milky Way, and the occasional satellite floating through space. Tonight, I fully understood Vince's passion for sailing and the beauty and freedom that comes with the sport.

Daybreak came rather quickly. I used every last bit of the coffee grounds left in the paper bag to brew our final pot of coffee on board. Wanting to stay on deck to relish in the break of daylight, we were both up early, feeling a tinge of sadness about leaving these unspoiled islands.

The divers on our neighboring boat seemed restless. The man who dropped the stern anchor, was back in the dinghy, trying to locate it for retrieval. Appearing confused, he returned to his boat without the anchor. The skipper stood waiting for him on the stern.

After what looked like a serious discussion between the two men, the skipper donned his wetsuit, dive tank, and goggles, and together they returned to the area where the stern anchor was tossed to the bottom of the sea. When the skipper dove into the water, I asked Vince, "Did they lose the anchor?"

"The skipper is down there looking for it, they should have had a trip-line and a marker on it. Now they will have to retrieve that anchor by hand. He'll be exhausted when he comes up," Vince explained.

Unfortunately, the skipper resurfaced without the anchor, and the men were forced to cut the line to free the stern.

"That's a chartered boat," Vince said with a look of concern. "I would hate to be the skipper who has to return that boat without the anchor. It'll be a black mark against his sailing record."

No matter how much we tried to deny it, it was time for us to head to Nanny Cay…*Poetry* was due back in a few hours. Our magical time in the BVI was over. Soon, we would be on solid ground on the way to the airport to catch our flight home.

Afterword

As cliche as it sounds, our adventure in the BVI changed my life. For ten days, I was out of my comfort zone, living a lifestyle I could have only imagined.

I fell head-over-heels in love with a sailor and the 3,000-year-old sport of sailing that formed his character. I loved feeling the wind in my hair, communing with nature, and the sense of peace that captured my soul in Manchineel Bay while I sat under a palm tree, staring out at sea.

To understand the basics, I enrolled in a sailing course and when we returned to the BVI the following year, I helped Vince raise the sails and we let the power of the wind take us from one magnificent harbor to the next. I was a true first mate who shared in the responsibilities and pleasures of sailing.

To overcome my fear of deep water, I learned how to snorkel. The following year, with Vince as my guiding force, we explored the Caribbean's colorful underwater world together. It was more beautiful than I envisioned or Vince could have described.

Over the years, the BVI has become the top sailing destination in the world, over-run with bareboaters, but we still returned often because it is a paradise of stunning natural beauty, warm winds, deep blue seas, secluded beaches, and waterside shacks for eating, drinking and soaking up the island's wonderfully unique, rich culture.

Accepting and facing my fears made it possible for me to conquer them. I emerged as a new person. Spiritually flourished, I discovered my heart's yearning for unknown experiences in unfamiliar places. Now, Vince and I travel to world-class sailing destinations, *Chasing Dreams in a Sailboat*.

French Polynesia
Arrival

Tahiti

After several years of bareboat sailing in the BVI, a charter sail in the French Antilles, and countless day-sails on the San Francisco Bay, sailing in the tropical waters of Tahiti; the largest island of the French Polynesian Society Islands tugged at Vince's heart. The adventure in the South Pacific sounded wonderful and exotic, and I looked forward to visiting a destination nearer to my birthplace of Surabaya, Indonesia than I had ever been.

It was the new millennium; February 2000. A bareboat charter in French Polynesia was an excellent way to start the decade! Vince looked handsome wearing the Aloha-style shirt I bought for the occasion. He loved wearing it and called it his 'blow in the breeze' shirt. Our hearts pounded with excitement as we boarded a commuter jet from San Francisco to Los Angeles to catch an overnight flight to Tahiti and a final flight to Raiatea. Vince booked a 46-foot sailboat for our two-week adventure!

After a delayed layover in Los Angeles, our flight on AOM Airlines finally departed just after midnight. It was our first time flying a French airliner. The interior of the plane was immaculate and the friendly, impeccably uniformed crew impressed us immediately. We had a vacant seat between us and appreciated the extra room to spread out during the long flight.

The crew provided the most outstanding service we ever experienced on any airline. Our gourmet meal was delicious; perfectly cooked, sliced beef with cheesy Au'gratin potatoes and steamed vegetables, a green salad, a French baguette with a wedge of Brie, dark chocolate, and a small bottle of Bordeaux wine. Following the entrée, the crew served a final course of smoked and poached fish with crackers, sparkling water, orange juice, and coffee. When it was time to sleep, each passenger was offered a cosmetic pouch containing a toothbrush, toothpaste, a moist towelette, and eye pads.

By the time we crossed the equator, Vince and I slept briefly and awoke somewhat refreshed.

On a bright, sunny morning, we touched down at the Faa'a International Airport in the capital city of Papeete on the island of Tahiti. Instead of a jetway, the ground crew rolled a staircase up to the door for an easy exit and a short walk to the terminal. The temperature was warm and humid, there was no mistaking, we were definitely in the tropics!

Dressed in typical island wear, serenading musicians playing a ukulele, a gourd, and a *pûni*; a small drum made from dried fish skin stretched over a coconut welcomed passengers with traditional Tahitian music. A native island girl dressed in a *pāreu (*or pareo) offered passengers *tiares*; a fragrant white flower to wear behind the ear. Instantly, Tahiti seemed like a friendly destination to visit.

Our final flight on a nine-passenger puddle jumper was not scheduled to board for another two hours. Although jet-lagged, we made the best of our long wait. Window shopping at the closed souvenir shops kept us occupied and when the bank opened, Vince exchanged our US dollars for Polynesian French Francs; the exchange rate was XFP1,000 to $10 US.

We looked on, as local women created lovely leis from flowers and shells at a makeshift market stand, but when the coffee shop turned its Closed sign to Open, we were the first in line to buy a cup of the rich, strong island brew.

Finally! The loudspeaker announced the boarding of Air Tahiti's Flight 384; our thirty-five minute trip to Raiatea. I crossed my fingers and hoped that our ground transportation agent would be there to meet us, we couldn't wait to head to the hotel.

Raiatea
'Apache'

The view of Tahiti from the air, was a knock-out, never had I seen islands as beautiful, encircled by incredible lagoons, water the color of emerald and aquamarine gemstones near the shore, transcending to cobalt blue toward the open sea. As Vince watched me take it all in, he explained that the jagged, verdant green mountains were *atolls* dotted with tropical rainforests, active and dormant volcanoes, surrounded by coral reefs spread across five archipelagos. The scenery was downright dramatic. Tahiti took my breath away.

To our disappointment, the ground transportation agent was not waiting for us at the airport. After traveling for nearly twenty hours, we were too tired to contact the marina and wait for another driver. Vince took control and hailed the first available cab to our hotel.

The short drive to the island's north shore was a sensory experience. With its white sandy beaches, thick rainforests, giant tropical ferns, and overgrown, jungle-like creeping vines, Raiatea was more lush than the Hawaiian or Caribbean terrain I was familiar with.

From my mother and grandmother's descriptions and photos, I imagined that the Indonesian landscape must be similar to these islands. When the driver opened his window, I caught the flowery, somewhat spicy-sweet fragrance of the brightly colored bougainvillea and hibiscus flowers the size of dinner plates wafting through the sultry air. Strangely, I felt a connection to this destination, I loved French Polynesia already.

Our accommodations at the Hawaiki Nui Resort, on the lagoon side of Tepua Bay, provided an impressive, tropical setting with a restaurant, tiki bar, and an on-site swimming pool overlooking volcanic mountains. The native language in French Polynesia is French. However, the cordial staff spoke fluent English as they welcomed us to the resort.

The front desk manager immediately reimbursed Vince for the cost of the cab and apologized for the agent who failed to meet us at the airport. While a receptionist checked us in, the manager ordered a cab to take us to Marina Apooiti in the morning to begin our charter.

Our accommodation was a lovely thatched roof cottage with an oversized garden view and tastefully decorated Tahitian-style furniture, and a king-size bed. The large shower in the bathroom drained into a rock garden with live ti plants. We both got a kick out of the elaborate tropical decor.

With the exhausting journey behind us, we were relieved to be in our hotel room. It didn't take long to undress and unpack just enough clothes to locate our bathing suits and flip-flops. Although we looked forward to having a wholesome meal, it was too early in the day to order lunch. Until the restaurant opened, we opted for snack foods and a coconut-y rum drink. Whenever we traveled, we found that adjusting to the new destination's time-zone was less unsettling if we followed the local rhythm of life as soon as possible.

A dip in the swimming pool was invigorating, and although the water temperature was surprisingly warm, after many long hours of sitting on an airplane, it still revitalized our bodies and spirits.

After an adequate swim, we relaxed on lounge chairs, sipped a local beer, and allowed our brains to take in our new surroundings. Motivated to learn more about these islands and the people who live here, I collected a few of the hotel's tourist information brochures and photographed the resort's flourishing grounds and the dormant volcanic mountains in the distance.

When the sun became too hot, we returned to our air-conditioned room for a much-needed nap with our bodies fully extended, instead of contorted in an airplane seat. Unfortunately, we didn't sleep long. Vince's anxiety to check out the marina and see our chartered boat was overwhelming. A few moments later, we ordered a taxi and headed for the harbor.

A small, highly efficient operation, Marina Apooiti, with approximately eighty slips for yachts up to 60 feet in length was impeccably maintained. Amenities included guest showers and toilets, yacht repair services, and a nice laundry facility. A paper map posted at the entrance highlighted several restaurants, a pub, and a well-stocked provisioning store located in Uturoa; the nearest village to the marina. While I studied the map, Vince stood on the dock and studied the channel markers.

"Heading out of the marina to Apooiti Bay will be a piece of cake tomorrow," he remarked.

"That's good news...I wonder where everyone is?" I responded, "The marina seems very quiet. Where is all the action? We seem to be the only people here."

"Maybe we arrived at an off hour, they work on European time here," Vince replied. That explained it, like in Europe, in French Polynesia, some businesses close for lunch at midday and resume at 3 or 4 o'clock until eight in the evening.

Suddenly, a dock-worker approached us and asked if we needed assistance. Vince promptly introduced himself and told him that we were starting a charter in the morning.

"Welcome, Captain," the dock-worker responded, "we are expecting you, your boat will be ready tomorrow." Thrilled that we were officially acknowledged, Vince asked to see the boat. The dock-worker paused for a minute, scratched his head, then raised his finger and said, "Of course, follow me."

We proceeded to the docks where the bigger boats were tied up, stopping at a sleek and sporty Beneteau 464. "This is your boat, Captain. *Apache* will be ready to set sail in the morning," the dock-worker reiterated.

Vince beamed with approval, this was the largest boat we ever chartered and she was a beauty.

"Great! We'll be here bright and early," Vince replied.

Society Island Hopping
Taha'a

Finally, after a more restful sleep, I woke up excited to explore our surroundings. Surprisingly, my shoulders were already a bit sore from laying out by the pool yesterday. The warm Tahitian sun really packs a punch.

Although it was still early, the morning light was perfect for wandering outside to admire the wide array of tropical flowers growing on the resort's well-manicured, artistically landscaped grounds. While Vince slept, I tied on my sarong and slipped on my flip-flops to take a stroll in the gardens around our cottage. A cluster of showy bird-of-paradise thrived profusely, tiara bushes exuded a subdued gardenia-like fragrance, but the show-stopper was a red torch ginger bloom, with its cone-shaped center and layered petals it resembled a graceful wax sculpture.

In one of the tourist brochures, I read that the *tiare apetahi* only grows on Mount Temahani, on the sacred island of Raiatea. Its five snow-white petals close at dusk and re-open with a soft cracking sound at dawn. It is one of the rarest, most extraordinary blooms in the world. I certainly hoped we would see it during our time here.

"Morning, Hon! Are you ready for breakfast?" Vince asked when I returned. "Look what room service delivered," he continued, as he led me to a tray ladened with a French baguette, two chocolate crescents, a wedge of ripe Brie cheese, a dish of rich creamy butter, strawberry jam, two hard-boiled eggs, a pitcher of guava juice, a pot of freshly brewed coffee and a bud vase with a bright red anthurium. It was a beautiful presentation and the food looked delicious. We dove in as if we hadn't eaten in days!

A few hours later, well-fed, showered, and dressed in comfortable beach attire, we waited for our ride to the marina when we noticed a small crowd of onlookers gathering at the end of a rock pier. Curious, we wandered over to see what attracted such interest. To our surprise, we watched the resort staff toss bucketloads of chum into the water to feed a large school of hungry bass, tuna, and gray reef sharks. Unnerving to watch, the aggressive fish gathered daily to participate in the morning feeding frenzy, compliments of the resort.

Our taxi pulled up to the curb precisely at the scheduled time. The driver stepped out, shook our hands, and loaded up our luggage, while the concierge placed shell necklaces around our necks, wished us smooth sailing, and thanked us for being guests at the resort.

When we arrived at the marina, the dock-worker we met yesterday opened our car door.

"Welcome Captain and Madame," he said, "it's a beautiful day for sailing. Please check in at the front desk."

During the past thirteen years of bareboating together, Vince and I instinctively shared the routine tasks of preparing the boat to leave the harbor as soon as possible. While Vince attended the safety and orientation meetings, unpacking, setting up, and organizing our temporary home for the next two weeks had become second nature to me. First, I assessed our living space on board.

However, with four staterooms, three heads, a large salon, and a galley-style kitchen, there was plenty of room. I valued the extra lockers to stash our clothes, unused bedding, and empty luggage.

The aft stateroom with a large adjacent head became our ensuite for the next two weeks, primarily because I imagined seeing glorious sunrises through the portholes and the large hatch overhead.

After I unpacked our bags, stowed away our belongings, and took an inventory of the galley equipment, I inquired at the Hospitality Desk about provisioning options. Simple enough, a marina staff member would drive me to the market in Uturoa and wait in the van while I shopped at my leisure.

Provisioning in Tahiti was quite a different experience. Unlike a well-lit grocery store with plenty of fresh vegetables, household goods, and other products attractively displayed, the market was a dim warehouse environment, with produce and other food items stacked in cardboard boxes. Household products stockpiled on warehouse shelves appeared as if they had just been unloaded from a cargo ship.

Long expandable tables displayed disposable bowls of noodles or rice, topped with vegetables, meat, or fish, covered with plastic wrap. At the end of each table, large aluminum containers dispensed an adequate amount of hot fish, lamb, or chicken broth over the contents in the bowls. Curious to try a bowl of this local deliciousness, I resisted the urge to buy one, since it probably wouldn't travel well on the boat.

Large chest-type freezers stored unrecognizable cuts of meat and seafood wrapped in layers of plastic. Handwritten paper labels identified the contents and weight of each package. I loaded up my grocery cart with frozen packages of fish, lobster tails, chicken parts, pork chops, a pound of giant prawns, and a half pound of langostinos. The irresistible, fresh-baked loaves of French bread cost only.35 cents each. It was difficult not to buy more than we could use during the first few days. Freezer space on *Apache* was limited and the high humidity would rapidly ruin bread and produce.

The availability of fresh local fruit was the best I'd ever seen. Large mangoes, fragrant star fruit, papayas, pineapples, coconuts, and lychee nuts emitted luscious ripe aromas. However, I was most excited to find rambutan; the spiny, red fruit was one of my grandmother's favorites. Similar to Lychee nuts, the taste of rambutan is more delicate, sweet, and less perfume-y. Oh, I wanted to buy everything but limited my purchases to a few papayas, two mangoes, a small bunch of bananas, a pineapple, a coconut, and to introduce Vince to this wonderful, exotic fruit, a small bunch of rambutans.

In addition to a six-pack of spicy tomato juice, a bottle of orange juice, a few pounds of coffee, and several basic household cleaning products, the cost of the provisions was the equivalent of $400 US. Vince pre-ordered an ample supply of bottled water, alcoholic beverages, and carbonated drinks for an additional cost of $250 US.

By late morning, Vince and I finally reconvened on deck. Pleased to see our belongings and provisions efficiently and properly stowed, he commented, "Good job, Hon, everything looks great." Happy and relieved, I beamed at Vince's approval.

"Are we cleared to leave the harbor?"

"Yep, we are checked out with the harbormaster, and we can leave anytime," Vince responded. Suddenly he noticed the bottle of French Crémant Champagne chilling in a blue ice bucket decorated with a red hibiscus, and the Welcome Card on the cockpit table. "This must be from the marina. Nice. When did this arrive?"

Not waiting for my reply, he popped the cork high up in the air, poured the golden, bubbly liquid into two glasses, and presented one to me. "Cheers, Love," Vince said, "welcome to Tahiti. I can't wait to start sailing."

Being in French Polynesia, I got a kick out of speaking the few words I knew in French. "*Santé*," I responded, "Here's to our South Pacific adventure. When do we leave?"

To answer my question in detail, Vince slipped below deck and re-emerged with the Cruising Guide in hand. While we sipped champagne and discussed our itinerary, he showed me an aerial view of the islands, depicting blue lagoons and enchanting *motus*; small islets formed by broken coral and sand.

"This afternoon we'll head to Apu Bay on the South end of Taha'a," Vince said, "since it's an easy passage, we'll use the *Iron Jenny*"; a slang nautical term referring to the engine. To begin a charter, I always preferred motoring to our first anchorage.

When just a dribble of champagne remained in the bottle, Vince decided it was time to leave. Underwater coral heads and unchartered reefs require boaters to be at anchor before sunset. Like an able-bodied captain and his crew, Vince drove the boat past the green and red markers, while I stowed the bumpers and organized the dock lines into neatly coiled bunches. Over the years, I developed into quite a helpful first mate.

Leaving Marina Apooiti behind was thrilling, I filled my lungs with glorious sea air and stretched out, leaning my back against the mast. I couldn't believe we were here. Suddenly, Vince shouted, "There's an activity in the water over there…there on the bow."

Quick as I could, I hustled to the front of the boat. To my sheer delight, I saw a large pod of dolphins bow-riding in the surf as if they were escorting us out to sea. Shrieking with excitement, I wanted to photograph these amazing mammals. Fortunately, my camera was on a lanyard around my neck. The dolphins encircled the boat, they were so close that I could almost touch them. There must have been twenty of them! I thought this only happened in Hollywood movies! What a fantastic way to begin our adventure.

Soon, Taha'a was directly on our bow, the lagoon was approximately 110–130 feet deep. While Vince scoped out an ideal location to anchor for the night, I soaked in the scenery, it was beyond breathtaking. Luminous, white sandy beaches, and picturesque slanted palm trees fringed the island famous for growing and producing most of the vanilla in French Polynesia. As we approached land, the unmistakable scent of vanilla orchids growing on host trees near the shore was ever-present.

Anchoring in a depth of more than forty-five feet of water, seemed the perfect spot to spend our first night. At a dead-slow boat speed, I controlled the helm while Vince released the anchor at the bow, returned to the helm, and reversed our direction until the anchor grabbed the bottom.

With the engine turned off, Vince lowered the swim ladder and, prepared to snorkel over the anchor to confirm that *Apache* was properly anchored. Almost immediately after he entered the water, he removed the snorkel tube from his mouth, and shouted, "This is the clearest water I have ever seen. There are schools of colorful fish right underneath our boat!"

Ordinarily, I would wait for his return to the swim ladder. However, this time, I was too impatient to get in the water. I knew how to snorkel now and loved being among the fish.

Gingerly, I climbed down the swim ladder with just my snorkel mask and tube. Holding my breath, I released myself and slipped into the water. A school of blue tang welcomed me to their world, they didn't swim away and stared at me curiously. In February, the average seawater temperature here is 80°F but somehow, I felt wonderfully refreshed.

We were truly snorkeling in paradise. The coral here was different; larger, more colorful, and more varied than what we had seen in the Caribbean. If this was a prelude to exploring the South Pacific's underwater aquarium for the next few weeks, we were ecstatic! We spent hours in tropical underwater splendor.

An hour or so before sunset, Vince mentioned how hungry he was, and frankly, I was too. Attending required meetings, boat preparation, and provisioning kept us occupied, and we forgot to eat a proper lunch. While Vince made MOC *(My Own Creation)* rum Mai-tai cocktails, I quickly grabbed a bag of taro chips, a can of mixed nuts, and sliced a fresh, fragrant pineapple to bring on deck for an impromptu snack.

Our first Happy Hour in Tahiti pulled together in a hurry but it was sufficient to still our hunger and…just in time. The sunset was spectacular, more brilliant orange and golden than we had ever seen anywhere. "Look at this glorious sky," Vince said as we walked up the companionway with our Mai-tais and snacks.

"Mai-tais for my pineapple spears…perfect," I teased and inserted a spear into each plastic tumbler.

"Let's stay up here until the sun goes down," Vince suggested as he reached for my hand and led me to the foredeck. In the open air, I heard the sound of music drifting in the breeze. I loved the rhythmic sound of Polynesian drums and the nimble tones of a ukulele.

"The music is the absolute, essential addition to watching our first Tahitian sunset," I commented, turning to lean into Vince's arms, feeling fortunate and grateful for this moment.

"I know, I can't believe we're actually here," he replied.

When the sun fell below the horizon, Vince hung a pendant light with a coconut-shell shade on the Bimini and fired up the charcoals in the kettle grill. Meanwhile, I tossed two lobster tails in a mixture of finely chopped garlic, lemon juice, olive oil, salt, and pepper to marinate while the charcoals burned to an even temperature and stopped smoking. Crispy skillet potatoes with onions and a fresh, sliced mango with a squeeze of lime juice completed the dinner menu for tonight.

Before long, we were sitting in the cockpit, enjoying our first meal on board. Although we were jet-lagged and weary, the stress of getting here was behind us now. For the remainder of the trip, we were free to relax, and tonight we dined on lobster, on a sailboat, in exotic French Polynesia!

"Wait, one minute," Vince said, as he ducked below deck. I heard the flip of a switch on the nav station. "OK, look up," he said.

Awhhh, Vince remembered to turn on the light at the top of the mast; my star. Now our first evening aboard *Apache* was complete.

At the end of the meal, I served a Tahitian Coffee specialty drink for dessert. Freshly brewed, with a generous splash of Irish cream, a drop of rum, and a pinch of cinnamon, the hot beverage smelled and tasted divine.

We were the only boat in the harbor, a goal Vince strived for. The lights on the islands around us created a magical setting. The evening was still, and it felt as if we were in a remote part of the world. Suddenly, we noticed a brilliant flash against the dark sky. There it was again and again. Vince recognized it as a dry lightning storm, beautiful electrostatic discharges among the clouds; no rain, no rolling thunder, just a phenomenal light show from God…

Taha'a
Motu Vahine
(Island of the Women)

When morning broke, the warmth of a sunbeam shining through the open hatch above our heads persuaded me to get up. Feeling energetic, I turned to find my already handsomely tanned husband still fast asleep. Carefully, I slid out of bed, tiptoed to the companionway, and stepped into the cockpit to meet the dawn. It was a spectacular morning, with no remaining evidence of last night's lightning storm.

The Cruising Guide noted that the number of tourists that visit the Hawaiian Islands in one day, visit the Society Islands in one year. Pleased to see that we were still the only boat in the harbor, I dared to stroll topless around the perimeter of the deck. Peering overboard at the water so clear it was translucent, I watched a variety of colorful fish swim near the boat, along with a school of strange-looking, ribbon-like jellyfish. I wondered what they were. Also distinctly visible was our chain and anchor lying on the sandy bottom of the sea. Everything looked amazingly pristine and clear.

As *Apache* pointed slightly west this morning, the views over the lagoon toward Taha'a and distant Bora Bora were on our bow. Raiatea was at our stern. The volcanic islands appeared somewhat mythical and dramatic, with green, spiked mountains jutting out from the earth, tumbling down to the blue South Pacific Ocean below. It seemed surreal, like scenery from a King Kong or Jurassic Park movie.

"Good morning, Island Girl," Vince said, as he joined me on deck. "How is it out there this morning?"

"*Bonjour, mon amour,*" I responded in French with a cheeky smile on my face, "this is the most beautiful place I have ever seen."

Pleased that I was so captivated by the islands, Vince came toward me for a morning kiss. "I agree, it is drop-dead gorgeous here," he commented, while he ambled to the foredeck for a better view.

I wrapped myself in a yellow sarong, tied the ends together above my breasts, and began to prepare a French-style breakfast; a few hunks of crusty bread, a smear of creamy, velvety butter and strawberry jam, two hard-boiled eggs, a bit of Brie, tiny pork sausage links, and a pot of hot coffee.

"Breakfast looks wonderful, and so do you. You look beautiful in your yellow pareo," Vince said as he helped me bring our meal to the table.

During breakfast, our conversation turned to the next anchorage, and although I couldn't wait to explore the islands, I also found it difficult to imagine a place more stunning than this one.

Our next destination was directly at our bow off the north shore of Taha'a. Motu Tu Vahine; known as the *Island of the Women,* was the location of L'Hotel Vahine; a private luxury resort with impeccable grounds and a coconut grove on one of the most picture-perfect lagoons in French Polynesia.

After breakfast, I tidied up quickly below deck, while Vince weighed anchor and headed west. Since the passage from Apu Bay to Motu Tu Vahine was less than two hours of motoring inside the lagoon, we decided not to raise the sails.

Vince's favorite position to steer the boat under power was from the stern's corner seat on the starboard or port side of the boat with his back against the stanchion. He pointed to the coral reefs on starboard, and as I cuddled up next to him, he explained how the reefs were natural barriers that formed the blue lagoons by separating the shallow bodies of water from the ocean. This created a haven for a large variety of tropical fish, colorful coral gardens, sea turtles, dolphins, and sharks. The scenery was magnificent, I had no words in my vocabulary to describe the beauty of this incredible tropical wonderland.

When we approached Taha'a's north end, Vince looked for a mooring buoy, which pleased me greatly. I always found catching a mooring line easier than manually setting an anchor. In preparation, I pulled the dinghy closer to the boat, walked up to the bow, fetched the boathook, and stood ready to catch the looped end of the mooring line on my first try. Success!

Motu Tu Vahine is an islet, separated by a rocky sandbar from the private Vahine Island.

"We can snorkel on that rocky area over there," Vince said, standing on the transom to release the dinghy line and lower the swim ladder.

Within moments, we splashed into the crystal-clear ocean water. However, there was no visible sea life, just endless blue water. With an arcing of his arm, Vince motioned for me to follow him to the boat. "It's too deep here, there's nothing to see. Let's take the dinghy to the rocky sandbar between the islands."

Aboard the inflatable, I took my position on the bow and coiled the anchor line so that when prompted, I could throw it toward my target in a tidy bundle or drop the anchor in a sandy spot, letting the line run smoothly and free. Between the two islands, Vince navigated to an area where spiny, black sea anemones, fragile coral, and rocks covered the ocean floor. When we reached the shallows, he shut off the outboard motor and pulled it up out of the water.

"The propeller blades will damage the live coral beds," he said as he grabbed both oars, placed them in the locks, and began rowing us to shore until he heard the dinghy's bottom scrape against the coral. "I can't row us any closer," he said, "and we can't walk on the coral, so stay in the boat, I'll tow us in."

What? Curious about how Vince planned to get us to shore, I did as instructed and remained seated. Holding himself steady against the dinghy, Vince strapped on his snorkel mask and fins and slid into the water. With the bowline in his right hand, he began to snorkel to the beach, towing the dinghy behind him with me on board; sitting pretty! Oh my god, although we must've been a comical sight, I felt like a Tahitian princess in a Polynesian canoe…this was awesome!

When we reached the shore, Vince removed his fins and assisted me out of the boat. "I can't believe you towed me to shore, that was incredible," I cooed. "You are my hero!"

Thank God for my reef walkers! Carefully, we walked on rocks and broken bleached coral to a clear spot on the sandbar. Vince tied the dinghy line to a shrub and gained his bearings.

"This is Vahine Island," Vince said, adding in a whisper, "I think the entire island is a private resort."

Standing knee-deep in the clearest ocean water imaginable, small, bright-colored fish swam between our legs, encouraging us to join them. Without discussion, we strapped on our snorkel gear, slipped into the surf, and pushed off with our hands until we floated into deeper water.

Mesmerized by the subaquatic world of wonder, we snorkeled together effortlessly. I loved snorkeling hand-in-hand with Vince. To direct his attention to something specific, I touched him on his shoulder and pointed to the underwater object I wanted to show him.

Suddenly, Vince noticed a flawless shell in the sand directly beneath us. With one hard blow through his snorkel tube, he dove down to retrieve the shell and brought it to the surface. Gleefully, I clapped my hands together and cheered when he showed me the elongated, spiral auger; off-white with pink, orange, and brown specks, the shell was a beauty, a true treasure!

Our first snorkel expedition in the South Pacific among schools of vibrant yellow striped butterflyfish, gray and white pufferfish, vivid green parrotfish, and brightly colored wrasse that hung out near the coral formations was indescribable, but the showstopper was a red and white lionfish, lying motionless on the sandy ocean bottom with poisonous spines extended and widespread, waiting to ambush its prey. I couldn't wait to write about all we encountered in my journal.

Ready for a break, we made our way to the edge of a coconut grove, removed our snorkel gear, and sat in the surf to catch our breath. Directly in front of us, *Apache* was at anchor. With no other boats around, we felt heavenly secluded on our tiny island.

Hand-in-hand, we strolled along the shore, Vince picked up a coconut husk and shook it close to his ear. "This is a good one," he said, as he looked for a solid surface to set it on while I searched for a rock to throw on the pointed end of the husk until it split open. Watching Vince crack the coconut, rip off the fibrous husk in the surf, and finally taste the white fleshy fruit was a pleasant reminder of our visit to Cane Garden Bay in the BVI years ago, where I first showed him how to crack a coconut.

With our eyes glued to the sand in search of seashells and other treasures from the sea, we continued our walk on the beach when a shark swam near me. Startled, I jumped out of its way but Vince assured me that it was just a gentle, baby reef shark that had no teeth.

On the sandbank, we came across a makeshift tiki bar; a charming place to order a cool drink and a bite to eat. Waiting for someone to appear, we hung around until a plus-sized, Polynesian woman dressed in traditional clothing approached us. "Would you like to order lunch?" she asked.

"You bet…two grilled fish sandwiches with fries, and two rum punches," Vince replied instantly, without looking at a menu or asking for one.

"Mauruuruu," the woman replied, meaning "thank you," in Polynesian. "I'll be back in a few minutes."

While we waited for our food, we checked out the surrounding area. Vahine Island Resort was a family-run, luxury hideaway with several over-the-water bungalows and a made-to-order gourmet restaurant specialized in French cuisine with a Tahitian flair. With no guests in sight, we made ourselves comfortable at a table under a large thatched umbrella with a panoramic view of the lagoon.

When lunch arrived, the over-the-top, elaborate food presentation impressed us and I couldn't resist taking a photo of the rum punch served in a green coconut husk, festooned with a red orchid, a paper umbrella, and a pineapple slice. The luscious grilled fish on a brioche bun topped with coleslaw and a generous serving of golden fried potatoes looked like a delectable feast!

"For you, my Island Girl," Vince said as he handed me one of the large coconut husks which I reached for with both hands. We bumped husks in a toast. "Santé, my Love," I said, "what a beautiful food presentation."

Not realizing how hungry we were, we consumed our lunch and guzzled down our rum punches; Vince readily ordered two more. When the bill came, he shrugged his shoulders at the staggering cost of $190! "The experience was worth every penny," he cheered.

On our way back to the dinghy, Vince collected three more coconut husks. Like a pro, he broke them open, pulled off the fibers, and tossed the cleaned nuts into our beach bag. "I'll store these in the freezer," he said, "we can have fresh coconut whenever we want."

By late afternoon, my arms, shoulders, and chest felt puffy and looked dangerously sunburned. Vince's neck and shoulders also looked painfully red. Although we strived to sport a Tahitian tan, it was time to stay out of the sun for a while.

The South Pacific Ocean is extremely high in saline, and it covered our bodies in a layer of gritty, dry salt. While I relished taking a long shower, moisturizing my skin and hair, Vince attached a bed sheet to the Bimini top with clothespins he found under the galley sink, turning the cockpit into a quasi-tent to shield us from the sun. Even though our beautiful view was lost, the shade made it bearable to stay on deck.

Delighting in our privacy, I began to prepare a Happy Hour charcuterie tray when two large catamarans approached and anchored on starboard. "Look at that," Vince grumbled, "there's a whole ocean out there, why can't they anchor somewhere else?"

I too felt frustrated, we enjoyed being the only boat in the area and wondered why other boaters didn't feel the same. Regardless of the invasion, we spent a few wonderful hours on deck with our drinks and nibbles, watching the sunset, and feeling mellow.

When the urge to eat struck, Vince flipped two juicy burgers on the grill. Honestly, I was not sure if the ground meat was pork or beef, but he grilled them perfectly and served with a spicy grilled mango instead of the usual salad, our meal was quite flavorful.

For dessert, I sautéd sliced bananas in butter with a pinch of brown sugar, a squeeze of orange juice, and a splash of rum. My creative concoction, topped with another drizzle of rum, looked quite decadent in the cereal bowls I found in an unlikely cupboard. The sweet ending was a hit with Vince, a fitting finish to an epic day on Motu Tu Vahine.

Taha'a
Marina Iti

For sailors, sunrise is an important part of the day, it's when the ocean starts to take on a character determined by the wind. This particular morning was stunning, with wispy pink and lavender clouds flung against a clear blue sky. Standing on the top rung of the companionway, I poked my head through the hatch to see Vince standing on the bow. "There you are…Morning Honey," I greeted.

"Close the hatches," he commanded in return, "there's a rainstorm fast approaching."

What? How is that possible? On starboard, the sky looked glorious, but on port, a wall of rain was swiftly moving toward us. I scurried to close the hatches and waited for Vince to head below deck. Instead, he asked for a bar of soap, which I handed to him through the hatch in the head. He darted to the transom, took off his swim trunks, and showered naked in the rain! How fantastic! In one split second, I tore off my sleep-shirt and panties and joined him.

Our slightly naughty, but invigorating outdoor shower was an enjoyable way to begin a new day. Refreshed and feeling happy, Vince studied the Cruising Guide while fresh coffee brewed on the stove, filling the cabin with that familiar rich coffee aroma. A locally grown papaya drizzled with lime juice, and two chocolate crescents warmed with butter in a skillet made a simple, tasty Tahitian breakfast.

"I think we'll head to Bora Bora tomorrow," Vince announced matter-of-factly. Oh my goodness, be still my heart! I was thrilled to visit this celebrated island, the most well-known island in the South Pacific…the epitome of natural beauty with its iconic peaks and dazzling blue lagoons.

The passage to Bora Bora would be our first one in open water and as such, Vince planned to make a quick stop at an inlet nearby, where a local market regularly stocked basic provisions. Accordingly, by mid-morning, we weighed anchor, motored the short distance to the inlet, re-anchored, and took the dinghy to shore.

Overgrown with lush foliage, tropical flowers, palm trees, papaya, and breadfruit trees, at the end of the dock, the roads to town were unmarked. Nevertheless, we meandered down an unpaved path until we saw a passerby and asked for directions to the *marche;* the market. The answer came in French, broken English, and sign language, directing us down the road to the village.

"Merci, au revoir," I said, smiling to myself, as I did every time I spoke a little French.

Though rustic and a bit ramshackle, the quaint local market offered a wide variety of meats, produce, and household items. Readily, I bought a few loaves of freshly baked French baguettes replenished our supply of chocolate crescents, and fresh tropical fruit. Again, I took pleasure in looking at the unfamiliar items in the market. Behind the cash register, I spotted a disposable underwater camera, outrageously priced at $33 US. I anticipated that Bora Bora's barrier reef would be worth the extravagant expense, so against my better judgment, I added the camera to my shopping cart.

Toting two bottles of wine and two large grocery bags, we walked back to the dinghy. On the opposite side of the road, an exotic, Tahitian woman wearing a brightly colored sarong artistically draped around her leggy, lanky body sashayed toward us. Neatly held in place by a red hibiscus, her shiny, jet-black ponytail, cascading down one shoulder, enhanced her seductive stature. Accompanied by a young boy and a small black dog, sprinting and darting around them, she pushed a bicycle by its handlebars as she approached. Mesmerized by her striking beauty, we could not take our eyes off the uniquely attractive woman.

Almost in unison, Vince and I greeted her and the boy as we passed them. *"Bonjour."*

"Bonjour, bonne journée," she replied in a deep, throaty man's voice! Oh my god, to our utter disbelief, the attractive-looking woman was a man, a

transvestite! Referred to as Rae Raes by the locals, transvestites are part of a Tahitian subculture and are considered to be Tahiti's third gender. We were flabbergasted!

When the transvestite and her entourage were well behind us, I turned my head to look at her one last time. To my embarrassment, she saw me looking back and blew me a kiss. I was stunned and felt my face glow red!

With our market purchases stowed away, we searched for a suitable overnight anchorage to relax and unwind before embarking on our 20-nautical mile passage to Bora Bora in the morning. On the South end of Taha'a near Marina Iti, Vince dropped anchor close to a lovely motu surrounded by a powder-white sandy beach.

"This is an excellent overnight spot," I shouted from the cockpit, "it's gorgeous here. I'll make a picnic lunch. Let's hang out on the motu for the rest of the day."

Lickety-split, I assembled two monster-sized sandwiches and packed them in a beach bag, along with a couple of bottles of Hinano Tahitian beer, water, wine, and all the essentials for being marooned on an island for an afternoon.

On the transom, Vince stood ready to help me board the dinghy. As I handed him the heavy beach bag, the view of a complete rainbow's brilliant spectrum of color perfectly arced high across the sky stopped me cold.

"I don't know if this day can be more beautiful," I remarked.

Vince drove the dinghy up on the beach, making it easy for me to step out onto the sand and look for the best picnic spot, with a splendid view. There was not another soul around, the motu was our private Garden of Eden with picturesque palm trees growing in every direction. The taller coconut palms along the beach bent toward the prevailing winds, trunks extending over the water while the shorter trees grew more inland. Strewn on the ground, coconut husks were in ample supply.

Vince picked up each one and shook it next to his ear in search of the ones that held water. Each time he found one that made a slushing sound, he announced, "This is a good one!"

There were so many good ones, he couldn't carry them all, but watching him search so diligently made me chuckle.

When I came to an extra scenic spot on the beach, with a clear view of the lagoon, I spread a beach towel on the sand, laid out our lunch, buffet style, and uncorked a bottle of wine.

"Lunch," I chimed out to Vince.

What is it about being alone on a tropical island in paradise that makes us want to undress? Taking my lead from Vince, I stripped off my swimsuit, grabbed a sandwich and the bottle of wine, and sat on a beach towel in the sand next to my naked hubby. For hours, we were the only two people on our secluded motu, savoring lunch, searching for seashells, spreading sunscreen lotion on each other's brown bodies, and taking a snooze in the shade. Pretending to be Adam and Eve was bliss!

Then, without warning, our solitude was shattered, rudely interrupted by the sound of people. "What is that noise?" asked Vince, as he emerged from his nap. I heard it too, people talking and laughing, and the sound seemed to be getting closer. To our amazement, a huge catamaran overcrowded with guests, flying a cruise ship pendant flag approached our tiny island! Oh no, the catamaran dropped anchor and began to ferry large groups of people to our beach. In lightning speed, we dressed, gathered our scattered belongings, and watched in horror as dozens of tourists invaded our remote island.

The first guests to reach the shore greeted us in a friendly manner, perhaps realizing that they were intruding. Accordingly, we greeted them in return, we exchanged casual conversation with several of the cruisers who appeared to be on a cruise ship excursion to have lunch on a private island. Our motu belonged to a cruise ship company! As the invasion continued, a chase boat also anchored in the vicinity. Moreover, the crew unloaded countless coolers, undoubtedly stocked with gourmet meals for their guests.

With long faces, Vince and I loaded up our dinghy and returned to *Apache*, our serenity annihilated by the oversized catamaran, the chase boat, and the crowd. On the bright side, when the tourist excursion was over, the entire crowd of people, departed at once, restoring our tropical oasis to its natural beauty. However, once our peace had been disturbed, we found it difficult to recapture the original ambiance of our solitude. So, we showered, dressed, and went ashore.

On shore, the Marina Iti Hotel offered simple hut-style accommodations to world-weary boaters. An enchanting open-air restaurant and a beach bar with big, blue, comfy sofas and a high-end sound system playing typical Tahitian music was just the kind of place we needed to get over the mass onslaught of tourists we encountered. Instead of spending our usual Happy

Hour on deck, we ordered drinks and appetizers to watch the sunset snuggled up on those big blue sofas.

Later in the evening, I prepared a light dinner of ground beef skillet steaks with onion *au jus* and a simple green salad.

On our bow, the cruise ships docked at Raiatea resembled giant floating cities, with all the hustle and bustle of city life. I felt fortunate that we were on our private yacht, with only eight other boats moored around us.

Bora Bora

"The Jewel of the South Pacific," "the most beautiful island on the planet," the Cruising Guide described Bora Bora as "geologically fascinating," "off-the-charts gorgeous," and "the ultimate alluring island in the Society Island chain."

Accordingly, Vince allocated three full days to this destination. We fully expected Bora Bora to be the highlight of our French Polynesian adventure. Weeks before our adventure began, I perused through countless brochures and studied stacks of travel magazines describing the island's blue lagoons, white sandy beaches, and tangerine sunsets. I was beyond excited to set foot on Bora Bora's sand and soil.

To prepare for our long sail, I emerged from our berth before daybreak to fix a hearty breakfast of fried eggs, oven-toasted banana bread, fresh bananas, and grated coconut. While the coffee brewed, I squeezed a couple of oranges into tall glasses filled with ice. If the wind stayed at our backs today, Vince estimated sailing the passage in six or seven hours, however, the weather channel reported light winds, so the voyage could take even longer.

When the meal was ready to be served, I gently nudged my captain and stroked his head until he stretched and softly purred.

"Morning Sailor, we're going to Bora Bora today. Get up, Sleepyhead," I said, waking Vince with a kiss.

During breakfast, we discussed our point of sail, while my stomach was a bundle of nervous anticipating the long trip. Up until now, we traveled only short distances, under power, inside the lagoons. However, Vince sensed my concern and told me not to worry.

An hour and a half later, we weighed anchor, and with the golden glow of a glorious sunrise on our bow, we entered the channel leading to the open ocean.

At times, we sailed at twelve knots, and Vince was in his element. When the winds were light, we sailed with only the jib moving us forward. Still, it was our first day of sailing in the South Pacific.

The long passage was uneventful, without a sign of marine life. After more than six and a half hours, we arrived at the entrance to Motu Toopua on the southeast end of Bora Bora. Fortunately, another sailboat on our bow, lead us through the channel. While I stood on deck to watch for coral heads, Vince gave a wide berth to the Southwest corner of the island where the reef stuck way out, and the currents easily pulled a sailboat in.

Immediately, the scenery became more dramatic as we navigated through Passe Teavanui; the well-marked approach to Bora Bora, where the two peaks of Mount Pahia and Mount Otemanu came into view. These remnants of an extinct volcano in the center of the island are the most photographed and recognized landmarks in French Polynesia. To be in the midst of the sublimely beautiful landscape, we had seen in travel books and films was astounding.

Safely inside the lagoon, Vince headed toward a cut in the landscape which he highlighted in the Cruising Guide. The area provided the best view of Bora Bora, while the cruise ships and opulent resorts were obstructed by hilly terrain. As we neared the cut, Vince dropped our boat speed down to nearly an idle. "Take the helm," he said, "I'll get the anchor ready to drop. When I give the hand signal, put the boat in neutral."

While I drove the boat forward, Vince prepared the anchor and stood watch on the bow for coral heads and the best spot for an overnight anchorage. When I saw his hand signal, I threw the gear in neutral, heard the anchor splash as it hit the water, and waited for Vince to take over. So far so good! Vince returned to the helm, reversed our direction until the anchor grabbed the sandy bottom, and moments later, *Apache* was safely secured.

In places, the water was twenty to thirty meters deep, hyper blue, with incredible visibility. After long hours of managing the helm in full concentration, Vince jumped in totally naked. I followed right behind him and without wearing a stitch of clothing, we played in the water like children; unencumbered and free.

"This is the best diving and snorkeling place in the world," Vince said, "let's get our gear and check it out."

Magnificent…spectacular…how do I describe the countless brightly colored fish and vibrant coral? A couple of large black and yellow striped angelfish with long dorsal fins were my favorite. Spellbound, I snorkeled above them and watched the couple swim gracefully past waving purple fans, brain coral, and stag horn coral formations. When I looked for Vince to show him the angelfish, I found him laying naked in the dinghy, with his back on the bench seat. His legs dangled in the water from his knees down, with his flippers on his feet.

"Hey Honey, whatcha doin'?" I called out.

"I'm just hangin' out," Vince replied with a big grin, flashing an OK sign with his thumb and index finger. Looking downright adorable, my heart fluttered at the sight of him.

Knowing he was content, I snorkeled away from the boat. The color of the water turned blueish green as it became deeper. Suddenly, I heard the muffled sound of something splashing. Unalarmed, yet curious, I looked up to see that Vince jumped from the dinghy into the water, swam to the boat, and climbed on deck.

Standing on the stern, he waved and watched me snorkel. All seemed kosher until I noticed a large, green, snake-like marine animal with a massive head and a wide gaping mouth staring at me from inside a crevice between the rocks below. Without moving, I drifted over it just in time to watch it strike out at a fish before swallowing the unfortunate victim in one gulp!

"Vince," I shouted, treading water to stay on the surface, "there is a giant snake down here, I saw it swallow a fish."

Doubting what I saw, Vince sped to my side, wearing his snorkel mask and tube. As he peered at the marine animal in question, he yelled out, "That's a moray eel, the largest one I've ever seen. Get back to the boat!"

With lightning speed, we made our way back to *Apache*. Curious about the eel, Vince referred to the 'Tropical Fish' reference book on board to read about the species. Apparently, we encountered a Giant Moray Eel; one of the largest coral reef predators in the South Pacific. This carnivorous fish can grow to be more than 10-feet long, ambush its prey, and swim out of its hole with immeasurable speed. Our encounter with the eel persuaded us to get back on board.

Just before sunset, I pulled together a few Happy Hour finger food items; mixed nuts, smoked fish on crackers, cubes of dry salami, and aged cheese. It was nice not to be traveling in the wind. I summoned Vince on deck just in time to see the sun slip below the horizon and when the last sliver of the orange globe disappeared; the sky became a shade of apricot, intensified in color, then turned lavender and purple. The day drew to a close; it was time to share a bottle of wine.

The meager hors d'oeuvres stimulated our appetite and foregoing a proper meal today made us hungry. Accordingly, Vince started the charcoal while I trimmed and seasoned two chicken breasts. A simple salad of sliced yellow tomatoes, celery, and cucumbers dressed with lime juice and olive oil became a quick and satisfying side dish when topped with garlic croutons made from stale bread cubes quickly tossed in a skillet with butter, herbs, and chopped garlic until they became crispy and golden.

We served ourselves in the galley and carried our plates, two glasses, and a bottle of wine up to the foredeck, where we ate our meal picnic-style, leaning our backs against the mast. The evening was quiet and we were tired.

When our plates were empty and the wine bottle had not a drop left, we pushed them to the side and reclined. Gazing at the stars, we fell asleep holding hands. Unfortunately, an hour later, the wine bottle rolled onto the floor and startled us awake. It was time to retreat to our cabin, where we spent the rest of the night sleeping soundly. Tomorrow was Valentine's Day!

Bora Bora
Vaitape; Valentine's Day

Waking up on Valentine's Day morning on a sailing yacht in the South Pacific…how fortunate can two people be? Although Tahiti is the largest of the Society Islands, Bora Bora is the most famous, visited, and beguiling. Dumbstruck by the natural beauty of these islands and the women who inhabited them, Captain Cook and Captain Wallace; 18th-century sailors found it difficult to leave. This morning, standing on deck, gazing at Bora Bora's magnificent mountain tops, I clearly understood their sentiments.

After a good, long morning stretch on deck, I ducked back down into our stateroom to snuggle in bed with my husband. I scooted in between the sheets next to him; it was Valentine's Day after all. We had silly cards and romantic little mementos to exchange and to decorate our breakfast table, I brought pink heart paper cut-outs, colored paper plates, and napkins from home.

After we climbed out of bed, I began to work my magic. First, I popped a 'Golden Oldies; Greatest Hits from the '50s music CD in the nav station's CD player and turned the sound down low. Out of the corner of my eye, I noticed that Vince acted a bit secretive as he made his way up on deck. Not wanting to pry, I smiled and continued on my mission.

To keep the sea breeze from messing up my paper decorations, I decided to set the table in the main salon. Singing along with the music, I unwrapped the red paper plates and folded the pink napkins into paper fans. Slipped into our glasses, they looked charming and brought dimension to my place settings. Randomly scattered pink paper hearts on the table and paper heart garland draped along the hatches looked like a party was about to take place.

At the top of Vince's plate, heaped with orange sections lightly drizzled with honey, I placed a Valentine inviting him to sit down and indulge. My special menu included: baked Brie on crusty French baguettes, perfectly cooked sunny-side-up eggs, pan-fried ham steaks, a pitcher of mimosas, a carafe of hot coffee, and a dark chocolate heart. When I stepped back to view the festive table, I was pleased with the result.

Ready to celebrate, I stood on the top rung of the companionway and announced that breakfast was ready, but to my surprise, Vince had created a little Valentine's Day presentation in the cockpit for me. On the table, a small stuffed teddy bear, a card, and a tiny gift-wrapped package waited for me to discover them. "Awhhh, Honey, how sweet…thank you. He's adorable. Happy Valentine's Day," I cooed, referring to both Vince and the teddy bear.

"Happy Valentine's Day, my love," he replied.

Not wanting to read the card or open the package until we opened our gifts together, I brought them to the salon and placed them near my place setting. "The table looks beautiful," Vince commented when he saw the decorations, "and breakfast smells delicious."

Our Valentine's Day morning was filled with love and romance. As we listened to our favorite songs, we exchanged our small gifts and opened our cards. The heart-shaped box of chocolate bon-bons Vince gave me, and the sweet teddy bear with a red bow around his neck, button eyes, and a stitched nose were precious and priceless. For dinner tonight, Vince surprised me with reservations at the Nao Nao Restaurant; a popular restaurant at the Black Pearl Resort in Vaitape; a town on the eastern side of the island.

After breakfast, we were ready to explore Bora Bora's legendary blue lagoon. Wearing only his snorkel gear, Vince lowered himself down the swim ladder first and waited for me to follow. I had my obscenely expensive underwater camera strapped around my wrist. Intending not to waste costly film on anything unworthy, I planned to be selective about what I photographed.

On this sun-drenched morning, we encountered colorful fish almost immediately. Floating in the deep, I wondered which world was more stunning; underwater, or above where the scenery has not changed much since the European sailors came in the 1700s and found paradise.

Hand in hand, naked as jaybirds, we snorkeled near the boat. It was grand to be nude and feel completely natural. In a jovial mood, I couldn't resist snapping a few pictures of Vince as he tumbled around in the blue abyss. When he caught me taking his picture, he shook his finger at me in disapproval. I merely snickered and swam away.

Sometimes, the sun's rays penetrated the translucent water, turning it opaque, and in areas too deep to see the bottom of the ocean, our vision became blurred.

Eventually, Vince suggested getting back on board and moving to a better location for going ashore tonight. Reluctantly so, we returned to *Apache*, weighed anchor, and motored to Vaitape in the Bay of Pofai to search for a suitable anchorage to spend the night.

As we approached the entrance to the bay, we were horrified to see an enormous cruise ship docked in the harbor. Its presence was grotesquely distracting. "Oh no," I moaned, "this means Vaitape will be swarming with tourists tonight." Dozens of launch boats unloading anxious, noisy passengers on shore validated my outburst. Nevertheless, continuing on our approach, Vince spotted a public pier with space for us to tie up.

"We'll dock at the pier for now," he said, "we can check out the town, get some provisions, and locate the restaurant where we are having dinner tonight. We can look for a suitable spot to anchor later."

As we neared the pier, a dock-man whistled through his fingers, called out to us, and pointed to a vacant spot at the end of the pier. When we arrived at the spot indicated, he assisted us with our bowline. *"Bienvenue à Vaitape,"* he said, then went on his way before I had a chance to thank him. With our bowline tied off, I grabbed the free end of the stern line, jumped onto the pier, and looked for a cleat.

"Good girl," Vince complimented, "loop it under the railing, and hold on to it until I get there."

Shopping bag and wallet in hand, we took off to do the shopping. A visit to Bora Bora would not be complete without a stop at Vaitape; the island's largest town with a picturesque harbor where all manner of watercraft, from Polynesian canoes and luxury yachts to cruise ships moored.

Regrettably, at first glance, the town appeared to have lost its charm due to the countless pop-up shops, strategically erected to accommodate the throng of cruise ship passengers focused on bringing home an island souvenir. Women sold flower leis, along with leis made from shells, and dried nuts, which they created on the spot.

In stopgap market stands, local artists displayed decorative items handcrafted from coconut husks, intricate wood carvings, and tikis representing the ancient statues found around the Polynesian Islands. A wide selection of colorful hand-dyed pareos and beauty products made with coconut oil scented with gardenias or tiare flowers lured tourists inside the arcade of temporary shops. As we elbowed our way through the hectic crowd, Vince and I promised each other never to travel with the masses.

At last, we reached the center of the village where brick-and-mortar shops sold luxurious black pearls in every size and color, loose, individual, or set in an array of gold jewelry styles. Black pearls from the Tahitian Black-Lipped Oysters are world-renowned for their quality, beauty, and iridescent black nacre. The pearls formed near the oyster's inner shell were darker in color, while those formed further away were lighter gray or silver.

As we window-shopped, Vince noticed the lust in my eyes and invited me to enter one of the shops. "Let's look at these beauties up close," he said, while I tried to control my outward longing.

Within seconds, a lovely blond saleswoman dressed in smart business attire warmly welcomed us, offered a cooling tropical drink in a stemmed glass, and encouraged us to feel at home as we looked around the shop. Although the exquisite creations from nature are said to be black, upon closer observation, they sparkled in the light with stunning color variations of olive green, silver, blue, copper, and purple. Ohhh…the ones with olive green and silvery-gray undertones were my favorite by far.

"Why don't you try something on," the saleswoman asked, "perhaps a pair of earrings?" Pulling out a red velvet chair, she offered me a seat at a glamorous vanity with a large mirror surrounded by stage lights.

"Go ahead, Hon," Vince replied, "try something on…You might as well, we're here…."

Oh, My God, I began to perspire as the saleswoman asked if I preferred pierced or clip-on style earrings. She showed me a lovely pair of black pearl studs and put them in my ears. When I moved my head just slightly, the pearls shimmered with the subtle undertones I adored. I loved the earrings but was afraid to comment or even look at Vince.

"They're beautiful on you," he whispered in my ear, "you make those pearls look stunning."

The saleswoman commented too. "The diameter is perfect for casual or dressier wear," she said, then added "Wait…I have an idea," and as if on cue, a colleague handed her a square-shaped, dark blue velvet box. "See if you like this," she continued, opened the box, and took out a delicate gold chain necklace with an exquisite, flawless, floating black pearl from which an equally exquisite, flawless white pearl fell from a flattering short length of matching chain.

It was a breathtaking piece of understated jewelry. Gently, the woman placed the delicately designed necklace around my neck, laying the black and white pearls proactively on my bare-skinned chest. I could hardly breathe as she closed the clasp and stepped back. "It is as if the necklace was designed for you," *(Oh my gosh, what a sales pitch, I thought)* "and the color of the black pearl matches the studs in your ears." *(Well, of course, they did…)*

Smiling, Vince looked at me adoringly, "Happy Valentine's Day, sweetheart," he said, "please wear them to dinner tonight."

What? Honestly? Speechless and thrilled beyond words, I realized that besides my wedding ring, I had never owned such lavish jewelry before. I couldn't believe Vince purchased the earrings and necklace…just like that…on a whim! They were beautiful and they cost a fortune, but I loved them, and I loved my husband most of all!

While the saleswoman drew up a certificate of authenticity and an insurance appraisal worth double the value of the jewelry, I wore my pearls and admired my reflection in the mirror. When the purchase was complete, the saleswoman presented me with a white paper shopping bag elegantly embellished with the store's logo, containing my velvet jewelry boxes. She thanked us for our business and offered us another drink, though we declined, shook hands, and left the store. I was over-the-moon filled with joy!

Shopping bag in hand, proudly wearing my Tahitian pearls, we continued toward the market where Vaitape became more charming. Colorful, wooden clapboard cottages and bungalows, randomly scattered about, lined the dirt road to the heart of the village. In driveways and front yards, displayed on fold-out tables or blankets spread on driveways, locals sold freshly picked fruit from homegrown trees. I couldn't resist buying a mango from one, a papaya from another, and a giant, fragrant pomelo from yet another villager on our route.

When we arrived at the market, I grabbed a shopping cart and enthusiastically pushed it down the aisles, taking my time, quizzically examining all the unfamiliar produce and merchandise on display. Even though we only needed some lunch meat, a few Happy Hour tidbits, a couple of French baguettes, and lots of ice, I made my way through the market at an easy-going pace, gazing at everything.

Vince waited for me near the exit doors, by the freezers filled with large blocks of ice and easier-to-handle bags of chipped ice. After paying for our selections, we realized that we had more than we could carry, consequently, Vince suggested loading up the shopping cart and pushing it back to the boat. Brilliant!

The tourist crowd near the harbor had dissipated, and our trip to the dock with a full shopping cart was more manageable. Onboard *Apache*, stacking the blocks of ice in the freezer was a daunting task, as it first required draining the dirty, melted ice water and wiping out the stinky freezer. While Vince took on that unpleasant chore, I stored the rest of our market items and once again, admired my new pearls in the mirror.

Once we returned the shopping cart to the market in town, we wandered back to the boat through the historic center of the village. Vince hoped we would discover a laid-back bistro or café where we could enjoy a proper, Valentine's Day lunch. However, it seemed that when the tourists returned to their cruise ships, the eateries stopped serving meals.

There was nothing else to do but move the boat to a picturesque spot in the lagoon and have lunch on board. Frankly, I couldn't imagine a more ideal place to be. We remained on deck for the rest of the afternoon. I composed journal notes, and Vince read his latest James Michener novel. It was blissful just spending some quiet time together.

For our Valentine's Day Happy Hour ritual, Vince had a different idea. "The Nao Nao Restaurant at the Black Pearl Resort is featuring live music tonight. Let's watch the sunset in the open-air lounge with a couple of 'fru-fru' drinks with pineapple spears and paper umbrellas," he said. That sounded like a lovely idea.

I showered quickly, washed and conditioned my hair with coconut oil shampoo, spritzed on a light floral-based perfume, and over my right ear, fastened a white plumeria in my long, dark hair. Wearing my black pearl studs and my beautiful new necklace, I was ready to share a romantic evening with the love of my life.

To my surprise, we both appeared on deck wearing red t-shirts and shorts. Vince reached for my hand. "Your chariot, my love," he said, as he helped me board the dinghy.

The Bora Bora Black Pearl Beach Resort was a Tahitian nirvana with beautifully landscaped gardens, the iconic over-the-water, thatched-roof huts on stilts, and a characteristic, torch-lit tiki bar. Stunning views of Mount Pahia, Mount Otemanu, and the white sandy beach below evoked authentic and picturesque French Polynesia.

An attentive bartender acknowledged our presence and invited us to sit at any vacant table. As the only guest in the lounge, Vince guided me to an outside table with an optimal view of the mountains. A barefooted waitress, dressed in a Tahitian pareo, wearing a flower lei came over to take our order. She was seductively attractive, with long, silky, pitch-black hair that shimmered with a dark blue hue.

"Welcome to our tiki bar, what would you like to drink?" she asked in a husky man's voice. Oh my god, our waitress was a Tahitian Rae-Rae!

"Good evening, which mountain is Pahia, and which is Otemanu?" Vince asked before responding with our drink order.

The waitress seemed pleased that Vince expressed such interest in Bora Bora and was forthcoming in her answer. "The smaller mountain is Mount Pahia. It is 2,100 feet tall, Mount Otemanu is 2,300 feet tall and forms the center of the atoll of the island," she replied. "The mountains change color throughout the day depending on the sunlight and the clouds," she added, pointing to the landscape and then to the faint orange hue developing in the sky by the gradually setting sun.

Vince ordered two banana daiquiris. While we waited for our drinks to arrive, we listened to a group of musicians playing harmonic tunes on ukuleles, mandolins, and a slit drum; a percussion instrument made from a hollowed tree trunk. When our drinks were brought to the table, the waitress invited us to stay for the after-dinner Traditional Polynesian Dance Show, touting it as the best on the islands. It sounded exciting and we looked forward to the musical extravaganza.

"Happy Valentine's Day, Hon," Vince said as he held up his banana daiquiri and looked into my eyes. "Please, be my Valentine forever."

"Happy Valentine's Day to you, sweetheart," I replied. "Yes, I will be…forever."

Our dinner reservation was in the main, open-air dining room under the stars, however before we moved to our table, I stopped at the Ladies' Room. I couldn't believe my eyes when I entered the upscale, cream-color, travertine stone room. There were fresh-cut, tropical flowers strewn around everywhere I looked. Counters were bedecked with hibiscus in every color, orchid leis were draped over the paper towel holders mounted on the wall, and vases holding elaborate bird-of-paradise flower arrangements were artfully displayed on tables at each end of the restroom.

Most impressive were the flower petals scattered on top of every toilet tank and the palm fronds decorated with loosely laid flowers placed on the floor in front of every stall. Honestly, it was unbelievable! I returned to the table and tried to describe what I saw. However, I could not adequately describe the overabundant decorations and suggested that Vince sneak a peek for himself.

The Nao Nao Restaurant was equally, beautifully adorned with flowers. Upon entering the dining room, a waiter greeted us immediately, showed us to a table near the center-front of the outdoor stage, and presented us with the dinner menus, only to return moments later with complimentary cocktails; a tall, iced, fruity, rum concoction with a slice of orange.

When the sky turned pinkish lavender and the sun was behind the mountains, the grounds of the Black Pearl Beach Resort and the Nao Nao Restaurant became a magical fairyland with tiki torches ablaze, and palm tree trunks, floral, fauna, and pathways illuminated by tiny white lights.

As I was unfamiliar with the local cuisine, I perused through the menu, looking for an authentic, local favorite dish. In French Polynesia, *Poisson Cru* appears on every restaurant's menu and is a must-try for serious seafood lovers. This healthy, flavorful dish made from yellowfin tuna is served raw; ceviche or poke style, marinated in lime juice and coconut milk with sliced tomatoes, cucumbers, and red onions.

Fresh-caught fish from this area is world-class and can include bonefish, tuna, mahi-mahi, Bonita, and ruby snapper. Since snapper was on tonight's menu, we both ordered it grilled, with island herbs, accompanied by seasonal roasted vegetables and coconut rice.

While our dinner was prepared, we enjoyed our complimentary cocktails and reveled in the magic of the evening. Soon, two waiters pushing an elegant serving cart, brought two whole fish dinners to our table, presented on domed silver trays. With expert finesse, the debonair waiters simultaneously removed the dome covers, "Your snapper, Captain, and Madame," one of them announced.

I almost applauded with delight, the delicate fish smelled amazing and looked wonderfully moist. While the waiters removed the bones and other inedible parts of the fish with long, thin knives and silver forks, I photographed the impressive ordeal. The food was top-notch, fine-dining, and every mouthful was a luscious treat. For dessert, Vince and I shared a decadent, mascarpone-filled macaroon with a scoop of coffee ice cream. This Valentine's Day dinner could not have been more perfect!

While we savored our dessert and coffee, one of the waiters brought us the check on a silver tray with two mint chocolates and a reminder that the show was about to begin.

Musicians filled the stage, tuned instruments and before long, we were entertained by melodic island songs, traditional chants, and colorful dancers. The power-packed, riveting evening show captured the music and culture of Fiji, Tonga, Tahiti, New Zealand, and Hawaii.

The exotic dancers were sensational to watch, although the dancer that caught our eye most was a darling young girl who couldn't have been more than five years old. As she performed the traditional Ote'a dance and wiggled her hips to the fast beat of the drums, her grass skirt kept slipping down below her waist but every time, she pulled it back up without skipping a wiggle. At the end of the performance, Vince purchased a CD-compilation of the music from the show.

Not wanting to leave when the performance was over, we stayed on the beach for a while and walked barefoot in the surf. Eventually, we boarded the dinghy and returned to the boat with the coconut light on deck and the light at the top of the mast; tonight was my Valentine's Day star.

Turned into the gentle breeze, *Apache* faced Bora Bora's famous mountains. Vince and I took a moment to stand on deck, gaze at the stars and kiss in the moonlight. Must this evening end?

Bora Bora
Motu Piti A'au (Two Hearts)

A few gentle raindrops found their way through the open hatch onto my forehead, causing me to blink and wipe my eyes. Careful not to wake Vince, I reached up to close the hatch above our heads and the other ones in the salon, then I crawled back into bed hoping to continue my dreamy dream about last night's Valentine's Day dinner. Unfortunately, when sleep didn't come, I found it difficult to remain in bed. It looked cloudy and wet outside.

Quietly, I stumbled to the galley and made a pot of coffee. While the coffee permeated the salon with that familiar, comforting aroma, I began to take down the paper heart garland to discard along with the rest of the Valentine's Day decorations. When the salon was orderly, I started breakfast by dicing a few strips of bacon, a ripe tomato, and a small white onion. The sizzling bacon would surely lure my sleepy-headed husband out of bed. I was right…

"Good morning, sweetheart," I said as Vince emerged from our cabin.

"Good morning, Hon, what did you do with the sun?" he asked, grazing my cheek with a kiss as he darted toward the nav station to turn on the *VHF* (Very High Frequency) radio. The weather channel's report confirmed Vince's prediction; rain most of the morning. Not a problem, I could hand-wash a few pieces of laundry, write in my journal, or sit quietly in the cockpit and watch the rain, while Vince could read his book and tinker with boat equipment. Honestly, we looked forward to spending a quiet morning on board.

Gradually, the gentle rain became more serious but it didn't distract me from cooking up a scrumptious breakfast. With the bacon, onion, and tomato, I created a luscious, light-as-a-feather, four-egg omelet, topped with a bit of *creme fraische* and grated cheese. In a covered skillet, I warmed up two buttery crescents to serve with orange marmalade. I delighted in "playing house" below deck while we were holed up in the rain.

After breakfast, Vince made decadent Irish coffees with double shots of Irish cream. The drinks made us sleepy and persuaded us to take a nap.

A few hours later, we awoke energized and refreshed, ready to begin the day all over again. Although the sky was still gray, the sun was desperately trying to break through the clouds. The rain left everything on deck drenched and soggy. From the forward cabin where we stored our soiled linens, I grabbed a wad of bath towels and tossed one to Vince.

Quickly, I wiped dry the cockpit seats and table while he swabbed the floor and foredeck. When everything was spic-and-span, Vince had a sudden urge to take a plunge. "Come on, let's go swimming," he shouted, as he leaped from the swim ladder before I could count to three. Wearing a tank top and panties, I took his lead. Splash! Entering the water took my breath away. Due to the rain, the temperature was unexpectedly cool, nevertheless, as we splattered around and played like juveniles, we hardly noticed.

Spending two nights in the same anchorage, with epic views of Bora Bora was heavenly but with only three nights of our charter remaining, Vince decided to position *Apache* closer to the charter base.

"After lunch, we'll head to the edge of the lagoon on the southeast side of Bora Bora. From there, we can easily make the long return to Taha'a," he said.

The Cruising Guide acclaimed the southern tip of the island for its stunningly beautiful shoals, inlets, motus, coral gardens, and ideal places to anchor for the night. During the orientation meeting, a local tour expert in this area suggested beaching the dinghy at Pt. Faaroone, walking a short distance around the corner, then body-floating back with the current. It sounded like an extraordinary experience.

With Vince already weighing anchor, I assembled a grab-and-go style lunch to eat on board before we snorkeled. Two apples, taro chips, substantial-sized sandwiches, and a large bottle of Hinano Tahitian beer to share sufficed. After our quick lunch, we pulled in the dinghy, started the engine, and raised the anchor.

Crossing the lagoon was challenging, although I stood watch on the bow looking for coral heads and sandbars, I found it difficult to judge how deep they were. Each time we scraped the keel, I apologized for missing the obstruction while Vince cringed. To add to his frustration, the channel markers in the Cruising Guide and the Navigation Charts did not match the true markers in the area.

When we finally reached Motu Piti A'au at the South end of Bora Bora, Vince let out a huge sigh of relief. "We are here," he declared emphatically, "let's find a spot to drop the damn anchor!"

The short passage under power was a nerve-wracking nightmare! Nevertheless, Vince was not ready to relax until he inspected the keel for damage. Without saying a word, he put on his fins and snorkel mask and swam completely around the boat to assess the situation. Fortunately, only a few areas where the anti-fouling paint had scraped off were visible. With his mind at ease, Vince was ready to enjoy our pristine surroundings, Motu Piti A'au; meaning *Two Hearts*...Vince's and mine.

Looking forward to checking out the highly anticipated coral gardens, Vince loaded up the dinghy with our snorkel gear, while I gathered our beach towels, sunblock, and a couple of bottles of water. Then, off we went in search of a picturesque, secluded strip of beach where coconuts dripped from trees, and the water was clear and calm.

Simultaneously, we spotted an open area that looked like an ideal spot to beach the dinghy while we snorkeled. We stepped out into the shallows with ease, and as I gave the stern a push, Vince tugged on the bowline to bring the dinghy high up on the sandbar where it wouldn't drift away with the tide.

We walked approximately a half-mile further up the beach, around the corner to Pt. Faaroone, where we sat in the surf to put on our snorkel masks and fins. Vince kissed me through my mask and offered me a hand in standing upright. We both giggled as we clumsily walked backward into the water until we stood knee-deep.

"Ready?" Vince asked.

"Ready," I responded. Together, we inserted the breathing tubes into our mouths, took deep breaths, and glided into the water.

Oh...My...God, the underwater scenery was simply jaw-dropping, it was so heart-wrenching and beautiful that I almost cried! It was not a particularly sunny day, but the water was the most translucent and crystal clear imaginable. The coral and fish were the most colorful anywhere and we saw a species of fish we had not seen before. Seven manta rays, captivated us as they skimmed past without making a rustle or a sound. I took several pictures with my underwater camera, being cautious to save a few pictures for a brighter day.

Drifting in the placid current, as we tumbled with our legs and arms out in front, and our eyes wide in our masks was wonderfully strange, completely effortless, and a uniquely spellbinding experience.

Eventually, Vince peered through his snorkel mask and spotted the dinghy patiently waiting for us on the beach. Reluctantly, he tagged me on my shoulder and said, "This is the end of the ride."

"Wow, that was truly the adventure of a lifetime," I exclaimed while I removed my mask and tube. "That was the most phenomenal snorkeling we have ever done anywhere!"

With the long nap we took after breakfast, the short passage we made crossing the lagoon, and the awe-inspiring snorkel excursion this afternoon, the hours had flown by although we experienced plenty today. It was time for dinner. However, Vince insisted on having Happy Hour cocktails on the deck before the meal, and I clearly understood that he needed time to relax.

While I took a quick freshwater rinse on the transom, Vince opened a bottle of French Champagne we bought at the market in Vaitape; a lovely, dry champagne that went down easy. Neither of us was in the mood for hors d'oeuvres, so we just sipped the festive bubbly until the bottle was almost empty and the sky changed from champagne-gold to a fiery red.

For dinner, I prepared an avocado, cucumber, and tomato salad, with a vinaigrette made from French Dijon mustard, a splash of champagne, and a pinch of salt and pepper. To accompany the salad, I boiled a pound of jumbo-sized shrimp in seawater until they just turned pink, took them off the heat, rinsed them in cold water, and served them whole, peel-and-eat-style with a buttery loaf of garlic bread, and another bottle of bubbly. Vince raved about our simple dinner and that always thrilled me.

After dinner, we moved to the foredeck, our favorite place to sit with our after-dinner, rum-fortified coffees. The ocean was dark, smooth as glass, the moon was full and bright, and it was a glorious evening. Overlooking Bora-Bora, an island of 5,800 inhabitants, we noticed that the city lights were no higher than the shoreline. I imagined the lights as a pearl necklace around the island. Motu Piti A'au was fast becoming my favorite anchorage in the entire South Pacific!

When the sun came up in the morning, I found Vince standing on the bow, looking through his binoculars at the edge of the lagoon. A sailboat appeared to be stuck in the sand or on the reef in the same area where we first scraped the keel on our approach to the southeast side of Bora Bora. "Hi there, Sailor!" I shouted, "Whatcha looking at?"

"I've been watching every boat enter the lagoon this morning, and I can't figure out the best way to cross through there," Vince answered, then followed with, "Morning Hon, never mind, I'll worry about it tomorrow, we're staying here one more night."

Happy to hear that we were not leaving today, my psyche relaxed instantly, although we were no longer in an unspoiled, secluded anchorage; another Beneteau 464 was moored nearby. Since sailing at night is prohibited in French Polynesia, we assumed our new neighbor arrived early this morning. Secretly, I hoped that we could follow them out to the open ocean if they left before us.

We decided to begin our day with another snorkel excursion at Pt. Faaroone. Yesterday's adventure left us speechless even on a cloud-covered day. This morning's bright sunlight would surely intensify the colors of the coral and fish. For a longer float trip back, we planned to walk a further distance away from the dinghy this time.

Again, the snorkeling did not disappoint, it was outstanding…extraordinary! Even where we stood in the shallows to put on our gear, tiny blue fish swam between our legs and followed us when we pushed off into deeper water. A wall of waving purple sea fans and the yellow stag-horn coral seemed particularly colorful.

Various flashy-colored fish looked as if they were neon bright this morning. A school of black, white, and lemon-yellow butterflyfish with black spots at the base of their tail fins appeared to be curious about us. A yellowtail snapper fluttered by an orange-spine unicorn fish, blue South Seas Devilfish with scattered white spots and translucent fins, and a rainbow-colored parrotfish enjoyed our presence and nipped at our legs and arms.

The current brought us back to our dinghy, but we were giddy with excitement and decided to repeat the experience one more time.

We finally returned to *Apache* when my camera roll was full of undeveloped photos. It was unbearably hot on deck, even with the Bimini top raised. With the hatches closed and the fans turned on high, it was more comfortable in the salon. Ughhh, my skin felt like dry leather. I couldn't wait to rinse the gritty, salty water from my body and hair.

While I showered, Vince searched the galley for a snack and settled for a banana. By the time I was dressed, it was nearly 1 o'clock and we hadn't had coffee or a bite to eat. So, with three cans of tuna, diced green and red onions, chopped pickles, a dollop of mayonnaise, some salt and pepper, and a long drizzle of lemon juice, I created two monster-size tuna sandwiches and called it 'brunch'. When Vince came out of the shower and saw the huge sandwiches, he laughed, that infectious, charismatic, joyful laugh I adored. "Those look great," he said.

Unhurried, we munched our sandwiches, a few handfuls of our favorite dehydrated, stackable potato chips, and washed it all down with a bottle of Hinano beer. In between bites, we reiterated how much we enjoyed snorkeling over the coral reefs and floating back to the dinghy. It was the pinnacle, the most amazing snorkeling experience of our lives!

In the late afternoon, after a few hours of just being lazy and content, Vince suddenly said, "We're sailing back to Taha'a bright and early tomorrow, who knows if we'll ever be here again? Wanna float one more time?"

Although we left the dinghy in the same spot, we walked up even farther on the beach this time. Surprisingly this time, there was a group of tourists at Pt. Faaroone who also appeared to be on a bareboat charter. Undoubtedly, they were given the same recommendation from the local tour expert during their orientation meeting and were here to experience floating over the coral gardens with the tide. We exchanged cordial head-nods as we passed them.

Searching for a shallow spot where we could easily enter the ocean with our fins and masks, we noticed a beautiful native woman standing in the surf. As if she was posing for a topless photo in a Tahitian travel magazine, she wore a flamboyant, wet, fabric headdress, and a lovely batik sarong tied around her waist.

In her right hand, she carried a paper Club Med shopping bag and in her left, she held a large fishing net slung over her shoulder. Gazing at the surface of the water, she prepared to cast her net. Feeling awkward, we avoided staring at her and, needless to say, I refrained from taking her picture. "Keep walking. I don't want to distract her," Vince said, guiding me forward by the arm. "She might be a Rae-Rae."

When we were a comfortable distance away from the woman and her fishnet, we entered the shoal with our masks and fins, gently pushing off into the crystal-clear water. Feeling comfortable and confident, Vince began to twist and turn like an acrobat floating with his arms at his side, walrus-style. Being buoyant made snorkeling almost effortless.

Without warning, the group of tourists we encountered on the beach; three men, followed by three topless women snorkeled in our vicinity. Their slightly sunburned, pinkish-red bodies hinted at their recent arrival on these islands. As most men would probably do in the same situation, I caught Vince hanging onto a rock, motionless, staring at the bare-chested women when they floated past us. I found him humorous and I chuckled at the sight of him suspended underwater.

We returned to the boat in time to catch a last glimpse of the sunset. With only a can of mixed nuts and the Gin and Tonic cocktails Vince quickly concocted, we sat on the foredeck, celebrated Happy Hour and life!

A joint effort, dinner was stress-free, an easy-peasy meal that came together in a snap. While I made a simple tomato, garlic, and dried herb pan sauce, and tossed in a can of smoked sardines, Vince cooked the pasta in seawater and opened a bottle of wine. Pasta, red sauce, and wine, what is more basic and satisfying when one has no will to cook?

After the meal, we washed and dried dishes together and tidied up the galley. "I'll meet you on deck," Vince said with a devilish grin on his face.

After all these years of sailing together, I knew what that look meant; it meant getting naked and laying on the deck in the dark. With our legs up in the air, as if our feet could touch the heavens, we gazed at the stars with the wonderment of a child. Although the sky was amazingly dark, observing the constellations in French Polynesia was unlike star gazing in the northern hemisphere, but soon Vince gained his bearings and pointed out the Milky Way. That visible stream of several hundred billion stars stretched across the sky was extra brilliant tonight.

Taha'a
Our Last Night on Board Apache

At barely 6 o'clock in the morning, the sky glowed an orange-to-golden hue, and…there he was again, standing on the foredeck peering through the binoculars. From the top rung of the companionway, I shouted out to Vince, "Morning, babe, whatcha looking at?"

"The grounded sailboat is off the reef and headed out to sea," Vince replied, keeping his eyes on the sailboat until he was convinced that the unfortunate vessel was indeed moving forward.

I slipped below deck, tied up my hair in a bun on top of my head, and began to take stock of our food supply when Vince joined me in the galley. "Morning, Hon," he said thoughtfully, "it's a long sail back to Taha'a. When the sun is a little higher, let's head out, make a quick stop at Vaitape, then sail straight through. OK?"

Although he asked for my agreement, by the tone of his voice, I quickly understood that his question was rhetorical. Vince was already engrossed in his plan to move *Apache* closer to the marina. Ughhh! Our French Polynesian adventure was almost over.

Quickly, we ate a banana, gulped a cup of coffee, and motored the short distance to Vaitape. Returning to a familiar destination was somehow comforting. Vince pulled up to the guest dock, where we were the only boat this time. With the bowline in my hand, I jumped off the boat and tied up to a cleat while Vince tied up the stern. Like an experienced crew, we operated in sync.

As this was our last visit to Vaitape, we agreed to explore the historic part of town without the multitude of cruise ship day-trippers overcrowding the charming streets. Near the entrance to the village, we visited the only three permanent shops selling tacky Tahitian souvenirs, coconut shell carvings, and artificial black pearls, among more civilized items such as mugs, postcards, and graphic t-shirts. I purchased a navy blue t-shirt depicting the Hinano Tahitian beer logo emblazoned on the back for Vince. He bought a beautiful, brightly colored pareo for me.

Wandering through the shops together, choosing memorabilia for our family and friends back home, was a joy. Our final purchase was a black coral pendant, set in a 14-carat gold encasement for Vince. It was the most ideal memento of our French Polynesian adventure. Hung on his Italian gold necklace, the charm looked very fitting for him.

During the walk back to the boat, I wondered if the local produce stands offered rambutan for sale. Not a fresh fruit I would readily be able to find at home in California. I was eager to buy it one last time. Alas, no one sold rambutan today.

Ordinarily overcrowded with boats and tourist activity, *Apache* looked forlorn as the only yacht at the guest dock. In preparation for our long sail, we locked up loose items, buttoned-down the hatches, shut off the toilet water intake valves and pulled the dinghy close to the boat. I released the bow and stern lines, jumped on board and we were off.

Slowly, Vince pulled away from the dock, aiming directly for the channel between Motu Tapu on port, and Motu Ahuha on starboard. Standing on the bow, I did my best to watch for coral heads and other obstructions, especially in the area where the phantom sailboat appeared to be stuck on the reef yesterday. Idyllic beaches epitomized serenity and seclusion as we followed the channel markers out to the South Pacific Ocean.

When we made it to deeper, wider water without a scrape, Vince almost cheered! In the lee of Motu Tapu, my assistance was requested. "Hon, hold the boat to weather while I hoist the main(sail)," he said.

Even after years of sailing, I hated holding the boat 'head to wind', while Vince pulled on the halyard with all his might until the mainsail went up without a snag. Nevertheless, the sail went up swiftly…we tacked, rolled out the jib, and…we were sailing!

Once the boat settled down, Vince programmed Auto to sail a course to Taha'a, inserted the Tahitian music CD he bought for me on Valentine's Day in the CD player, and turned the music up loud. Sailing at a comfortable four to six knots was marvelous…invigorating…liberating, and Vince couldn't stop smiling! He was thrilled to be sailing, it was his passion.

On the ocean side of the reef, a large school of dolphins swam out to meet us for a bow-ride escort out to sea, making our departure from one of the most beautiful islands in the world a surreal phenomenon!

Six hours after leaving Bora Bora, Taha'a appeared on our bow and another hour later, we anchored at Marina Iti, near the open-air restaurant and beach bar with the big, blue, comfy sofas that we visited earlier in our charter. From here, the passage to the base would be a quick trip and, with our provisions almost depleted, we had the option to eat meals on shore. Luckily, there were a few vacant moorings in the harbor and we hooked one without a problem.

After the long sail, Vince was understandably tired, and since our lunch consisted of only a bag of chips and an apple, I suggested going on shore for drinks and a bite to eat. Vince jumped at the idea.

"Welcome back, *Apache*," the bartender greeted us, to our surprise. "What can I get'cha?" Being remembered and referred to by our boat name made me smile.

"Two tall *Gin and Tonics*, an order of *Chevrettes a la Vanille,* and a French baguette to sop up the sauce," Vince said. Chevrettes a la Vanille; a rich, full of flavor, a decadent local favorite dish made with shrimp, coconut milk, vanilla, rum, and cream is an appetizer ideal for sharing.

Ahhh, relaxing with an adult beverage, and lounging on a comfortable sofa, with nowhere to go for one full day, was bliss. We stayed at the bar until the sunset and it was time to plan dinner. For a split second, Vince's invitation to dine at the restaurant sounded tempting but we still had a half-pound of langoustines in the icebox, that I was eager to cook. So, somewhat reluctant, we returned to *Apache* where I urged Vince to take a nap while I prepared dinner.

In a large skillet on the stove, I added butter, garlic, and thyme. When the butter melted and the thyme became fragrant, I added a cup of seawater, dropped it in the langoustines, seasoned them with pepper, and the juice of one lemon. Then I covered the skillet, turned the heat down low, and let them simmer for twenty minutes. In another skillet, a bushel of canned white asparagus browning in a bit of butter made us salivate. "I'm starving!" Vince cried out when a whiff of the seafood cooking tickled his nose.

"By the time you set the table, dinner will be ready," I replied, as I placed a cold bottle of white wine, two wine glasses, napkins, and utensils on the top rung of the companionway hoping Vince would get the hint. I plated our meal, wrapped the beautiful pareo that Vince bought for me in Vaitape around my waist, and checked myself in the mirror. My reflection made me smile, I hoped Vince would like how I looked topless, with my dark Tahitian tan, and wearing my new pareo. After sailing all day, I planned to spoil Vince as much as possible this evening.

"Bon appétit, mon amour, " I said as I placed a plate in front of him.

"Wow, come here you…you are beautiful…forget dinner," he teased as he gave me a bare-chested hug.

The succulent langoustines and the flavorful asparagus were a wonderful light meal at the end of a long day. To serve with the last of our Irish coffees, I created my version of a tropical dessert; two pineapple and chocolate crepes with whipped cream.

Our dinner conversation about the Society Islands, French Polynesia, and the South Pacific made us silly with excitement, anticipating a return trip in the future, to visit parts we didn't explore this time.

Unexpectedly, a loud splash in the water near the boat startled us. It was too dark to identify what made such a noise. Vince was concerned and brought up the flashlight from the nav station and aimed the beam at the water's surface in the direction of the splash. When we heard it again, we saw three large remoras nipping at the langoustine shells we threw overboard.

Watching the fish swimming in circles, waiting for us to throw more food, was entertaining. I searched our galley pantry for something suitable to feed them. "Will they eat chocolate chip cookies?" I shouted out to Vince.

"They're scavengers, they'll eat anything," Vince replied, "bring the cookies up…quick…before they swim away."

For quite a while, we entertained ourselves by feeding chocolate chip cookies to the bottomless-pit remoras. When the last cookie crumb was gone, it was time for us to retire.

Waking up in the morning, we both felt a bit melancholy. We were the only boat in the area and the marina was exceptionally tranquil. We stood on the foredeck together, Vince behind me, gently stroking my shoulders, "How should we spend our last day?" he asked.

I turned around to face him. "Let's just stay here and enjoy our surroundings," I replied, knowing it was the answer Vince was hoping for.

"We'll head back to Raiatea early in the morning. Our check out at Marina Apooiti is 9 AM."

Oh, I was crestfallen, the thought of leaving these beautiful islands and the long flight home was not at all appealing. Taking a deep breath, I shrugged off the negative images in my brain of crowded airports and flight delays and made a pot of coffee. Using up the remaining breakfast items on hand, I displayed every leftover food choice on the salon table, buffet-style; a melange of cut fruit, a toasted crescent split in half, and the minutest piece of Brie.

"Breakfast is served," I called out to Vince, who was already gathering a few of his clothes to fold and stow in his travel bag. Without much conversation, we ate our meal in the cockpit, each of us engulfed in our thoughts about our time here in the South Pacific.

"Honey, we have all day…let's have one last unforgettable snorkel together, even if it is just around the boat," I said, trying to lighten the mood. "Then we'll think about our long journey home."

Vince smiled, kissed me, and said, "You're right, let's not waste our last day sulking." While I washed the dishes, he gathered our snorkel equipment, along with two towels, and placed them on the transom.

"When we're done, we can rinse off right here," Vince said, pointing to the outdoor shower and neatly stacked towels. He was so thoughtful. The shower at the top of the swim ladder was a wonderful convenience but we rarely used it.

Sitting next to each other on the transom, with our fins on our feet and our snorkel masks on top of our heads, Vince held my hand and led our jump into the clear blue water. We plunged in over our heads, popped back up, adjusted our masks, and off we went. A few inquisitive fish swam toward us. Unfortunately, the water was too deep to see more than a few feet in front of us. Occasionally, two giant sea turtles swam in our vicinity, but when they dove down to feed on the ocean floor, they disappeared.

Suddenly Vince directed my attention to a school of manta rays swimming ahead. During high tide, these extraordinary creatures enter the lagoons from the ocean where they eat plankton, shrimp, krill, and crab larvae. Like B-52 bombers with wingspans that stretch up to twenty feet wide, the manta rays staggered our imagination.

Upon closer look, we noticed that one had a fishhook with a long length of line attached embedded in a brachial slit under its belly. It was so sad to see and we felt an overwhelming urge to catch the ray, remove the hook and relieve it from pain and discomfort. Seemingly not bothered by our presence, the manta ray squadron moved gracefully through the water, and for nearly an hour, we swam behind these gentle giants. It was a heart-stopping encounter!

When the rays disappeared into the blue beyond, we returned to the boat, rinsed off with the outdoor shower hose, and sat on the transom with our feet dangling in the water. Gazing at Raiatea on our stern and the faint silhouette of the other Society Islands in the distance left us with a lasting vision. There wasn't much to say. Our French Polynesian adventure was nearly over.

Mid-afternoon, I assessed our left-over perishable food situation for the last time and wondered how I could create an appetizing lunch. A thinly sliced cucumber tossed with a diced green onion and canned pineapple chunks became an imaginative salad when drizzled with lime juice and olive oil. A can of black beans combined with a few tablespoons of red salsa turned into a tasty dip for a half bag of taro chips, and a dozen celery stalks filled with peanut butter completed the menu. Regardless of what meager delights I served, they paired well with a bottle of white wine.

After our meager lunch, it was time to work. As this was Vince's seventh time chartering with the same company, it was important for his charter-history file to return *Apache* in a clean, cared-for condition.

While I swept the floors, stripped the bunks, cleaned the heads, washed everything in the galley, wiped counter tops, and stowed our dirty linen in pillowcases, Vince swabbed the deck, re-furled the mainsail and jib, tidied up the sheets, rinsed our snorkel gear with fresh water and organized boat equipment in the hatches. When we finished, *Apache* sparkled from bow to stern.

Without a morsel of food on board, we decided to eat dinner at our familiar, open-air restaurant at the Marina Iti Hotel. Expats from France and renowned for their excellent French cuisine, the restaurant owners loved cooking for boaters. We looked forward to having a full-course meal tonight.

"Nice to see you again, *Apache*," the owner-chef greeted us upon entering the restaurant. "Sit wherever you like."

There was no menu but the chef's special dishes this evening were: *moules avec frites;* mussels with fries, Poisson Cru, or mahi-mahi with vanilla cream sauce. On-the-house, freshly baked bread and a homegrown salad accompanied every entrée.

Vince ordered Poisson Cru to share, followed by the mahi-mahi with vanilla cream sauce, while I chose the mussels and fries. Cooked with heart and soul, the food was indeed delicious.

As sundown paled our surroundings and the bay became a radiant, lovely pool of golden liquid, Vince made a toast to officially end our French Polynesian adventure. "This has been an incredible trip, my love," he said, as he raised a glass of wine in my direction, "you were a wonderful first mate. Let's promise each other that we will return here one day."

Tahiti

Papeete

I adore waking up with a kiss from my husband. "Morning, sweetheart, are you ready to go?" he said sweetly. That's how our day began, no coffee, no breakfast, but a kiss.

At 8 o'clock, we slipped our mooring and headed for the charter base at Marina Apooiti; a quick twenty-minute motoring trip. When the harbor was in sight, I radioed the base to alert them of our return while Vince navigated around in circles.

Within minutes, two pilot boats came out to meet us. Several deckhands grumbled a greeting of good morning and jumped on board. Vince and I moved quickly out of their way while they took over the boat handling. Watching the professional crew operate the gears to reverse the boat into a slip without touching the dock was quite impressive.

When Vince settled the bill, he confessed to scraping the keel during our approach to Motu Piti A'au. The charter company agent appeared unconcerned and did not ask for details.

With our travel bags at our side, we waited in the lobby for our shuttle to the airport. Unexpectedly, a concierge informed us that our flight to Tahiti was delayed by six hours due to mechanical problems. As a result, we were invited to be guests at the Hawaiki Nui Resort until it was time to head to the airport. The opportunity to relax at the beautiful resort where our adventure began was too good to be true and I looked forward to taking a leisurely, warm shower in a full-size bathroom with a stable floor!

The hospitable staff at the Hawaiki Nui Resort seemed pleased to see us again, welcomed us warmly, and offered towels, full use of the pool, and a complimentary room for our short stay. Although we had been in the ocean almost every day, being immersed in a pool of chlorinated water was refreshing, luxurious, and almost cleansing. This was an ideal way to while away the hours until our departure.

When the snack bar opened for lunch, Vince ordered an oversized shrimp and avocado salad and tropical drinks made with rum, vanilla syrup, and lime for us. The salad was scrumptious and the rum cocktail packed a yummy punch. Lunch hit the spot!"

Eventually, we withdrew to our room for a power nap; it's astonishing how tiring spending a day in the sun can be. After our nap, we showered together and took a walk on the beautiful landscaped hotel grounds among tropical flowers, avocado, mango, and breadfruit trees.

At 7 o'clock, our airport shuttle arrived, and a jovial, charismatic driver greeted us with a sing-song voice. "Good evening, I am at your service," he said. During the ride to the airport, the driver talked non-stop about Tahiti's facts and trivia and surprisingly we learned that:

- Two years after arrival in French Polynesia, one may apply for permanent residency with a sponsor.
- After ten years, one may apply for citizenship, and after fifteen years, one may purchase a property.
- By 2005 or 2010, French Polynesia will be independent of France.
- Tahitian explorers discovered the Hawaiian Islands.
- French Polynesia is drug-free and crime-free.
- All healthcare and personal-care products, from lip balm to prescription drugs, must be purchased at a pharmacy.

In jest, the driver added, "And no one in the Society Islands knows how to make a proper rum cocktail." Vince and I strongly disagreed with his last statement, as connoisseurs, we consumed excellent rum cocktails at tiki bars and restaurants all over the islands.

Our thirty-five-minute flight to Papeete landed at 8:30 PM and it was well after 10 PM when we checked into the Tahiti Tiare Hotel, located in an undesirable part of the historic center. Our unattractive, dingy room smelled musty. However, the staff was friendly and the bed and bathroom were clean. Most importantly, there was a shower with good water pressure. Fortunately, due to an early morning flight, our time at this hotel was limited.

Eager to check out our dining options, we dropped our luggage on the bed and left the room. Due to the late hour, the restaurants near our hotel were already closed for the evening, however, Vince noticed an open-air food truck market located a few blocks away. "Look," he exclaimed excitedly, "our favorite type of restaurant, Food Trucks!"

I have fond childhood memories of eating at food trucks. When my sister and I were young, my mother and grandmother delighted in patronizing these mobile kitchens to buy freshly prepared tacos, burritos, and other Mexican delicacies served on paper plates from a side window for $1 each. Early in our relationship, I introduced Vince to this unique style of dining, eventually trying various ethnic specialty dishes, always cooked from scratch, with excellent quality, seasonal products. Since then, we found food truck cuisine difficult to resist.

"Oh my goodness," I replied, as I grabbed Vince's hand, leading the way, almost running in the direction of the trucks.

More than a dozen, brightly painted trucks congregated at the *Roulettes* (French for *Caravans*) *Food Market* on Papeete's waterfront. Immediately drawn in by the festive atmosphere, café lights, music, a stockpile of billowing smoke generated by a plethora of open-air grills, and the aroma of mouthwatering, exotic cuisine, we strolled through the pop-up food market to explore our menu choices. Several roulettes offered makeshift outdoor seating, while others served their prepared specialties in paper wrappers for consuming on-the-go.

"Where do you want to start?" Vince asked enthusiastically.

I chose *Chez Marie;* a quaint, wooden roulette with lace curtains and a simple handwritten menu featuring a wide variety of sweet and savory crepes. Vince ordered a ham, egg, and cheese-filled crepe topped with diced tomatoes. I ordered a seafood crepe, stuffed to the brim with fresh crabmeat, shrimp, and a drizzle of rich, herbed cream sauce. Both tasted out-of-this-world delicious and left us wanting more.

Next, we shared a heavenly coconut-cream-filled crepe, topped with caramel sauce, and lastly, my always-the-hopeless-romantic husband ordered a bottle of French Champagne from yet another roulette. While long-time friends, locals, and tourists mingled seamlessly around us, we sipped our perfectly chilled bubbly from plastic cups and engaged in our favorite past-time of people-watching. Being in the midst of such a unique social environment was a wonderful way to experience Papeete on our final night in Tahiti.

We returned to our hotel room after midnight, fatigued, and a little tipsy from the champagne. In just a few hours, we would be on our way to the airport. There was barely time to sleep.

The shrill tone of the cheap hotel alarm clock shocked us awake at the set hour. "Morning, sweetheart," I murmured, turning toward Vince, "I can't wait to sleep in our own bed tonight."

After a quick shower, we departed our less-than-standard hotel room. With an hour to spare before the airport shuttle arrived, we wandered outside in search of a cup of good strong coffee. In the daylight, we noticed that Papeete s historic district exuded an old-world European vibe with French cafés lining the streets. At a corner bakery, we ordered coffee and crescents which we consumed at a stand-up table as we watched the city come alive with rush hour activity.

To mark our final moments in French Polynesia, I asked a passerby to take a parting photo of us toasting each other with our crescents. Just then, our shuttle pulled up to the curb, the driver stepped out and called our name.

Afterword

Sailing in French Polynesia was astounding. Unrivaled in scenic beauty, it was a privilege to be in a fragment part of more than a hundred islands, and a myriad of motus that stretch over a thousand miles of the South Pacific Ocean. It was soul-enriching to be among Tahiti's jagged, emerald green mountains, terrain left mostly wild as nature intended, and water so clear and brilliant blue, there are no words to describe it.

At every opportunity, we embraced the French Polynesian's expressive, rich culture by interacting with the locals, dining on traditional fare, and immersing ourselves in daily island life.

Tahiti's people, customary music, and colorful legends touched our hearts so much that seven years later, we returned for another bareboat charter, giving credence to the impression we formed on our first visit, that the Society Islands truly are hauntingly, stunningly, intensely beautiful.

This part of the world gave us a lifetime of dreaming about a glorious tropical paradise. A gift from God and Mother Nature, French Polynesia is a true heaven on earth.

The Tyrrhenian Sea
Arrival

Procida *'A Kind of Blue'*

Approaching Vince's sixtieth birthday in 2005, I asked Vince how he wished to celebrate the milestone event.

"Let's go sailing," he replied almost instantly, and then added, "*in Italy…just the two of us.*" Oh my gosh, my heart skipped a beat, my eyes grew big as saucers. I was overjoyed. We started planning immediately. Vince chartered a 40-foot sailboat on the tiny island of Procida; in the Bay of Naples off the Southwest coast of Italy. He plotted an exciting 7-day course on the Mediterranean, along the Amalfi Coast. I have always dreamed of sailing past timeless history, ancient castles, and mighty fortifications. I imagined it would be a fairytale-like experience.

We flew from San Francisco to Florence, rented a car, and drove to Naples where the charter company arranged for our thirty-minute transfer from the Capodichino International Airport to a ferry dock in the quaint seaside village of Pozzuoli. The driver holding a sign with our name met us promptly at the car rental return counter when we arrived.

After cordial introductions were made, he assisted us with our luggage, lead us to his Mercedes taxi, and drove to the harbor without much conversation. There, matter-of-factly, he handed us two tickets for the ferry, pointed to our departure dock, and wished us a *Buon Viaggio* before disappearing into the crowded flow of traffic.

The weather was ideal for a ferry boat ride. We were the only passengers on the top deck. As we left the harbor and Naples grew small in the distance, the Isle of Capri and the distinctive outline of Mount Vesuvius came into focus.

Procida s silhouette appeared quickly. Vince recognized it from the charts and photos he studied endlessly while planning our trip. Through the haze, a large stronghold emerged on the island's highest point. It looked like a desolate age-old fort or a timeworn castle. Built at the edge of a cliff, it was quite an impressive sight.

Looking ever so charming, the faded pastel colors of the Moorish-style buildings that lined Procida's picturesque waterfront were reminiscent of ice cream flavors in subtle shades of pink, white, yellow, and orange with brown or green shutters and blue doors; in the same blue hue as the fishing boats in the marina.

As we approached the dock, I saw brightly colored, flourishing oleander trees, restaurants with wicker chairs, and pennant flags suspended from rooftops across the narrow streets. Scooters and small cars buzzing along the town's main street were a flurry of activity. There was a prominent yellow church and a piazza with a children s merry-go-round. Procida seemed like a friendly place with wonderful energy. We loved it at first sight and couldn t wait to disembark.

An agent from the chartering company met us at the end of the ramp and welcomed us to the island. We squeezed into her tiny red truck and drove a short distance to the office. I was dying to see our boat, but there were a few formalities to take care of first.

To my delight, I finally met Valentina; the agent who booked our charter and made our travel arrangements to the island. We exchanged emails for months and in the process, developed a friendship.

When we saw each other, we hugged as if we had always been friends. Valentina was young, had a delightful disposition, wore short punk-red hair, and spoke adequate English. She smiled often and seemed genuinely pleased to meet us. The staff served ice water and potato chips while Vince filled out forms. Valentina offered us a bowl of chocolate truffles that her mother made. They were outrageously decadent!

While our paperwork was processed and Vince attended the orientation and safety meetings, I bought a polo shirt and a belt embroidered with the charter company logo for him. He was thrilled and couldn t wait to wear them.

Once we were properly checked in, an agent escorted us to our boat. Home for the next seven days was a sporty, nearly new, 40-foot sailboat named '*A Kind of Blue*'. The cockpit table was set with a bottle of *Limoncello* on ice, two glass flutes, and a handwritten note from the chartering company wishing us 'smooth sailing'. We always appreciated this heartwarming gesture to welcome us aboard.

We moved into the port-aft cabin, leaving the two forward cabins as the usual storage spaces for empty suitcases, extra linens, towels, and large beverage bottles. Having ample space on board was always a luxury. As on all our bareboat charters, I unpacked and stowed our clothes in the hanging lockers and drawers provided and arranged our toiletries in the head so that we could easily access what we needed, even under sail.

In small-town Italy, businesses open in the morning, close midday, and reopen from 4 o'clock until 8 or 9 o'clock in the evening. Anxious for the shops to open in the afternoon, we wandered into town to buy a few provisions. Although our sailing itinerary included plenty of time to sit idly in cafés and intimate restaurants to soak up the local culture and enjoy the Italian cuisine, we also planned to prepare meals on board.

At an *alimentari;* we bought unlabeled bottles of homemade red wine, olives, fruits, and vegetables. At a bakery, we picked up loaves of freshly baked bread, and at a small *supermercato,* we stocked up on prosciutto, salami, cheese, and coffee. Since no one spoke English, Vince made his selections by pointing to the bountiful display of cured meats behind the counter, holding up his fingers to indicate the desired number of slices, and raising the palm of his hand to indicate 'stop' or 'that s enough'. He was extremely assertive and quite comical to watch.

Since our lack of Italian language skills was quite evident to the other customers waiting for their turn at the deli counter, they eagerly helped us communicate. Our shopping experience with the locals was a community effort and we enjoyed it immensely.

On our way back to the boat, we stopped to admire the exquisite, true-to-life detail of several oil paintings on display at an art studio in a cave-like dwelling on the ground floor of a historic building. When the artist appeared, he introduced himself as an island native. Speaking only Italian, he invited us into his studio to view his artistry painted on plywood. His use of vivid colors was eye-catching and appealed to us immediately.

Vince chose a still-life depicting oranges and lemons and I chose one with green figs, purple and yellow grapes, and a pomegranate split in half. We were thrilled with our €20 purchase of original art, the first souvenirs acquired on our trip!

As in most of Europe, restaurants don't open for dinner until 8 o'clock. Famished and impatient, we sat on the deck in the harbor, facing the waterfront, watching for the locals to patronize the restaurants so we could follow suit. We chose a charming *trattoria* with wicker chairs, white tablecloths, and café lights strung up around the outside dining area and seated ourselves at an outdoor table facing the harbor.

A waitress approached us promptly. *"Buona sera,"* she said, with a lovely lilt in her voice and a friendly smile as she handed us the menus written only in Italian, evidence that Procida was an undiscovered island gem, without international tourist crowds.

We have always enjoyed the challenge of translating a menu. If our attempt to pronounce our selection was not understood, we pointed to the item and waited in suspense until the food was brought to our table. We were often surprised but never disappointed. When the waitress returned to take our order, Vince attempted to pronounce the names of the seafood dishes he chose for us to share. The waitress smiled and said, "OK."

We waited in hungry anticipation. When the food was served, each dish smelled and looked delicious! The smoked fish, grilled octopus, and fried calamari were to-die-for and the seafood linguine was out-of-this-world. To pair with our outstanding meal, Vince ordered an excellent bottle of red wine. While we enjoyed our romantic dinner, I realized that this was our first opportunity to relax in more than forty-eight hours. It was wonderful to eat and drink among the island's residents while we talked about exploring the Amalfi Coast. This adventure seemed surreal.

Before returning to the boat, we stopped at a coffee bar for a local favorite dessert. A *Rum Bubba* is a luscious, yellow, cakey pastry, drenched in aromatic rum. We asked the man behind the counter if we could take it to-go. *"Si Signora, no problemo,"* he replied.

With a pair of silver tongs, he transferred the delicate dessert to a gold paper tray, wrapped the tray in purple and gold paper, sealed it with a gold sticker, tied it with a curly ribbon, and handed the pretty package to me. I was in awe! It was as if I had been given a precious gift. I couldn t believe how beautifully this €1.25 purchase had been packaged. It was a true testament to the Italian lifestyle. Sitting at the cockpit table on the deck, we ate and enjoyed the divinely delicious Rum Bubba in less time than it took to wrap it.

Vince was anxious to begin sailing, and although we were officially cleared to leave the harbor, he reluctantly decided that we would spend our first night on board in the harbor. It was late, we were tired, in unfamiliar territory, and Vince became increasingly concerned about docking or anchoring in the dark. So, we deviated from our original schedule and planned to set sail bright and early the next morning.

Our heads hit the pillows in our cozy cabin, we were asleep within minutes. Unfortunately, I was restless and woke up intermittently throughout the night. When Vince also stirred, I looked at my watch, it was only 3 o clock in the morning! Ughhh! Getting acclimated to the local time was never easy.

We were dying for a strong cup of coffee. I rolled out of bed, stumbled into the galley, and searched for the strange coffeemaker I discovered earlier when taking inventory of the cooking equipment on board. I had never seen a coffee maker like it and fumbled around with the two-part contraption, but could not figure out how to use the darn thing!

In desperation, I folded several layers of paper towels into a cone shape, held it over a glass pitcher to serve as a makeshift coffee filter. It worked like a charm. The water easily dripped into the pitcher without making a mess and the coffee tasted surprisingly good.

Later that morning, Vince was determined to learn how to use the strange coffee maker. Eventually, his persistence paid off and we were rewarded with an excellent pot of espresso.

Breakfast on board was an ample selection of the outstanding quality deli items we bought in town; chunks of salty, nutty, pecorino cheese and a few slices of prosciutto, spicy salami, and the melt-in-your-mouth mortadella with pistachio. We shared a beautiful, fragrant peach and a glass of blood-orange juice was the perfect pairing beverage for our first meal on board. Why doesn t food at home taste like this?

With the sun peeking over the horizon, Procida woke up in a flurry of activity. The morning light indicated that it was going to be a glorious day for sailing. We intended to leave the harbor right after Vince handled his financial matter at the bank.

Rush hour on Procida was quite an experience as a constant, chaotic flow of pedestrians, mini-buses, scooters, and tiny (sometimes dilapidated) cars dispatched down the narrow streets toward the waterfront. We walked up the main road to the center of town and each time we heard a motorist approaching;

we held our breath while we flattened our backs against the wall until the vehicle passed. We found life on Procida entertaining and downright charming.

Capri
The Faraglioni Rocks

By 11 o clock, we were finally ready to leave the marina. I was excited, yet slightly nervous at the same time. However, Vince commanded perfect instructions for me to release the bowlines while he released the stern lines and motored the boat out to sea. Determined to be an exemplary first mate, I did my best to follow orders, stow the fenders, and kept a watchful eye out for the unexpected.

Somehow, it all felt as if we were living in a fantasy, sailing in the Tyrrhenian Sea; the part of the Mediterranean on the western coast of Italy. I captured our departure from Procida on camera, although each image was already a memento of my heart and mind. The first spectacular sight, the stronghold on the cliff, was exactly the site I imagined seeing, as we sailed away from an ancient city somewhere in Europe.

When we were safely out of the harbor, Vince asked me to hold the boat head-to-wind while he hoisted the mainsail. No matter how many years we've been sailing, the clanging of the rigging always made me uneasy, but once the boat settled into a proper heading and we were sailing smoothly, it was completely exhilarating. No fluky winds, no luffing sails, Vince was in his glory again, constantly trimming, adjusting cleats, and coiling lines.

The deep blue water of the Mediterranean was iridescent and the sun was wonderfully warm. An ideal spot on deck invited me to stretch out, lower my blood pressure, and work on my suntan. Completely relaxed, I felt peaceful and content. Marking the true beginning of our sailing vacation, my Italian husband changed from his cargo shorts into his sexy, tight-fitting Speedo swim brief.

Unfortunately, there was not enough wind to keep the sails filled, moreover, we were fighting back a rising tide. Moving forward at only three knots, it would take forever to reach our first anchorage, near the Faraglioni Rock formation towering 100 meters above the sea off the coast of Capri. Other boats in the area also seemed to be struggling to sail in the light air. After ninety minutes of trimming for optimum boat speed but going nowhere, Vince acquiesced and turned on the motor while the humming sound of the engine lulled me to sleep.

Startled awake by a sudden wave that came at us from a passing power boat, I couldn t believe my eyes! We were on the southern coast of Capri, where the steep rocky cliffs plunged straight down to the ocean floor making it possible for us to venture close to the shoreline. The dramatic beauty of the Italian coast was undeniable, seeing the beaches and tiny fishing villages at close range was truly jaw-dropping.

Soon we came upon a pink and orange structure on the cliff. We recognized it as the Punta Tragara Hotel; a memory indelibly ingrained in my brain. Instantly, I reflected on our visit here two years prior, when we stood in front of that hotel gazing in envy at the yachts moored below. Vince declared that if we ever sailed in these waters, we would anchor in the same spot. Now, here we were, preparing to anchor. It was a *pinch-me* moment for both of us. We realized how fortunate we were to experience this opulent lifestyle.

Vince chose an ideal location for us to spend the night. When the boat was settled, he turned off the engine, put on his snorkel gear, and swam over the anchor to visually affirm that *A Kind of Blue* was secure.

The water is crystal clear," he exclaimed, "you can count the grains of sand on the bottom. There are no fish, but the water is clear as a bell."

I hurried to put on my snorkel and mask and cautiously, lowered myself partially into the water from the swim ladder. The refreshing temperature took my breath away. I needed a few minutes to adjust before I released my hand from the ladder. It was exhilarating to be immersed in the Tyrrhenian Sea, feeling jubilant and daring, we snorkeled around the boat. Although we saw only a few harmless, minute jellyfish, we didn t care, we were in the *Med* for goodness' sake, laughing and splashing, acting like children. It was grand!

After a playful swim, we rinsed off, changed into comfortable clothes, and relaxed on deck. Absorbed in our surroundings, our life in California seemed like a million miles away. Vince opened a bottle of wine and we nibbled on fresh fruit, sliced salami, and toast with marmalade. In the late afternoon, when the sun ducked behind a cloud, we grabbed two blankets from our cabin and took a dreamy nap on deck. In the evening, with no desire to eat at any of the restaurants on shore, we made sandwiches for dinner and dined on board our beautiful yacht.

Two monster-size commercial cruise ships, en route to Amalfi, sailed by. We couldn t imagine being a passenger among such a multitude of tourists. As we watched the sun turn the sky from brilliant orange to bright shades of pink and purple, before it dipped below the horizon, I felt that God must have painted this seafarer s sunset for us. "Red sky at night is a sailor s delight."

In the distance, a vintage power yacht at anchor looked particularly romantic with deck lights reflecting in the water. As our day concluded, I wrote in my travel journal: *Today was a most spectacular day!*

Still feeling quite jet-lagged, unable to sleep through the night, we woke up hours before sunrise. Vince suggested going on deck for a breath of fresh air. It was a balmy evening, and the scent of Italy and the sea in the air was intoxicating. The imperious cliffs of Capri and the granite terrain illuminated by moonlight against the starry sky appeared prehistoric, almost supernatural. As Vince observed closely, he noticed the inconspicuous spotlights suspended in the hillside s indentations that enhanced the landscape's natural beauty. Italian engineering is truly impressive.

In the distance, we saw the mast lights of the surrounding sailboats at anchor and the cabin lights on the vintage yacht were still aglow. We appeared to be anchored closer to the other boats, but in the darkness of night, I was comforted by their company. "Wait a moment," Vince suddenly said, "let's turn on your star."

With a flip of a switch, my star appeared at the top of the mast and everything was even more perfect.

Eventually, we ducked back into our cabin and slept until 8 o clock. I hoped that the long slumber helped us acclimate to the local time zone.

Though warm, the morning was cloudy and gray. I decided to serve coffee and a light breakfast in the main salon.

Off our stern, the town of Anacapri was shrouded in mist and barely visible. Our inflatable dinghy was tied up on the foredeck and an outboard motor was affixed to a wooden board at the stern. Vince was compelled to take the dinghy for a test drive, but I was reluctant and suggested that we save the experience for a brighter, sunnier time. Nevertheless, Vince lowered the dinghy into the water and in a matter of minutes, we were headed to the Faraglioni Rocks.

As we approached the imposing stone giants, they appeared even larger, and at their base, the water was even a deeper blue. While I photographed our side-trip, Vince skillfully navigated between the rocks and through the narrow passage of the arch. In hindsight, I was grateful that we didn't give in to my reluctance to go. It would have been a shame to miss getting so close to these massive stones. We returned to the boat just as it began to rain.

On board, we sprang into action to close the hatches but all was in vain. Just as Vince turned the last latch, the rain stopped, and the day became sunny and warm.

The Amalfi Coast
Amalfi

Ahhh, Amalfi! Today we were headed to Amalfi. I was nearly giddy with excitement just hearing Vince mention the romantic name of this ancient town on the famous coast road. Two years ago, we passed through Amalfi on our way to the airport, stopping only to take a picture of me posing at the entrance to the historic city center by the statue of Flavio Gioia; inventor of the sailor's compass. We didn t have time to explore, and for that reason, we were particularly looking forward to arriving at this destination.

Rather than hauling the dinghy on board and storing it up on deck where it encumbered Vince s forward vision, he decided to tow it behind the boat as we did on previous bareboat charters in the Caribbean and South Pacific. Tilted up and locked into position for towing, we also kept the motor attached to the dinghy.

When everything was shipshape and secured, Vince appointed me to take the helm while he raised the anchor with the windlass. We cleared the other boats in the area quickly and raised the sails. Once the boat was properly trimmed and we were sailing smoothly, Vince dropped his Speedo, and with a playful, boyish smile on his face, did a gleeful little dance. Adorable! I loved my naked skipper!

Unfortunately, again, there was not enough wind to sail. Ughhhh! After several frustrating hours of perpetually trying to catch a breeze, Vince lowered the sails, turned on the engine, and locked on the autopilot. With our old and trusty friend Auto steering to Vince's predefined course, we were free to snuggle up together, naked, incline into a comfortable position, and enjoy the scenery.

Suddenly, Vince pointed to a winding road that snaked through the landscape on the side of the cliffs. Look! That's the Amalfi Coast Road," he shouted.

Was that honestly the magnificent road we toured by a car two years ago? I remembered how the buses pulled in their side-view mirrors to pass on a curve.

Oh, My God, it looks so different seeing from the water," I replied. From this distance, we saw how crowded and congested the traffic was. We preferred our current mode of travel. Our expansive panoramic view from the boat was unobstructed and it was quite impressive to see the picturesque narrow highway from a different perspective. The Amalfi Coast Road is indeed one of the Wonders of the World.

As we continued past volcanic, mountainous terrain, lush vineyards, olive groves, and lemon orchards typical of the Italian countryside, charming villages among illustrious villas of distinction, ancient churches, and the remains of medieval castles spilled down the hillsides. Scattered among them, ruins of magnificent Saracen Towers still stood watch for invaders.

Eventually, Vince directed our course to a shining white village on a distant shore.

That s where we're headed," he said. "Amalfi! We will be there in about two hours."

As we approached the harbor, Vince became increasingly more concerned about executing his first Med-tie; the European way of securing a boat to the dock with the stern tied to the quay. He studied the process thoroughly and saw it carried out in the Caribbean, but he had no first-hand experience. We talked through the maneuvers, formulated a foolproof plan and although it appeared to be a complex undertaking, we were confident that we could accomplish the task without a problem.

Not knowing what obstacles we might encounter, I attached fenders to both sides of the boat. Then, without warning, I noticed a sporty, inflatable speedboat, flying a large Italian flag, rushing out to meet us. I alerted Vince that someone appeared to be heading our way, threw him a t-shirt and his Speedo, and took over command of the helm.

Vince dressed just in time. Within minutes, the speedboat pulled up alongside and a handsome man with a gorgeous tan, wearing fancy

Hollywood-style sunglasses welcomed us and inquired in a thick, Italian accent, Ciao Captain! Do you want to come into the harbor?"

Si," Vince answered.

Do you want to stay overnight?"

Si, Grazie."

"OK, come…follow me." The speedboat made a wide turn behind us and as it jetted out in front, the handsome Italian arched his arm forward and shouted again, Follow me!"

Vince and I looked at each other. Oh, My God!" I said. Welcome to Amalfi!"

We followed quickly, relieved that we had an escort who could show us the ropes. When we entered the harbor, Vince slowed our boat speed down considerably. Two men, who appeared to be waiting for us, stood on the dock with lines in hand, ready for a toss.

Vince, he wants you to go over there," I shouted, indicating where the men were standing. Vince turned the boat toward them, proceeded, then cautiously backed the stern into the slip.

Buon giorno," muttered the men as they stepped on board, focused on the job at hand. In an instant, one secured our stern lines while the other controlled the helm. It was quite hectic as the experienced men exerted with accuracy and precision. Although I was oblivious to what was happening, Vince paid heed to everything they did. At our bow, the man with the Hollywood-style sunglasses stood in his boat, signaling for my attention.

Signora," he called out as he grabbed a long, thick rope out of the water, handed the looped end to me, and pointed to a cleat.

It's beautiful here," I commented while I reached for the loop and placed it over the designated cleat.

Yes, it s not like America!" he replied.

When I heard those words, I suddenly realized where we were. Looking at the shore, I was stunned into silence by the breathtaking beauty of Amalfi. Tears filled my eyes and I choked up with emotion. Before me, jagged mountains sloping toward the sea made a dramatic backdrop for what appeared to be an imposing monastery built below the ancient remains of a castle. Charming, white buildings among pastel, cream-colored houses piled high on a rocky shore surrounded a predominant church boasting an extraordinary majolica dome.

On the cliff above the harbor, the ever-present traffic on the famous coast road proceeded at a snail s pace as it entered the resort town through a tunnel dug into a giant granite boulder. This was the magnificent Amalfi Coast!

Vince and the harbor crew were still busy tidying up lines and making crucial adjustments to ensure that we were safely and securely tied up to the dock. Soon, the crew vacated the boat. *"Ciao! Buona sera,"* they shouted, as they disembarked and tipped their hand in a saluting wave.

"Ciao, Grazie!" Vince replied and waved back.

"Prego. Arrivederci."

Finally, Vince stepped out of the cockpit and came to the bow, where I stood anxiously waiting. I just assisted in my first Med-tie," he bragged, with a lofty little attitude.

 I am very proud of you, Honey," I responded, "but look…look at this…look at Amalfi. Can you believe how beautiful this is?"

Amalfi looked like the classic Mediterranean coastal town I always imagined. I needed a minute to take it all in.

The Med-tie made it convenient to step from the boat to the dock by way of a plank. We had not been on solid ground since we left Procida, and I found it wonderful to feel surefooted. The man with the sexy Hollywood-style sunglasses walked toward us and introduced himself. His name was Giulio; he was the harbormaster. Vince asked how much we owed him.

 No, you don t pay now," Giulio said in a masculine, melodious voice with that to-die-for, wonderful Italian accent.   You pay later. How long you stay?"

 One night," Vince answered.

 OK, no problem, you pay tomorrow."

That was easy! With the formalities taken care of, I couldn t wait to explore the village.

We showered and dressed quickly. It was a short, 10-minute walk along the waterfront to the center of town. Upon entering the village the ninth-century, in-your-face, massive *Cathedral of St. Andrew* wedged smack dab in the tiny main *Piazza del Duomo*, stopped us in our tracks immediately.

The impressive cathedral was unlike any other we had seen. The uniquely Arab-influenced exterior loomed over the historic center, inciting us to climb the sixty-two steps to the immense medieval bronze doors. The Duomo is the religious heart of Amalfi and Saint Andrew is the patron saint and protector of the village.

As we anticipated, the village was dense with swarming tourists. It was difficult to walk through the narrow street lined with souvenir shops. Rather than elbowing our way through the throng of people, we settled on sitting in an outdoor café on the piazza where people-watching was prime, with a cup of coffee and a *cannoli* until the crowds dissipated. It was nice to relax amid the action, without being a part of it.

Before returning to the harbor, we stopped at a market to buy a few provisions. It was a relief to be back on the boat, where it was quiet and we were alone. Vince opened a bottle of wine and, with the cushions from the benches in the cockpit, arranged comfortable seating for us on the foredeck. While we sipped our wine, launch-boats ferried guests back to their cruise ships, tour groups returned to their buses, and independent tourists ducked back into their grand hotels for dinner.

Hours later, when the town was peaceful and quiet, we meandered back to Amalfi, this time to enjoy the genuine charm and beauty of the most famous village on the Italian coastline. We dined at a cozy *trattoria* and visited an antique stationery shop where a man created a sheet of paper from wood pulp, the way paper was made hundreds of years ago.

We strolled through the narrow main street, past souvenir shops, and the typical grocery markets displaying long braids of garlic and red peppers by the front doors. We walked to the edge of town, through a splendid arch in a charming red *palazzo*, seemingly marking the entrance to real-life Amalfi; a friendly, humble neighborhood where the locals lived undisturbed.

Eventually, we found our way back to the Piazza del Duomo, the lights of cafés and shops washed the ancient village square in an amber-colored hue. With only a few locals and a handful of tourists mingling around the *Fontana Sant'Andrea* fountain and gathered on the steps of the cathedral, the evening was filled with romance. The balmy air enticed us to stay in town a little longer, to linger somewhere leisurely with a *gelato* or a final cup of coffee.

I took pictures of the elaborate street lights; like beautiful chandeliers mounted on posts, they lined the Amalfi Coast Road on the outer edge of town and near the water along the wharf leading the way to the harbor. It was lovely to stroll hand-in-hand at an unhurried pace.

We entered the marina through the security gate, *A Kind of Blue* was the only boat at the docks. After we stepped on board, Vince led me to the bow for a parting look at Amalfi by night. My amateur photographs could not do justice to the image of this evening I would never forget.

Waking up to a sun-drenched morning, I rose up the companionway and peaked through the hatch to seize the day. The parking lot in town was still empty, an indication that Amalfi was not yet overrun by tourists. While I gazed in every direction, I caught a most endearing sight on the beach; a short and stout, bald, elderly gentleman wearing a red Speedo, belly hanging over his waistband, stood in the water up to his knees, reading a newspaper with his back toward the sun. It was quite a comical, but oh-so charming sight.

Buon giorno, my love," Vince said affectionately as he approached me with open arms for a morning hug.

Buon giorno, sweetheart," I replied.   It s a beautiful day. Come look, isn t it gorgeous?" Vince joined me on the companionway and also poked his head through the hatch. Something caught his eye as he pointed to a path in the mountainside above the Amalfi Coast Road.

Look, there s a donkey trail up there," he said, pointing in the direction of interest. A young workman led a pair of donkeys carrying baskets laden with sand to a path on a higher ridge in the mountain. We watched as several minutes later, the donkeys returned with empty baskets, only to go up again with another load. It was a typically old-world Italian way of accomplishing a heavy task.

Our itinerary today would take us west to Positano, although not without taking one last walk into the village before the tourists arrived. We hurried to the café in the piazza, found an outdoor table facing the cathedral, ordered a cappuccino, and cherished our last few moments in Amalfi. Ahhhh…the simple pleasures of life in Italy; sipping coffee in a piazza while soaking in the morning sunlight. What a beautiful moment!

When we returned to the boat, Vince was antsy, eager to settle our bill and head out. The cost for an overnight stay in Amalfi s harbor was surprisingly reasonable. After Vince and Giulio shook hands on the dock, I released the bowlines. Giulio released the stern lines while Vince steered us out of the harbor. "*Ciao,* Giulio, *Grazie!*" Vince said as we waved goodbye.

Giulio shouted back,   *Arrivederci, tutti*! Say hello to America!"

Positano

Due to the short distance to Positano, much to my delight, Vince decided not to hoist the sails. The coastline between Amalfi and Positano was truly magnificent and we marveled at the drop-dead gorgeous landscape as we motored by. This particular section of the Amalfi Coast is world-famous for the luxurious hotels scattered among quaint little villages, expensive restaurants, and prominent villas, one more extravagant than the next.

Soon, the recognizable church with its dominant majolica dome, uniquely distinguishing Positano from other villages on the coast, came into view. Without a true harbor, there were no guest docks at this waterfront, and securing a mooring was expensive. Accordingly, we cruised around in search of a suitable place to anchor in the bay.

Eventually, Vince settled on a spot near the South end where we would be sheltered from the wind and the onslaught of ferry boat traffic. I always wait to breathe a sigh-of-relief until the anchor is set, the engine is turned off and we are settled because I've come to know that is when we can relax and enjoy our new destination.

The expansive, sweeping panorama of Positano was an outstanding example of a Mediterranean landscape. The picturesque, historic village appeared to spill down to the sea in a cascade of sun-bleached, pink, peach, and white terracotta houses adorned with clusters of flourishing bougainvillea with its brilliant crepe-paper-like flowers, and trusses of sweet-scented wisteria.

I recognized the view of Positano from photographs in magazines, postcards, and film. The *Spiaggia Grande;* the Grand Beach at the foot of the *Church of Santa Maria Assunta* on the eastern shore is the most iconic scene on the Amalfi Coast.

The temperature in Positano was slightly warmer than in Amalfi, and the crystalline, ink-blue water looked inviting! "Let's take a swim. I bet we can make it to the shore," Vince said, "wanna give it a try?"

We snorkeled to a beach with coarse black sand and a rough stony shore, ideal for roaming topless, collecting beach glass and shells, and frolicking until we were famished.

When we returned to the boat, we were ready to explore the village. A short while later, we were all dolled up, and ready to venture to shore. What a total disaster!

Vince stepped from the boat into the dinghy. As he held it in position with one hand, he offered me the other to step aboard, however, the swells in the sea made it difficult for me to judge when to take the initial big step into the dingy. Despite Vince s urging me to 'just do it' without over-thinking it, I was apprehensive.

Eventually, I took the graceless 'leap of faith', and landed in the dinghy with a heavy thud! My butt was wet and became more drenched from sea-spray as we motored to shore. Once there, I stepped out of the dinghy into the shallow water, while Vince waited on board for a wave to push the dinghy ashore.

In theory, that sounded like a simple undertaking. However, after I stepped off into the shallows, a strong wave hit the back of my legs. I lost my balance and fell end-over-tea-kettle into the salty water. When Vince saw my predicament, he came to my rescue, but he too was thrown off balance into the surf by a breaking wave. He emerged just slightly short of being soaking wet! Here we were, in full view of everyone on the beach, getting tossed around like paper dolls in the tide.

Eventually, Vince stumbled to shore holding the dinghy's dock line, when a kind gentleman ran toward him to offer assistance, although, by then we were in control of our conspicuous, nightmarish circumstance.

Vince walked up the beach to secure the dinghy. Regardless, I could not explore Positano dressed like a drowned rat! Furthermore, my shoes squished water when I walked. I pleaded with him to take us back to the boat, where we could dry off and change our clothes. We were a mess!

Back on board the boat, we gained composure, fixed ourselves up, and tried again. This time Vince motored to a stationary commercial dock. Once we were on stable ground, Vince walked the dinghy to a proper place, tied it up, and said, "OK, we are here. Now, where do you want to eat?"

We chose the first restaurant with an available outdoor table facing the sea and ordered a bottle of wine. After our miserable ordeal, it was just what we needed.

Here s to us," Vince said. His toast marked a new beginning to the remainder of the day. We were in Positano…on the Amalfi Coast. How fortunate can two people be?

After a long lunch, wine, and light-hearted conversation, we walked up the winding road to the top of the village. Along the way, we bought souvenirs for family and friends, postcards, and a gelato for the walk to the South-end of town to see the most recognized view of Positano; the Church of Santa Maria Assunta, the Spiaggia Grande, and the shimmering, blue Mediterranean in the background.

As we gazed out to sea, Vince pointed to *A Kind of Blue* at anchor when he noticed that the winds had grown stronger. He became concerned about getting stranded on shore and suggested that we return to the dinghy. I dreaded boarding that darn thing again. However, there was no alternative way back to the boat.

Happy to be safely on board in time for Happy Hour, we shared a bottle of wine in the cockpit and watched the sunset. Later in the evening, Vince cooked a delicious pasta dinner with seasonings we bought in Amalfi. Sheltered from the weather, snug-as-a-bug, we ate in our comfy salon.

The wind grew stronger, and I became exceedingly anxious. While I focused on cleaning the galley and washing dishes, Vince kept a constant watch on the distance between our boat, the shoreline, and the other boats anchored nearby. I tried writing postcards and composing journal entries, but the persistent howling wind was distracting and wearing on my nerves.

Although the stars were out and the moon was bright, the sky turned dark, ominous, and eerie. Vince often made vigilant walks on deck to ensure that our windlass was holding and we were not drifting. Our anchor chain was stretched out to its maximum length. Suddenly, we heard a loud, frightening sound that Vince could not identify. He jumped up on deck and discovered that the bowline of one of the small local wooden boats became entangled with our dinghy line.

In the strong wind, the unfortunate small vessel must have broken loose and kept banging into the side of our boat. Vince tried desperately to untwist the two wet ropes while I held a flashlight's beam directed at the tangled mess. In the process, our dinghy flipped over! What a horrific situation! Vince struggled and struggled. Eventually, he separated the lines and pulled the dinghy up to the transom, where he was able to turn it upright. Thank God the motor was still attached.

With the stress of the flipped-over dinghy behind us, I prepared to hunker down in our cabin to get some rest. However, Vince had another idea.

We have to move the boat," he commanded.

What?" I replied in shock. You mean re-anchor in the dark? In this wind storm? Are you kidding me?"

Yes, we have no choice. The wind is too strong here, we have to move."

Without further discussion, Vince started the engine and while he pulled up the anchor, I reluctantly took the helm. As a novice sailor, I was petrified of moving the boat in the howling wind and the sound of the idling engine made it nearly impossible to hear Vince s commands. I watched for his hand signals and prayed that I was doing as he ordered. God watched over us as we re-anchored the boat in extremely dangerous conditions.

By the break of dawn, the wind became calm and it was finally safe for us to fall asleep. We were completely exhausted!

Positano
Our Wedding Anniversary

I woke up feeling excited and happy down to my toes. Today was our wedding anniversary and I was in a celebratory mood. "Happy Anniversary, sweetheart," I gushed, soon as Vince opened his eyes.

I threw my arms around his neck and gave my husband a loving hug and a passionate kiss. During breakfast, we exchanged greeting cards, sipped sparkling mimosas, and discussed how to spend the day honoring our seventeen years of marriage. Since I coordinated the travel details for this trip, I assigned the planning of our day to Vince. It was sunny and warm, and I was looking forward to doing whatever he planned.

While I took a long, luxurious shower, put on make-up, and dressed to go to town, Vince made several attempts to start the outboard motor. However, when the dinghy flipped over last night, gritty seawater seeped into the motor and ruined the engine beyond repair. With no other alternative, he finally detached it from the dinghy and mounted the inoperable motor to its storage location on the boat, where it stayed for the remainder of our charter.

By late afternoon, we stood on deck, pondering how to go ashore. Several water taxis shuttled passengers to the beach from the other boats around us, and although we had a ship-to-shore radio on board, we didn't know who to call for a launch service.

Out of desperation, Vince waved his arms ferociously in the air when the water taxis went by us, hoping to attract the pilots. When one finally came within earshot, Vince shouted,   We need a lift to shore!"

Thank God, the pilot acknowledged our plea and said that he would pick us up in an hour. Mission accomplished! An hour later, the cost of the short one-way trip was well worth the €4 each.

It was a picture-perfect day for celebrating! Positano was lively, and oddly, it felt festive to be among the tourist crowd. We spotted an *Enoteca; a* wine bar with a great atmosphere and a table facing the sea. The sun was low and the sky was becoming those glorious streaks of fiery orange and red. When the waiter came to take our order, Vince selected a luscious cluster of purple grapes on ice, a freshly baked *focaccia* bread with olives, anchovies, and *pancetta,* and a lovely bottle of *Pinot Grigio.*

 Happy anniversary," he said, when the wine was poured, "these past seventeen years have been the happiest of my life."

"Happy anniversary, Honey, here's to us," I responded, as we clinked our glasses, and kissed. At our leisure, we discussed our dreams for the future, made more toasts, watched people passing, and held hands across the table until the sun dipped below the horizon.

When the first star appeared and the glow of our star on top of the mast became visible against the early evening sky, to my surprise, Vince pointed to a waterfront restaurant and said it was time for our dinner reservation.

Upon entering the elegant establishment, a Maître d' welcomed us, acknowledged our reservation, and led us to a table with a panoramic view, topped with a white linen tablecloth and a vase of white flowers and baby's breath.

Grazie Signore," Vince said while the Maître d pulled out my chair and helped me scoot in place. In an instant, a waiter appeared at our table, Vince ordered a bottle of dry *Prosecco* on ice and I felt like a princess.

As we studied our menus, a small group of performers set up near our table, discreetly tuning three mandolins and an enormous harp. I loved the harp; a medieval, graceful instrument, quintessential to the Mediterranean sound. With delight, I anticipated being serenaded during dinner by these local musicians.

After the Prosecco was presented at our table, Vince did the honors and, as if on cue, the music began to play when he raised his glass in a toast. Happy anniversary," he cooed sweetly.

When he leaned over for a kiss, everyone sitting around us applauded. I was surprised and puzzled, but when I looked at Vince for a clue, his gaze was fixed on a stunning bride and groom who suddenly appeared in the dining room, followed by an elaborate entourage. Ahhh! That explained it! For a fleeting second, I assumed that the flowers, music, and applause were all for us, but now I understood that it was in honor of a wedding celebration. We laughed at our good fortune and Vince's precision timing!

After we ordered appetizers and the main course, we noticed groups of people with drinks in hand, standing on the beach, waiting to board a fleet of traditional wooden fishing boats decorated with strings of old-fashioned Christmas lights fastened to the masthead, draping down to the bow and stern. The enchanting lights lent a fairytale setting to the evening as the boats drifted into the bay and turned a corner.

I wonder where they're going," I questioned.

"They look like party boats," Vince replied. "They must be going to a beach party."

While we waited for the appetizers to be served, a clamoring noise moving toward the restaurant caught our attention. It sounded like the loud voices of demonstrators, although we also heard music and laughter. Suddenly, a conspicuous, merry group of locals marched down the hill carrying rudimentary signs, playing tambourines, percussions, an accordion, and a grinding organ. The epitome of a local hometown marching band stopped outside the restaurant, directly in front of our table.

Oh my gosh!" I exclaimed while I quickly snapped random photos of the free-spirited group. What is going on? What are they doing here? What do their signs say?"

Happy anniversary, Honey," Vince replied.

No way! Vince, did you have anything to do with this? Are they here for us?" I asked, as I swiftly searched for my Italian dictionary to translate the meaning of the homemade signs. I was so excited! Just then, our waiter came to our table to serve the appetizers.

Good, eh? Do you like?" he asked, as he nudged his head toward the band.

Yes, I love them. Who are they?" I asked, What do the signs say?"

In broken English, the waiter explained that the restaurant was hosting a fish festival on a private beach around the corner. The uproarious marching band carried signs to promote the event, tempting guests to board the party boats headed to the festival.

Ahhh! That explained it! For a brief moment, I assumed that the band was for us. Instead, the band was there to promote a fish festival! It didn't matter, I thoroughly enjoyed the experience and felt as if we were at a neighborhood party. Vince asked the waiter to bring our dinner courses at a leisurely pace so we could linger in the evening s festive atmosphere.

Our meal was top-notch delicious and we savored every bite. Afterward, we shared a decadent dessert, ordered coffee and Limoncello, before taking a dreamy walk along the north shore for a view of Positano at night.

From the top of the cliff, the twinkling lights of the village looked magical against the mountainside, and on the beach below, the colored lights of the boats illuminated the fish festival in full swing. We watched as the enticing aroma of fresh fish grilling over an open fire lured hungry guests to dining tables arranged in the sand. It seemed as if the whole world was celebrating something special tonight! I didn't want the evening to ever end.

Eventually, Vince suggested heading back to the water taxi for our pre-booked return trip to the boat. Reluctantly, we started our slow descent down the rocky path to the beach, when a dazzling display of fireworks lit up the sky. Dumbfounded, I couldn t believe what I was seeing, but then, there it was again, another explosion of brilliant color and light. Was this honestly happening? What a tremendous surprise!

Oh, My God, Vince!" I exclaimed. Are you kidding me? Wow!" The enormous bursts of fireworks kept coming, one more beautiful than the next. The loud booms and hissing sounds enhanced every explosion, and I could barely contain my excitement.

Happy anniversary, Honey!" Vince said with that familiar juvenile twinkle in his eyes.

Oh, sure," I replied, "I don't believe you anymore. You didn't arrange this…"

Sometimes, it just pays to be lucky," Vince chuckled as we hugged and kissed and laughed about the entire evening's serendipitous timing of events and circumstances.

The fireworks continued during our walk to the beach where our water taxi stood ready and waiting to take us back to our boat.

On board, I changed into more comfortable clothing, while Vince offered another drink before we went to bed. Settled into a comfortable position on the foredeck, snuggled in each other's arms, we sipped Limoncello and stared at a moonlit Positano until midnight when the last fireworks display marked the end of the fish festival.

We were tired, but our hearts were full. It had been an extraordinary day and an anniversary celebration we would remember forever!

Capri
Marina Grande

Positano was a rough anchorage. The boat was unsettled all night long, which made sleeping difficult. However, still reeling from our amazing anniversary celebration, I woke up refreshed and happy. During breakfast, I couldn't stop talking about the unplanned, lucky coincidences that made our day uniquely special. The adage of 'being at the right place, at the right time' certainly applied to yesterday's events.

Fortified by a hearty breakfast and several cups of strong Italian coffee, Vince was antsy to head to the Marina Grande; Capri's main harbor was on the Northside of the island. I took some last-minute photos of Positano while Vince programmed Auto for a course to our next destination. Before long, Positano was in the distance and our conversation turned to the adventures we anticipated on the alluring, romantic island of Capri.

After traveling for more than four hours with the annoying noise of the motor, our approach to the harbor was a happy event! When the legendary harbor came into view, I knew we were among the glamorous, elite boaters of the world. Vince pointed out the sleek, luxury yachts. Look at those masts! There's some money here. I feel like we'll be the smallest boat in the harbor."

Indeed, there were several multi-million-dollar, mega-yachts, over 80-feet in length docked here.

Wondering what the procedure was for securing a slip in the posh Marina Grande, Vince slowed our boat speed down and asked me to take the helm. As he prepared the stern lines, I stayed the course and kept an eye out for a dockhand or harbormaster signaling us toward a vacant slip, but no one came out to meet us or guide us to the docks. Vince returned to the helm, making dauntingly slow circles in the confined area near the harbor entrance trying to avoid the commercial boat traffic.

Finally, I heard someone on the dock whistle at us and point to a vacant slip in the front row. Relieved to be directed, Vince backed the boat into position while I threw the stern lines in a neat little bundle to the dockhand. Looking like professional sailors who had done this a million times, we executed our Med-tie without a problem. Vince was proud of our teamwork and complimented me on my boat handling. I was pleased that I had been helpful.

After everything was in order and the excitement of our flawless docking performance faded, we prepared to go to town.

Like Amalfi, Capri was swarming with hordes of day-trippers who arrived on ferries, tour buses, cruise ships, and private yachts. It was exasperating, fighting our way through the hectic crowds to buy a ticket to board the *funicolare* for a cable car ride to the main piazza at the top of the cliff. The ten-minute journey through the island s natural lemon groves was the best way to arrive at the center of the city. It was a beautiful day and the spectacular views at the top were worth fighting the crowds.

Despite the multitude of people, we were thrilled to be back on the island of Capri. Vince remembered exactly which bakery made the scrumptious, over-the-top delicious *pinoli* cookies we discovered two years ago. He walked right into the shop and bought a half dozen to devour while we window-shopped on the glamorous Via Camerelle; Capri s world-famous glitzy walkway.

Few places we have been to boast such a high concentration of expensive, exclusive designer shops and artisan showrooms. Vince bought a delicate Murano glass pendant for me and we enjoyed a lovely late afternoon lunch at a posh restaurant. By the time we returned to the marina, the crowds thinned out considerably.

Capri was most tranquil before dusk when the stark beauty of our surroundings was much more prevalent and the island looked like a picture postcard.

As usual, we opened a bottle of wine, prepared a few appetizers, and positioned ourselves in a comfortable spot on the foredeck. It was Happy Hour on the boat and Vince loved relaxing on deck to watch the other boats come into the harbor before nightfall. Since the Marina Grande is considered the playground of the elite, we anticipated some world-class yachts to enter the harbor. *Strangelove;* a sexy, sleek 60-foot sailboat, and a 108-foot powerboat from London were already here.

Basking in the marina s vibrant activity at twilight, we suddenly noticed that everyone around us appeared to be looking toward the horizon. Quite curious to see what caught their attention, we climbed up on the Bimini top just in time to see one of the largest privately owned yachts in the Mediterranean anchor near the seawall. The dark blue, 240-foot four-masted sailboat was the most luxurious vessel I had ever seen.

Our sailing adventure was almost over. Sadly, we were scheduled to return to Procida tomorrow. Impulsively, Vince suggested having a romantic parting dinner at one of the cozy restaurants on the Via Camerelle. What a wonderful idea! The restaurants along the waterfront would surely be overcrowded. Besides, I looked forward to riding the funicolare to the top of the cliffs at sunset.

As we walked toward town along the docks, past all the luxury yachts that now filled the harbor, we peered inside the lavish salons. Nearly all had an elaborate lounge, furnished with a large-screen television and posh furnishings.

Onboard, teak tables were elegantly set with white linen cloths, flowers, and formal dinnerware. Uniformed crew pampered guests serving cocktails and hors d oeuvres from large silver trays, while personal chefs prepared scrumptious gourmet meals fit for an admiral. Still, something about that kind of life did not appeal to me. I wouldn t trade *A Kind of Blue* for a mega-yacht.

At the funicolare station on top of the cliffs, the magnificent sea view enhanced by the brilliant colors from a glorious sunset was perfect for taking my parting photos of this world-famous, intoxicating island.

The restaurant we selected for our farewell dinner was located under a graceful old magnolia tree, with an inviting courtyard overlooking the exclusive shops on the Via Camerelle. A properly attired waiter welcomed our arrival, ushered us to a frontside table, and offered us a glass of Prosecco. Just as we took the first sip of our sparkling, celebratory drink, he opened a bottle of 2004 Gewürztraminer from a local winery that we didn't order.

"How did you arrive in Capri?" he asked, as he pulled out the cork, analytically sniffed it, and handed it to Vince. We readily told him that we sailed from Procida and talked about the highlights of our entire adventure, and we admitted that we selected his restaurant to commemorate the end of our trip.

While the waiter listened with genuine interest, he poured a touch of the wine into Vince's glass and asked him to taste it. When Vince approved, he presented us with the bottle free of charge. We were taken aback by his kindness and generosity. To pair with the wine, our waiter suggested a main course of grilled local fish prepared with roasted potatoes, green olives, and lemon. Our meal was delicious, the wine heavenly and the service impeccable. Every aspect of our last evening on Capri was unparalleled, thanks to our waiter who made it exceptional.

When we returned to the Marina Grande, the Rich and Famous yachtsmen wined and dined on their private vessels, congregated on the docks, or socialized on deck. Boisterous men wore light-colored slacks with navy blue blazers, smoked fat cigars, sipped aperitifs, and made exaggerated hand gestures as they engaged in swaggered conversation. Alluring women wore slinky gowns, glittery jewelry, and smoked long cigarettes in sexy, elegant holders. We wondered who these 'Captains of Industry' were as we walked past the affluent crowd to our modest sailboat.

The mild evening temperature was perfect for sharing one last Limoncello nightcap under the stars. Our trip to the Amalfi Coast would not have been complete without a stop at this ultra-glamorous island in the Mediterranean. Capri was the most extravagant and opulent destination we have ever visited.

At 4 o'clock in the morning, we were fast asleep when an obnoxious, noisy group of German-speaking men stomped across our deck as they docked their boat. They were giddy, clumsy, loud, and oblivious that they had so rudely awoken us. Exasperated and seething with anger, we glared at them through an open hatch. The rookie sailors had obviously been drinking. Fortunately, after they secured their boat, the crew stumbled into town and we were able to fall back asleep for a few more hours.

Today was shaping up to be 'Vince s Day'! Although this charter had been the experience of a lifetime, due to the constant lack of wind, the sailing conditions had been less than favorable.

However, today the weather looked promising and Vince anticipated an excellent day for sailing. Knowing how eager Vince was to leave the dockslip, we appeared to be tightly wedged into the harbor by the mega-yachts.

Reluctant to navigate in such a limited area, we waited until someone on the port side boat appeared on deck. Eventually, a disheveled-looking man emerged on deck with a cup of coffee and a newspaper.

Buongiorno!" Vince called out to the man on the neighboring boat. *Parla Inglese?* Do you speak English?"

To our relief, the reply was in English. When Vince expressed concern about potentially damaging our boats as we left the dock, the man immediately confirmed our lack of space and offered to fend us off.

Vince fired up the engine, I released the stern lines, while other yachtsmen suddenly appeared on decks and docks to watch Vince flawlessly, skillfully maneuver through the maze of magnificent yachts without a scratch. My heart burst with pride as I realized that all who witnessed were impressed with my husband's ability to get out of such a tight spot.

Once we cleared the marina, we raised the sails like professionals, set our heading for Procida, and engaged the autopilot. We sailed past *Phocea,* the four-masted beauty anchored on the other side of the seawall. As we looked back at her, she was even more elegant and impressive than she appeared at first glance. The wind was excellent for sailing and for a few hours, we cruised smoothly at the comfortable speed of 6 knots. It was exhilarating to feel the motion of the boat and the wind in my hair but best of all was watching Vince experience the joy of finally sailing in the Mediterranean.

When the Procida harbor was in sight, Vince asked me to contact and announce our approach to the charter office on the ship-to-shore radio. I located the proper channel, held the button on the mouthpiece down and called out, I called out, "Harbormaster, harbormaster, this is *A Kind of Blue*…over."

Afterword

In later years, we welcomed opportunities to share further explorations along the Amalfi Coast with family and friends. It was a pleasure to take them for a walk on Capri's glamorous Via Camerelle for an afternoon of world-class window-shopping, watch their eyes grow wide at our favorite bakery as they tasted the best pinoli cookies in the region, and point out the breathtaking views from the top of the cliffs with the hope that their visit too would be the experience of a lifetime.

On an early autumn vacation in 2007 with long-time friends, we rode a chairlift to the foot of Monte Solaro, three kilometers from Capri s historic center to Anacapri on the highest part of the island. Saturated with the color, fragrance, and essence of the Mediterranean, this charming town is the only other municipality on the island. Quieter and less touristy, Anacapri is a welcome breath of fresh air after spending time in a bursting-with-life Capri. We spent hours perusing through more modest ceramic shops and relaxed on a park bench with a lemon granita.

In the spring of 2012, we hosted our twenty-year-old niece Meghan and her friend Alison on a sailing vacation along the Amalfi Coast. Everywhere we visited, the beautiful, seductive girls attracted admiration from young Italian men. Meghan and Alison embraced being in a foreign country and wholeheartedly immersed themselves in the Italian culture. Enthusiastically, they sampled the local food and wine, made an effort to speak the language, and explore on their own. Watching them seize their Italian adventure was a gift and a memorable experience for us.

So captivated by Italy were Vince and I, that in 2011, we jumped at the chance to buy a second home in the exquisite medieval village of Morcella, located in Umbria; the Green Belt region of Italy.

Now we divide our time between living in the United States and Italy; where we share the Italian *Dolce Vita* lifestyle with the locals. We are truly fortunate.

The Turkish Riviera
Arrival

Istanbul

In the spring of 2010, wanderlust tickled our fancies and Vince mentioned that sailing in southern Turkey lured his interest. In particular, the sun-kissed Dalaman Coast along the Fethiye Gulf, nicknamed the 'Turkish Riviera', seemed like a pristine sailing destination, unlike anywhere we sailed before. World-renowned for its magnificent natural beauty, ideal weather conditions, bright sun, and deep blue sea this enchanted region is also steeped in archaeological history.

Vince researched the area between the Mediterranean and the Aegean Sea, while I contacted a friend who frequently visited Turkey. A fellow sailor, Avner knew us well and recommended the best Must See and Dos based on his first-hand experience and our interests.

Avner insisted that on our way to the coast, a visit to Istanbul, located at the crossroads of Europe and Asia, was paramount. Thus, we planned our Turkish adventure accordingly. I gathered and read every magazine and internet travel article about Istanbul I could find, and based on Avner's recommendation, we also hired a private tour guide to help us explore this culturally diverse city.

On September 9, filled with excitement, we began our journey aboard an early morning flight from San Francisco to Istanbul with a connection in Munich. The flights were long and tiresome, but at 11 PM the following day, we finally arrived at the Atatürk International Airport in Turkey.

From the moment we deplaned, we realized that we were in an unfamiliar part of the world. Although Turkey is not a Middle Eastern country, everything about it looked Middle Eastern, foreign, and exotic. The bustling airport was crowded and the confusing signs in Arabic and English did not clearly direct us to the exits.

Eventually, we found our way to the arrival area, where (thank God) an agent from our hotel stood waiting on the curb, ready to transfer us to the Ottoman Hotel Imperial. So far, so good! Unfortunately, the drive from the airport at night was not the best opportunity to take in the sights to form a first impression.

A small, luxury, boutique hotel in the heart of Istanbul's Sultanahmet District, the Ottoman Hotel Imperial was keenly located directly across the street from the famous Hagia Sophia Grand Mosque and near all the signature historical and cultural sights.

After our long journey, we were thrilled to arrive at the hotel where the staff warmly welcomed us despite the late hour. The check-in process was speedy and efficient, and we were assigned a modest, yet comfortable room with a view of the enormous mosque. Within moments of unpacking only the essentials, we slipped into the king-sized bed and fell into a deep sleep!

Waking up on our first morning in Turkey was exciting. It even smelled different here! Refreshed and eager to explore, we showered quickly and wandered to the hotel's self-service restaurant for an authentic Turkish breakfast.

The ambient restaurant with an unencumbered view of the hotel's historic garden boasted a spectacular stained glass rotunda. "What a beautiful room," I commented to the hostess. She responded merely with a smile, seated us at a table by the window, and invited us to help ourselves to the attractively displayed bountiful buffet.

"Oh my goodness," I whispered as I reached for Vince's hand, "what a lovely restaurant." The stained-glass dome ceiling reminded me of the Garden Court at the Palace Hotel in San Francisco.

At the buffet tables, I was not shy about lifting the stainless steel covers to closely examine what was on each of the platters. The mostly cold buffet included an ample selection of Mediterranean olives and ripened local cheeses, hard-boiled eggs, *Sucuk*; a sliced Turkish sausage made of cured beef with garlic, and spices, fresh and dried fruit, sliced cucumbers and tomatoes, honey, mixed nuts, and several different types of yogurt.

This certainly was not a typical European breakfast buffet. Beverages included freshly squeezed pomegranate juice, pineapple juice, orange juice, milk, American coffee, and Turkey's most ubiquitous morning drink; hot black tea. Vince and I eagerly filled our plates with selections from the wonderful buffet.

After a good night's sleep and a hearty meal, our jet lag seemed to fade and when the hotel concierge announced the arrival of our private tour guide, we were raring to go. A short, stout Turkish man and an Istanbul native, Celotti greeted us with a huge smile and a welcoming handshake. Speaking fluent English, he told us that he lived in Arizona for many years, until his older brothers recently ordered his return to Turkey to care for their aging father. Turkish tradition dictates that the youngest family member shall care for the oldest.

Celotti planned an incredible day of touring the signature sites, beginning with the Hagia Sofia Grand Mosque. Suddenly, we heard an announcement in Arabic over a public loudspeaker. The monotonous sound droned on and surprised us. "What is that?" I asked emphatically.

"That is the *salat*," our guide answered, "it happens five times a day; it is the Muslim call to prayer."

Vince and I had never visited a mosque, so we did not know what to expect as we entered the Hagia Sofia. Our mouths dropped at the sight of the impressive gold and black pillars and tall ceiling in the entrance hall. First constructed in 360 AD as a Greek Orthodox Christian church, the structure embodied Byzantine architecture.

The mosque's third design was completed in 537 AD, and until 1520, the Hagia Sofia remained the largest cathedral in the world. Fascinated and wide-eyed, we roamed through each large room past Ottoman tombs, mosaics, and galleries while Celotti expertly explained the history of each.

We toured the mosque for several hours. Eventually, Celotti suggested stopping at a popular eatery for lunch before the mid-day rush started. Located nearby, we entered a pub-style restaurant and took a seat at a counter overlooking the town.

Since we were not familiar with Turkish cuisine, Celotti offered to order his favorite menu items for us. The lamb stew with eggplant, tomatoes, peppers, and Mediterranean spices, and the grilled lamb kebab with yogurt sauce burst with flavor. Our first typical Turkish meal out on the town was excellent and Celotti was outwardly pleased that we enjoyed it. During lunch, Celotti described how Turkish culture has evolved over the years. Although it is influenced by the Greeks, Arabs, Eastern Europeans, and Armenians, to name a few, it is vastly becoming more like Western Europe.

Next on Celotti's agenda was a tour of the underground Basilica Cisterna; the largest of hundreds of cisterns beneath the city. As we marveled at the ancient columns and arches, he explained that the cistern was built in the 6th-century to reserve water for the Imperial Palace and its neighborhoods.

With our tour guide leading the way, we strolled to the Hippodrome constructed in 200 AD for chariot racing, and past the Obelisk of Theodosius erected in 390 AD. Soon, we arrived at Istanbul's premier treasure and most magnificent structure; the Blue Mosque; a downright mosaic work of wonder.

In the 17th century, Sultan Ahmet vowed to build an Islamic place of worship, even grander than the Hagia Sofia. With a splendid center dome surrounded by stained glass windows and intricate blue and white mosaic patterns, the Blue Mosque is considered to be the most beautiful mosque in the world and one of few to have six minarets. Indeed, Celotti saved the best tour for last.

On the way back to our hotel, we meandered through an ancient bazaar filled with unique handicrafts created by local artists. We admired glazed tiles, pottery, copper and brassware, shoes made of leather, embroidered boots, meerschaum pipes, and handwoven carpets made of every kind of natural fiber.

At last, we arrived at the hotel, and honestly, the timing was perfect for us. We received a tremendous amount of history today and our travel-weary brains could not absorb another bit of information. It was high time to take a break and relax with an adult beverage.

Ahhhhh! Just a few hours of chilling out with a cocktail at the bar, followed by a few minutes of laying down in our hotel room, gave us the second wind we needed. However, our body's internal time clock had not yet adjusted. After our big lunch, we were surprised to be hungry again. In fact, we were famished! The hotel's concierge suggested the Sultanahmet Fish House, promptly phoned in a reservation and although the restaurant was just a few blocks away, hailed a taxi for us.

When our driver pulled up to the restaurant, the manager opened my car door, gushing with gratitude for choosing his establishment. He introduced himself as Oktay, and with a snap of his fingers, turned us over to an eager-to-please waiter. The waiter shook Vince's hand vigorously before escorting us to a romantic table with a yellow tablecloth set with votive candle lighting and a small vase with yellow roses. We began to anticipate a memorable evening.

When the waiter presented the menus, instead of browsing through them, Vince asked for the evening's dinner recommendations.

"Sir, our fish is always hours fresh," the waiter responded. "Tonight, I suggest a first course of grilled anchovies, and for the main course, sea bass stew with saffron and vegetables."

"That sounds excellent," Vince replied in a spirited tone of voice, "we'll share an order of the grilled anchovies, then we'll both have the sea bass stew, with a bottle of your local white wine."

"Perfect! Allow me to show you our display case of fresh fish on ice so you can choose your fish," the waiter said as he moved my chair out from under the table, gesturing me to rise.

What? Choose our fish? We've never heard of such a thing! At the display case, our waiter named each whole fish, explaining its taste and texture before showing us the selection of sea bass. With quizzical expressions on our faces, Vince and I looked at each other and handpicked the anchovies and sea bass for our meals.

When we returned to our table, a sommelier stood ready to pour several pairings of wine for us to taste. "Turkey is the fourth largest wine producer in the world," he informed us with his chest slightly puffed with pride. After tasting a few of the wines, Vince chose a crisp, dry white wine; perfect for our meal.

As predicted and anticipated, dinner was delicious, and the quality of the food may have been the best we have ever had. For an after-dinner cordial, our waiter brought two cordial glasses and a bottle of *Raki*; a liqueur made from grape residue; a Turkish version of Italian Grappa, with a subtle taste of anisette. While Vince sampled a sip of the Raki, I ordered a Turkish black tea with honey.

The waiter smiled when he brought a tray with two glasses and a copper teapot to our table. He handed a short tulip-shaped glass to Vince and on the table directly in front of me, he placed a glass, similar to a juice glass, on a small plate with a lemon wedge and a teaspoon. With his left hand, he raised the copper tea pot above his head and, with expert finesse, poured the hot liquid straight into my glass in one long steamy stream.

When the glass was half full, he picked it up by the small plate and handed it to me. "Your tea, ma'am…Do you care for some honey?" he said, as he stepped back and offered me a charming, silver honey pot.

The traditional ritual was mesmerizing to watch, and we couldn't help applauding this unique way to serve tea. Lastly, the waiter turned his attention to Vince, filled his glass half full with Raki, and added, "*Serefe*, Cheers! Please enjoy…compliments of Mr. Oktay; the manager."

Dazzled by the impeccable service and outstanding cuisine, this was an unforgettable dining experience and we were appropriately impressed.

"Let's walk back to the hotel," Vince suggested after the bill was paid. "It's a beautiful, starlit evening, and the hotel is not far from here."

The next morning, Celotti met us in the hotel lobby at 9AM for a brisk walk to the Topkapi Palace. The entrance gate was overrun with bus-loads of tourist groups! Accordingly, Vince quickly requested to move on to the next historic site.

Unfortunately, the Grand Bazaar was also swarming with sightseers. One of the tour books I read stated that 300,000 to half a million people visit the Grand Bazaar daily!

We were adamantly not interested in pushing our way through the crowds just to see sea sponges, clothing, perfumes, purses, fabrics, piles and piles of colorful spices, and the ever-popular *Turkish Delights*. Turkish Delights are confectionary pieces made with nuts and dried fruits bound together by a rosewater or bergamot orange flavored gel made of starch and sugar, sprinkled with cream of tartar to keep the pieces from sticking together. Locals buy them by the bags full.

Without an alternative plan to continue touring, today turned out to be a short day for Celotti, which suited us fine. We were happy to be on our own for a while.

Unescorted, we walked back to the hotel, in search of an out-of-the-way place to eat lunch, when we stumbled upon a café advertising freshly made Turkish *pides*. Our curiosity inspired us to try one.

"This must be a popular snack," I commented, "look how busy this place is." A Turkish pide is similar to a pizza, with a thinner crust, shaped into an elongated oval, and topped with fried eggs, chopped fried onions, minced beef, or lamb. We ordered a minced lamb pide with onions and diced mint. It was unexpectedly spicy but extremely tasty!

While we enjoyed our first Turkish street-style food, Vince noticed a large, golden, puffy pastry shaped like a football, being served to diners sitting around us. "I wonder what that is," Vince questioned our waiter, pointing to one of the culinary masterpieces.

"Oh, that is *lavash*, made with yeast, flour, a bit of sugar, water, and salt. When it bakes, it becomes a light-as-air, pillow of bread. Served piping hot, brushed with butter, and sprinkled with toasted sesame seeds on top, we eat it with goat cheese or butter," the waiter replied as he tossed a joyful kiss of his fingertips in the air. We ordered one immediately.

When it came to our table, puffed-up and crispy, I snapped a photo before the thing of beauty deflated. While it was still hot, Vince tore a piece off and offered it to me. "Tell me what you think," he said. Even without goat cheese or butter, it was scrumptious.

After savoring these wonderful foods, we wandered back to the hotel in plenty of time to take a nap before dinner.

One of Avner's suggestions was to have Turkish coffee at the Pierre Loti Café while watching the sunset over the Golden Horn. The famous café was named after a French novelist who used to go there in the 1800s for coffee and inspiration. We loved the idea and wished that Avner could have been our tour guide, or joined us there for coffee.

Just before sunset, we took a taxi to the Eyüp District, where the coffee shop was located off the beaten path on Pierre Loti Hill. Surrounded by trees, Pierre Loti Café's exterior reminded me of an English cottage with leaded glass windows and charming planter boxes swaddled in fragrant white jasmine vines.

Adjacent to the café's entrance, we paused at the outlook point to admire the view of the Golden Horn where the Bosphorus Strait meets the Sea of Marmara. Although the sun would not set for another hour, an orange-y, golden glow was beginning to fall on the Asian and European sides of the Bosphorus and as we gazed at the panorama in front of us, I knew that we would never forget it. I realized where we were in the world, and it was indeed inspirational and somehow spiritual.

When Vince opened the front door to the café, an intoxicating nutty coffee aroma enveloped us. The building's interior resembled a library or a reading den in a Tudor-style home. The walls, covered in rich, dark-hued wood panels, displayed vintage frames depicting photographs of Istanbul's historic past and bookshelves filled with leather-bound books and long wooden, church pew-style benches lined the rooms.

Newspapers and periodicals were strewn about on tables inviting visitors to sit and read with a cup of Turkish coffee prepared the traditional way, from beans ground fine with a mortar and pestle and brewed three times for that perfect, rich, pure cup of wonderful, coffee flavor. We sat on one of the church-pew-style benches against the wall, sipped the strongest coffee I ever tasted, and took pictures to document our experience.

Feeling the effects of a coffee-buzz, we hailed a taxi to the Khorasani Kebab and Grill; another recommendation by the hotel s concierge for excellent food. Upon arriving at the restaurant, the host met us in the same welcoming manner we encountered at the Fish House last evening. Was everyone in Turkey so outwardly cordial?

The restaurant's interior was sultry-smokey, yet romantic, and loaded with ambiance enhanced by a charcoal grill in the center of the dining room. Soon as the host seated us, a server brought a steamy-hot lavash to our table. Then, the manager came over, introduced himself as Aagha, and asked if we would like to partake in the evening's special tasting menu. Eagerly, we accepted his invitation.

All at once, our table became a gastronomic display of Turkish cuisine. Grape leaves stuffed with ground beef and rice, lamb, chicken, and beef kabobs, raw sliced onions sprinkled with sea salt, and falafel balls represented the appetizers. The main course included boneless chicken in a coconut milk sauce, grilled lamb chops with spicy balsamic rice, beef cooked in a creamy yogurt sauce, and eggplant cooked in a fresh tomato sauce with yogurt and roti. Side dishes of chickpeas and beans, and a grilled cheese-filled pita bread completed the menu! It was an impressive array of food.

In disbelief, Vince discreetly giggled in his fist and whispered, "I hope this is it...please tell them not to bring any more food to our table. Who's going to eat it all?" I knew he was joking. We were happy to taste every single dish.

As we worked our way through the feast, the manager, our waiter, and the other table attendants each inquired how we enjoyed tonight's tasting menu. We gave everyone the same answer. "It was outstanding!"

After we couldn't eat another morsel, our table was properly cleared and Aagha reappeared at our side. "Are you ready for dessert?" he asked. "Tonight, we present our freshly baked *Baklava* and *Helva*."

Baklava is made by alternating layers of nuts and honey between thin sheets of crispy, flaky pastry. Helva is a starchy custard made with sesame seeds and nuts.

"To digest the meal, we have Raki, and for the grand finale, you must have our Turkish coffee or black tea," he added. Oh, My God, I couldn't breathe! Stuffed to the gills, I thought we'd explode, but Vince didn't want to insult the staff by refusing dessert. Reluctantly, he ordered a Baklava to share and I ordered a cup of black tea. Tonight's meal was a showstopper. I didn't know how many more of these we could endure….

On our return taxi ride to the hotel, Vince and I chatted non-stop about the impeccable service and the extraordinary Turkish cuisine.

The next morning, we arose, feeling physically fit, rested, and eager to begin our new day. This was our last one with Celotti, accordingly, we requested to do an all-important activity that Avner said we shouldn't miss; a boat cruise on the Bosphorus.

From our hotel, we meandered to the Eminönü District; a commercial area on the waterfront, where we boarded one of the many tourist boats that cruise the strait between the Sea of Marmara and the Black Sea, separating the European continent from Asia Minor. The two-hour cruise began at the Galata Bridge; the bridge that joins the two continents.

Leaving behind a splendid view of the New Mosque on the southern end of the bridge, we cruised past lavish summer mansions built in the Ottoman-style, opulent palaces, museums, fortresses, and quaint villages. The weather was ideal for cruising, and since the boat was not swarming with tourists, I wandered around the deck freely to photograph the views.

When we returned to the dock, Celotti met us at the embarkation ramp, energetically waving, he seemed enthused. "We have a lunch reservation at the best restaurant in Istanbul," he said, "come, follow me."

Through the hustle and bustle, we walked to the Hamdi Restaurant in the center of the city, renowned for mouthwatering Turkish cuisine, and magnificent views of the Golden Horn, the Galata Bridge, and the Bosphorus. Upon entering the dining room, our jaws dropped at the ostentatious floor-to-ceiling windows that provided a 360-degree, panoramic view of Istanbul.

Celotti approached the Maître d' who motioned for us to follow him to a beautiful table in the middle of the restaurant. The restaurant was crowded with groups of tourists and other private guides with their guests. "This restaurant has the best view of the city, and the food is fantastic," Celotti said. "Soon the tour buses will come and it will get very crowded." Oh my goodness, I thought it was crowded already.

When it came time to order lunch, Celotti did the honors, and once again, our table became a gastronomic display of Turkish cuisine. As if on cue; an array of platters heaped high with delectable fare appeared, followed by a luscious roasted eggplant salad, a fragrant gazpacho, and several types of juicy, flavorful kebabs served with rice, pita bread, and a green salad.

As we indulged, every dish tasted divine. However, my favorite was the spicy *birecik* kebab; a beef kebab named after the place where it originated. To complement the meal, Celotti ordered a pitcher of *Efes Pilsen;* the most popular Turkish beer among the locals.

Like the other meals we've had here, this one was also outstanding. Extremely high quality, lean meats, along with a wide variety of seasonal vegetables, sauces made with yogurt, and no heavy carbohydrates, Turkish cuisine appeared to be a healthy diet.

After lunch, it was time to say farewell to our wonderful, eloquent tour guide. Tomorrow, we planned to pick up a rental car to begin our road trip to Göcek; a small town on the coast where most bareboaters start and end their Dalaman Coast and Turkish Riviera adventures.

Together, we took the elevator down to the street level, where we thanked Celotti, paid him for his excellent service, and wished him luck in caring for his aging father. After we parted ways, Celotti stepped into a cab and, moments later, disappeared into the horrific maze of traffic. Istanbul s biggest urban problem is the congested traffic flowing in and out of the city.

When we returned to our hotel room, ready to relax and let our lunch settle, Vince noticed that his jacket was missing. Tracing back our steps from the last time he remembered wearing it, he realized that he left it at the Khorasani Bar and Grill last evening. Determined to retrieve his favorite jacket, Vince decided to walk back to the restaurant, while I stayed behind to organize our belongings and prepare for an early check-out in the morning.

It was hours later when Vince returned wearing his jacket. He was outwardly excited. "Hi Hon, you will *not* believe what happened to me. I had lunch with Aagha and his dad!"

"What? What do you mean? You just had lunch…what happened?"

Vince was almost breathless as he spoke. "When I arrived at the restaurant, Aagha was sitting at a table with another gentleman. He saw me immediately and said, 'Hey, I remember you…you left your jacket here, it's on the coat rack over there.' Then he introduced me to his father…his father invited me to join them for lunch. When I said that I had already eaten and that you were waiting for me at the hotel, Aagha said it was a grave insult to refuse his father's invitation. So, I had no choice…I had to stay for lunch."

Ahhh…I loved Vince's heartwarming story. It was a testimony to the Turkish people's innate hospitality and kindness.

On our last evening, a sign in the hotel lobby advertised a Happy Hour live performance of zither music with complimentary appetizers. There was no better way to say goodbye to Istanbul, than to sit in the hotel's candlelit courtyard, sipping wine, and overlooking the city at night while we listened to the soothing sounds of the zither. We loved our time in Istanbul!

Road Trip to Göcek
Bursa

Foregoing breakfast to beat the rush hour traffic, we checked out of the Ottoman Hotel Imperial and said goodbye to the staff who made our stay in this lovely boutique establishment so memorable. Although it was not a long distance away, the taxi ride to the car rental agency took almost an hour due to the heavy, hap-hazard traffic flow. Vince and I realized immediately how confusing the directional roadsigns were and anticipated a challenging drive out of the city.

Obtaining the rental car was relatively a smooth process. We were assigned a comfortable Mercedes sedan. Looking forward to discovering what lay ahead, we were eager to begin our road trip to Göcek.

Vince programmed the car's GPS (Global Positioning System) for the shortest route to the Kitap Evi Hotel in Bursa, where we reserved a room for our first night on the road. After converting the system's language to English, he punched in the hotel's address and we were on our way.

Almost rudely so, Turkish drivers were extremely aggressive. Nevertheless, Vince was not intimidated and matched their driving style. Before long, we crossed over the Galata Bridge and left Istanbul behind us in the distance.

The landscape in Asia Minor changed rapidly. The occasional mosque was less grand, there were tree-lined streets, nicely maintained public parks with benches, and most noticeably, the Asia Minor side was much less populated and chaotic.

Two hours later, we felt more relaxed, being away from the chaos made it easier to breathe. "I could use a bite to eat," Vince said, "all the stress of getting out of the city has given me an appetite." A convenient roadside gas station, with an outdoor café advertising a Trucker's Lunch for ₺126 *(Turkish Lira)*; the equivalent of only $7 seemed like a nice place to eat.

We seated ourselves at one of the four tables, and almost immediately, a friendly attendant, dressed in a mix of European and typical Turkish clothing came over and spoke to us in English. "Welcome, we have no menu, we cook our food fresh every day," he said. "I will bring you what we cooked today."

The first course was a bowl of chicken wing soup. "Made from boiled chicken wings, we simmer our broth for hours to pull out the true flavor of the chicken, then we remove the bones, shred the meat and garnish the soup with crispy, fried chicken skins," the server explained. *"Afiyet olsun…*eat it in good health," he added, as he placed two bowls of the savory soup on the table.

"Wow, this is delicious…chicken wings and fried chicken skin…what could be better than this?" I commented after my first sip from the plastic spoon. The depth of flavor was robust, and the crispy chicken skin was to-die-for!

The main course was a plate of fried calf liver and crispy potatoes, white rice, and a cucumber salad with tomatoes and red peppers. Freshly baked, rustic bread and bottled water came with the meal. The quality of the food was outstanding and every mouthful was packed with flavor. "I can't believe we're eating gourmet food at a roadside gas station," Vince remarked, "why can't American gas stations serve food like this?" When we paid our bill, we thanked our waiter and asked him to give our compliments to the cook.

Another 90 minutes later, we arrived at the edge of Bursa. At first glance, the town resembled a small village somewhere in Mexico, with dirt roads, desert plants, and men leading donkeys carrying baskets ladened with goods. Although Bursa is Turkey's fourth largest city and the first capital of the Ottoman Empire, to our western eye, the significance of Bursa was not outwardly apparent.

However, as we approached the historic city center and saw the *Ulu Cami;* the Great Mosque at the foot of Mount Uludag, we began to understand the city's importance in Turkey's history. The mosque was large enough to accommodate 5,000 worshippers!

Unfortunately, our car's GPS could not locate the Kitap Evi Hotel's specific address. Testing our patience, the system led us down roads that became narrower and narrower. Suddenly, I noticed an insignificant sign marked with the name of our hotel nailed to a telephone pole. Since there was no direction indicated, I asked Vince to stop the car while I walked up the small street to investigate. The street became a dirt path and the hotel was nowhere in sight.

Without hesitation, I approached a young pedestrian woman and asked for directions to the hotel. She spoke only Turkish but tried to be helpful. I showed her my reservation slip, pointed to the name of the hotel, and shrugged my shoulders, hoping she would understand that I was lost and could point the way. From her hand gestures and body language, I gathered that she wanted me to follow her.

Vince perceived what was happening, parked the car, and stepped out to keep an eye on us. At the end of the path, the woman turned left and lead me to what looked like a questionably safe neighborhood. Immediately, I became concerned about the hotel I had chosen for us until I realized that we were walking on a medieval castle wall. When the woman pointed out the beautiful view of the Bursa Valley and our hotel just a few feet away, I was relieved. The hotel was gorgeous, and I was thrilled!

I thanked the woman for her time and kindness and ran back to Vince, who stood anxiously waiting for me. Quickly, I rattled off my experience with the woman and told him how gorgeous the hotel was.

"What a pleasant surprise and kind act," he said, "everyone we've met in Turkey has been extremely nice and friendly." I wholeheartedly concurred.

The Kitap Evi Hotel was located on the largest bastion of the ancient city wall and provided a fabulous view of the Great Mosque. Upon entering the lobby, a woman and her toddler greeted us. In broken English, she welcomed us and informed us that the hotel was a former bookstore and coffee shop. The toddler was her 2-year-old daughter. Some years ago, she and her husband bought the business and converted it into a Bed and Breakfast-style hotel.

After Vince signed the guest book, she presented us with a charming skeleton key to a beautiful suite with an unexpected, oversized bathroom and a clawfoot bathtub. The floor-to-ceiling windows overlooking the mosque at the foot of the mountain provided quite a view, especially at twilight when the mosque and the city seemed to bask in the pinkish glow of twilight.

Once we dropped our luggage on the bed and loosened our clothes, it was high time to have an adult beverage. After driving all day, Vince was more than ready to indulge. Dinner was served in the garden under the canopy of a magnolia tree and the soothing sound of a trickling fountain and a tranquil pond; home to live turtles and snow-white water lilies.

At the garden gate, a waiter extended his hand. "Two for dinner?" he asked. We followed him through the garden, along a pathway illuminated by tiny fairy lights. Throughout the garden, topiaries tastefully decorated with the same fairy lights marked table placements, and café lights strung across the courtyard to a center candlelit chandelier created a magical atmosphere.

"Ohhh, this is beautiful," I whispered, "this is a magic garden."

Near the center of the courtyard, underneath the chandelier, the waiter stopped at a round table adorned with taper candles and a vase holding a single white flower. "Your table," he said while gallantly holding out a chair for me.

"This is the perfect setting for a romantic dinner," Vince commented. "Will you please bring us each a glass of your local wine?"

"Of course, sir." The waiter left, returning promptly with two menus and a tray with two glasses of red wine, and two glasses filled with sparkling water over ice, garnished with a cucumber spear and a sprig of mint. We didn't know what kind of wine it was, and it didn't matter. We were more than ready to take a sip, feel the tickle in our throats as it went down, and relaxed our weary spirits.

Although the food selections sounded delicious, we were too tired to eat a heavy meal. We selected the grilled chicken with fresh tomatoes and basil for dinner, along with a bottle of *SARAFİN* Cabernet Sauvignon. When the wine was brought to the table, and the glasses poured, I raised mine to make a toast, "Congratulations on getting us to Bursa safely, Honey. Getting out of Istanbul and finding our way here was no easy feat." I clinked my glass with Vince's and kissed him on his cheek.

After dinner, we didn't linger over coffee or an after-dinner glass of Raki this time. We were ready to call it a day…

Selçuk

After a good night's sleep, we woke refreshed, re-energized, and ready to tackle the next leg of our road trip to the coast. However, having a hearty breakfast was our priority this morning! We barely ate our dinner last night, so we were ravenous, and since Vince was antsy to put some distance behind us before we stopped for lunch, we headed to the garden where the morning meal service was underway.

The same waiter who attended to us last evening greeted us at the door. "Good morning," he said, "would you like to sit at your same table?" Of course, that suited us perfectly.

We looked around for the usual buffet, however, before we could ask questions about the meal service, our waiter returned with a pot of coffee, two cups, and saucers. Another server followed behind him, pushing a cart with an array of specialty breakfast items on small plates.

While our waiter poured the coffee, the server methodically placed the small plates in front of us in a tidy display; goat cheese with walnuts, a mix of warm marinated olives, dried figs, sliced cucumbers drizzled with green olive oil, diced tomatoes with basil and peppercorns, thinly sliced cured meats, dried apricots filled with cream cheese and a basket with warm bread rolls sprinkled with toasted seeds. To add to the elaborate spread, a third server brought fresh orange slices and cheese omelets to our table!

"May I bring you anything else?" our waiter asked, while the other two servers disappeared. Oh my goodness, what else could we possibly wish for?

After that sensational breakfast, we settled the bill and checked out of the hotel, complimenting the owners on the meticulous service they and their staff provided during our stay. As a token of appreciation, they presented us with a luxurious, linen hand towel, embroidered with the name of the hotel. Their gesture touched our hearts and the towel was a treasure that I would proudly display in our bathroom at home.

Our next overnight destination was Selçuk; a town in the Province of Izmir, in western Turkey. Selçuk was the gateway to Ephesus; our primary goal. We planned to travel the seven-hour drive at a leisurely pace and Vince promised to stop for taking pictures along the way.

As we drove through the hot and desolate terrain, we waited for the scenery to become more appealing. Vince remarked, a bit in jest, "I'm waiting for the countryside to get pretty. So far it's *pretty ugly!*"

His comment made me laugh, it was exactly what I was thinking but didn't verbalize. In addition to the dry landscape, countless unsightly satellite antennae, randomly attached to homes and apartment buildings, detracted from anything pleasing to look at. However, thinking positively, I replied, "I'll hold my opinion until we get to Göcek, hopefully, the scenery on the coast will be phenomenal."

Driving for hours through nothing but the same barren landscape was grueling, we needed a stretch, a bathroom break, and before long, we also needed gas. Apparently, in this part of the country, gas stations were far-and-few-between.

"We'll stop at the first gas station we see," Vince stated. As luck would have it, the first one we came to advertised a daily lunch menu. Since breakfast was more than four hours ago, and our previous lunch experience at a gas station had been delightful, I suggested that we get something to eat.

For a gas station, the dining room was quite stylish, with 1950s cafeteria-style tables and chairs and a daily menu handwritten on a blackboard on an easel. I stepped up to the counter and ordered two beers, a small green salad, and a skewer of grilled chicken for us to share. Again, we were astounded to see the large selection of cooked-to-order, oversized portions of home-style, local cuisine presented at our table.

In addition to the green salad with tomatoes and peppers, an attendant brought a basket with freshly baked pita bread, a colorful mix of grilled vegetables drizzled with peppery, green olive oil, six skewers of grilled chicken, and three hand-formed patties of grilled pork! As if that wasn't enough, we were served a hefty portion of ice-cold watermelon slices for dessert.

"How much food did you order?" Vince remarked. "There's enough here to feed an army." I promised that all I ordered was a salad and a chicken skewer! As if prepared in an award-winning restaurant, the food tasted delicious!

Sufficiently fortified and ready to tackle the last few hours of our drive to Selçuk, we paid the nominal bill and continued on our way.

Getting off the highway was a pleasant change, but now we looked forward to arriving at our hotel and getting out of the car. Alas, to our frustration, the GPS failed to locate the hotel again and the internet map on our mobile phone was no better at directing us. At our wit's end, I called the hotel to explain our predicament. The young man who answered the phone calmly asked me to describe our car and our surroundings. Understanding that we were in the vicinity, he offered to drive out on his scooter to meet us so we could follow him to the hotel.

Once again, the kindness of the Turkish impressed us. Before long, a young man on a beige Vespa appeared in front of our car, and gave us a thumbs up, followed by an arc of his arm as if to say, "Follow me." The Urkmez Hotel was just a few minutes away.

The cost of our accommodations was only $35 per night, and I began to feel a bit apprehensive about the quality of the hotel I had chosen. However, we only planned to stay for one night, so if our room was clean, with a shower, a toilet, and a comfy bed, I wouldn't object. Thank God, we were pleasantly surprised.

Upon entering the front door, we were immediately struck by the bare-bones establishment, but the hotel staff was friendly with a jovial demeanor, so it wasn't long before we recognized that something was charming about this place.

For the past twenty years, the hotel was owned and operated by two brothers. One of the brothers was the young man who came out to meet us on his Vespa, the other promptly carried our luggage to the room, opened the windows, and pointed out the beautiful view of the Selçuk Castle on top of Ayasuluk Hill. Soon as he left, we let out a sigh of relief that the long drive was behind us. We changed into more comfortable clothing, splashed water on our faces, and headed into town.

Selçuk won us over instantly. With several interesting shops and restaurants, the walkable historic center exuded a friendly, social vibe. Near our hotel, we spotted a park with stone benches and a place to buy a cold beer. Perfect! While Vince bought the beers, I snagged a bench for us to sit, people-watch and seriously decompress.

As we began to unwind, we noticed that the center of town evolved around the ruins of an ancient Roman aqueduct with pillar remnants that provided nesting places for storks. The enormous nests reminded us of our visit to Strasbourg, France, years ago. The leggy, long-necked birds nested there too, but just like in Selçuk, we didn't see them because, by the end of August, the storks migrate to Africa.

When evening fell, Selçuk became even more charming as the town transformed into a livelier, communal place for local diners and shoppers. Suddenly, the aqueduct metamorphosed into a beautiful fountain, enhanced by ice-blue lighting.

"Let's explore this town," I cheered, forgetting how tired we were. "Let's check out a few of the shops." Ordinarily, Vince wasn't thrilled about shopping, but after driving most of the day, he welcomed the opportunity to walk and stretch our legs.

The first shop that caught our eyes sold lovely gauze, cotton, and linen clothing in styles that reminded me of yachting or resort wear. I loved the men's loose-fitting shirts and pants, the women's long, sleeveless dresses, and broomstick-style skirts. Without prompting him, Vince bought a black gauze shirt for himself and one just like it in white. In another shop, he bought a white flowy sun dress for me, and in still another shop we purchased hand-painted bowls as souvenir gifts for our mothers.

As we searched for a restaurant, we discovered a shop selling exquisite woven scarves and pashminas in every color imaginable. Reasonably priced, the soft luxurious fabric felt expensive to the touch, and I couldn't resist buying several of them in various colors. Our first shopping spree in Turkey was a hit and a success!

It was well after 9 o'clock when we came to Wallabies Restaurant; located near the aqueduct fountain at the edge of town. The outdoor tables, crowded with local diners, indicated how good the food must be. A waiter acknowledged our interest in his restaurant and pointed to a table where the guests were about to leave.

"Welcome, I'll have this table cleaned right away," he said, "my name is Aydin, we have no menu, but we feature a typical Turkish, Mediterranean cuisine tonight…would you like to join us for dinner?"

The idea of not having to decide what to order appealed to us. Moments later, Aydin brought a basket of warm lavash, a dish of sliced cucumbers in a yogurt and herb sauce, and a bowl of *baba ganoush*; a thick spread made from pureed eggplant, olive oil, sesame seeds, and a pinch of salt. The main course was a platter of fresh fish kababs floating in a piquancy, rich sauce made with red bell peppers and black olives.

Dessert was an impressive fruit sculpture made from orange slices, green grape clusters, and watermelon wedges sprinkled with pomegranate seeds. The creation, held together with long wooden skewers and toothpicks, was served with a selection of medium-soft cheese and crackers.

"Wow, that is beautiful," I cheered. We'd never seen such a wonderfully unique way to serve fruit! I asked Aydin to take our picture with the fruit sculpture on our table. No one at home was going to believe this!

Ephesus

A wonderful whiff of fresh ground Turkish coffee brewing and eggs frying aroused us from our slumber. I peeked through the window and saw a glorious sun rising over Selçuk Castle on the hill. This morning was shaping up to be a beautiful day for exploring Ephesus; once considered to be the most important city in Greece.

Built in the 10th-century BC, near a harbor in western Asia Minor, Ephesus was a significant center of trade. According to local belief, it is also said to be the last home of the Virgin Mary. While visiting this part of the world, Vince did not want to miss touring Turkey's most important cultural heritage site. So, after having breakfast on the rooftop terrace, we checked out of the Urkmez Hotel. I hugged the two brothers, thanked them for rescuing us when we were lost, and off we were, headed for Ephesus.

While Vince drove, I read a few of the historical highlights from the Ephesus tourist brochure out loud. A newly excavated exhibit called The Slope Houses has only been open for public viewing since 2006. The importance of these typical Hellenistic and Roman settlements of the rich has been compared to the 1st-century villas of Pompeii. Vince looked especially forward to seeing the intricate mosaic tile work and frescos in these timeworn homes.

Upon entering the Magnesia Gate entrance, freelance guides hoping to be hired on the spot, handed out more free literature about the ancient city. Nevertheless, we preferred to take a recorded, self-guided tour with portable headsets. It was phenomenal seeing marble ruins and relics indicating a civilization dating back to 7000 BC, when Ephesus was a powerful political, cultural, and financial capital, exuding wealth. So that Vince would not miss a single artifact, we explored the ancient site at a snail's pace for hours and although he could not get enough of Ephesus, my interest shifted to refreshments and souvenir shopping.

"Hon, I'll meet you at the Visitor's Center…take as much time as you want," I said to Vince, not hinting at my desire to cool off and do some shopping.

With temperatures nearing 90 degrees, the afternoon was hot and dry, ideal for sipping an ice-cold beer and snacking on chilled fruit. The Turks consume an abundance of fresh fruit, served in single-use containers. Cold orange sections, quartered nectarines, watermelon wedges, and even lemon slices sprinkled with a salty-sweet, sugary substance that tasted a bit like tamarind, are popular snacks among the locals. Preparing to settle in for some serious people-watching with a large glass of beer and a dish of cold mixed fruit, I pulled out a chair at a bistro table under a date palm tree.

Immersed in observing the tourist crowd, among visitors dressed in European and western style garb, I was intrigued by folks dressed in Islamic-style clothing. Women wearing *hijab* scarves, *burqa* veils, *abaya* cloaks, and men wearing *kurta* tunics were fully dressed according to the teachings of Islam. It was an international fashion feast for the eyes. Without being conspicuous, I photographed a few of the most interesting passers-by.

Before I realized it, more than an hour elapsed and it was time for me to shop! Another broomstick skirt caught my eye immediately, this one in a lovely terra-cotta color. I bought a linen tablecloth, a long can't-live-without-it celestial blue scarf, and another one in corn yellow, and I couldn't resist buying another pashmina as a thoughtful present for a friend, or…to wear with my black wool coat should I decide to keep it.

Some vendors willingly bargained for prices, while others strictly adhered to the handwritten price on the sales tags attached to the merchandise. Nevertheless, I thoroughly enjoyed my shopping spree.

Eventually, Vince finished his extensive tour and, apparently happy to see me, found me at the Visitor's Center.

"Hi sweetheart, sorry I took so long, but Ephesus was mind-blowing! Can you believe that the Library of Celsus was built in 135 AD? The Gate of Augustus with its massive arches was my favorite," he said feverishly, followed by, "What did you do? Did you go shopping? Where can I get a cold beer…" Honestly, Vince's passion for Turkey's history was admirable and almost contagious.

"I'm pleased that you took your time," I replied. "Look, I have been shopping," but raising my shopping bags to show Vince caused little reaction.

Together we sat at the bistro table under the date palm tree, while Vince was refreshed with a tall glass of beer. After I showed him a few of my purchases, we ordered *shwarma* wraps for lunch. A shwarma wrap is a pita-pocket stuffed with a thinly sliced chicken, pork, lamb, garlic, and onion mixture, which has been slow-cooked on a rotating spit. Drizzled with yogurt and mint sauce, this typical, succulent Middle Eastern street-food-style sandwich was uniquely delicious.

Göcek

Marina Skopea

After finishing our shwarma wraps, we continued on our daunting six-hour drive to the coast. If Vince adhered to the speed limits, we hoped to arrive before dark. When we approached the Dalaman region, the landscape became indeed more scenic and by the time we reached the coast, the drive to Göcek was stunningly beautiful.

Located in the heart of the breathtaking Turkish Riviera, Göcek is at the head of Skopia Limani; set on the Gulf of Fethiye. Yachtsmen and bare-boating enthusiasts from all over the world choose this quaint bohemian town as a place to organize, plan and unwind before leaving the harbor in search of adventure. By the time we arrived at our hotel, our excitement to explore this popular sailing destination, dotted with picturesque secluded bays and small enchanted islands, was difficult to contain.

Our charter company booked a room for us at the Efe Hotel, located in the center of town and within walking distance of Marina Skopea. Although the hotel was an older establishment with slightly outdated decor, it was well-appointed, with a swimming pool, lush gardens, and a friendly staff. We were delighted that the driving-part of our Turkish adventure was over and looked forward to relaxing by the pool until our charter started tomorrow afternoon at 1 o'clock.

Although it was late, after unpacking and settling in our room, I phoned the concierge to ask for a restaurant recommendation; one where we could enjoy an unhurried, easy-going dinner with a bottomless bottle of wine. The concierge recommended taking a stroll to Marina Skopea where a plethora of restaurants, outdoor cafes, and food trucks were always open. That proved to be an excellent recommendation!

Situated on the water's edge, Marina Skopea was a long, well-lit promenade; a walkway illuminated by lanterns and café lights, lined with food trucks, outdoor bistros, restaurants, and vendors pushing handcarts selling local favorite, take-away snacks. Behind the restaurants, an attractive market square with shops selling handmade crafts appeared to be the center of local activity, while the promenade buzzed with boating community excitement. The area radiated a welcoming, festive vibe.

"I love this marina! It feels like a party!" I nearly shouted, grabbing Vince's hand, leading him to the action.

"Well, then…let's party," Vince replied enthusiastically. Meandering past the restaurants, we stopped to read the menus and savor the aromas of Middle Eastern cuisine wafting through the balmy, evening air, when a vendor with a pushcart feeding a hungry crowd drew my interest.

"Let's see what he is selling," I said, "whatever it is, the locals seem to love it." Upon closer inspection, we saw the vendor selling large, fresh-off-the-grill *midye dolma*; mussel shells stuffed with rice, seafood, and herbs. A handwritten sign on his cart advertised one stuffed shell for ₺1. Almost pushing my way through the crowd, I bought two and gave one to Vince. Before we got the mussel shells to our mouths, the vendor squeezed fresh lemon juice on two more shells, placed them on a paper napkin, and rather insistently, pushed them toward us. Not that we minded…

"Do you want to try them with hot sauce?" he asked. Of course, we did, again, another two shells were presented immediately. Without realizing it, we ran up quite a bill devouring these delicious, on-the-spot appetizers! Street food-style eating always seemed to be our favorite way to dine.

We continued our romantic walk on the promenade along the harbor. There were so many foreign people and unfamiliar boat styles to look at and admire. Built on the Southwest coast of Turkey, gulet boats seemed to be a popular charter boat here. Although Vince was familiar with this classic, wooden boat style, I was not, and found their exotic beauty and craftsmanship fascinating.

When we read the menu posted outside the Restaurant Marinara, the whole grilled fish with lemon inspired us to sit at one of the outdoor tables facing the promenade and the marina. When the waiter came over to greet us, we both ordered the fish without considering another menu option.

While we waited for our meal, the waiter brought a bottle of white wine from Bodrum to our table. "This wine is one of the oldest, and best known from this region," he said, as he presented the bottle to Vince so that he could read the label. "This dry wine will pair nicely with your meal." Vince tasted the wine, smiled approvingly, and asked the waiter to proceed pouring and leave the bottle at the table.

The meal was superb! The fish was delicate but flavorful and the crispy potatoes cooked in a skillet with butter, rosemary, and garlic were the perfect accompaniment to the fish.

By the time we finished dinner, it was late in the evening and the dinner crowds everywhere on the promenade began to die down. Boaters in the marina disappeared below deck, and tourists migrated to their hotels. Bone-tired from a full day of exploring, driving a long distance, and the relaxing effects of our dinner with wine, we also decided to return to our hotel.

With barely an exchange of words, we prepared for bed, stretched out on the comfy mattress, and turned out the lights!

Ahhhh! What a difference a good night's sleep makes! We woke up invigorated and felt like new people!

During a slim breakfast of fresh fruit and coffee, we shared our excitement at finally getting on the boat this afternoon. "I can't wait to start sailing!" Vince confessed. Although lounging by the pool until it was time to check in for our charter was enjoyable, we were impatient and unable to fully relax.

At last! The hotel concierge informed us that our shuttle to the ferry dock had arrived. We were scheduled to be on the next ferry from Göcek across Büngüs Bay to the Marina Skopea location where most bare-boat charters begin.

With a mooring capacity of 195 yachts, the marina was much larger than we expected. Upon our arrival, a charter company agent introduced himself as our host, welcomed us, managed our luggage, and escorted us to the office. The check-in process was quick and efficient and Vince was pleased to see that our documents were in order, and ready to be signed.

For the next eight days, our home on the water was an Oceanic 43 named *Juliette,* a sporty sailboat with two heads, three staterooms, a large galley, and a comfortable salon. Soon as we boarded, the customary bottle of champagne on ice and a welcome card addressed to Captain Vince and Crew were delivered, marking the official beginning of our charter.

The 'Turkish Riviera'
Sarsala Bay

Instinctively, Vince stepped into his role as skipper. While he attended the safety and orientation meetings, I opened the hatches, stowed the usual pre-ordered supply of water and other libations, evaluated the galley equipment, unpacked our bags, stored our belongings in the lockers and drawers in the stateroom, and made the bed.

The weekly farmer's market and various neighborhood grocery stores, all accustomed to delivering to bareboaters on Marina Skopea, were excellent places to stock up on provisions of frozen items, eggs, snacks, lunch meats, produce, and an ample selection of fresh bread and cheeses.

With our requirements met and chores completed, we were cleared to leave the harbor. Vince was ecstatic to be on the water! Although the winds were reasonably pleasant for sailing, we motored the quick forty-five-minute passage to Sarsala Bay.

Surrounded by turquoise water, lush vegetation, and a picturesque, long stretch of pebble beach, the bay appeared almost secluded with only a few gulet boats moored in the coves near the north end. The jetty was vacant and Vince aimed directly for it. Mooring in Med-tie fashion was a piece-of-cake. With expert precision, Vince dropped the anchor, backed into position, and turned off the engine.

When I received the signal, I jumped off the boat onto the uneven, wooden timbered dock, tied off our stern lines, and placed our gangplank across the open space between the stern and jetty to provide easy access to dry land. To fend off potential neighbors, Vince tied bumpers to our lifelines. There were no boats on either side of us, and although I crossed my fingers hoping that no one would arrive, Vince was a realist.

"I bet we'll have port and starboard neighbors before dinner," he warned. Located near most of the major marinas in Göcek, many boaters spend their first night in Sarsala Bay, so Vince was probably right.

The beautiful bay's focal point was Sarsala Restaurant; with covered seating and a stunning view of the bay. For a more casual dining experience, tables and chairs were also arranged on the sand on the beach. Two rickety, charmingly quaint, wooden jetties led to a wider, more substantial dock and a footpath up the hill to the restaurant.

There was a weathered shack with a shabby sign dangling from a doorknob advertising a shave and a haircut, and another sign pointed the way to makeshift, outdoor shower stalls. Sarsala Bay looked like a delightful place to spend our first night.

According to the guidebook, the restaurant served outstanding, fresh-caught, local fish. "I'll call in a reservation for tonight," Vince said. Great! I couldn't wait to have dinner on shore.

After we investigated our surroundings, a highly anticipated that a swim took immediate priority. Without snorkel masks or a floating device, we lowered ourselves down the swim ladder and into the shimmering, translucent water for our first swim in the Turkish Riviera. *Somebody pinch me!* A bit cooler than I expected, the water temperature was wonderfully refreshing and it was a sheer joy to splash around and play together between the mooring ball and the dinghy, at *Juliette's* bow.

As Vince predicted, eventually more boaters entered the bay to anchor, pick up a mooring, or tie up before sunset. A friendly, bare-boating couple from Brittany tied up to starboard, and a small yacht with a six-person crew from England tied up to port. To minimize bumps and scrapes to the hulls, we assisted each skipper as they maneuvered into position until they were safely secured and settled.

With all the goings-on, Vince and I found a comfortable place on deck to sit and watch the action with a glass of wine, a can of salted nuts, and a basket of cheese and crackers. It was our first Happy Hour in Turkey and watching many foreign yachtsmen exert different sailing and docking techniques reminded me of the Happy Hours we spent in the Caribbean watching boaters drop anchor or pick up a mooring. Some were experts, while others were quite comical to watch.

When the sky became a glorious shade of orange with streaks of lavender and red, the Sarsala Restaurant illuminated the pathway up the hill, as if to say, "We are now open for dinner."

Suddenly, the entire bay transformed into a romantic backdrop of fairy lights, flaming torches and softly glowing café lights artistically strung between trees. A brilliant starlit sky, flickering fireflies, and the subtle sweet scent of pine in the air accentuated the scene. As the evening progressed, yachtsmen and their guests began to gravitate toward the beach where strolling musicians playing traditional Turkish string instruments serenaded and lured people inside.

When it was time for our dinner reservation, we meandered to the restaurant's spacious covered terrace. I spotted two vacant seats with a vast view of the bay and the illuminated beach below. A waiter came over to welcome us, "Good evening. thank you for joining us for dinner…what may I bring you?"

Vince ordered two *gin and tonics*, with a follow-up order for two more when the first ones were consumed. In no hurry to dine, we enjoyed being in the moment, we were happy to relax, and engage in lighthearted conversation.

Taking in the unfamiliar sites around us, we were surprised to see the large team of cooks in the open-air kitchen, including minors not more than sixteen years old. Minors stirred large, charred aluminum pots, cut meat with cleavers, and pulled freshly baked bread out of hot stone ovens. We wondered if there were child-labor laws in Turkey.

As ordered, when our first cocktail glasses were nearly empty, the waiter brought two more and told us about tonight's dinner specials. "The fresh catch this evening is grouper, we grill it over charcoals and serve it with grilled peppers and rice. We also have our very best baked sea bass. It is delicious! Or I can offer you a hamburger, cooked to order." The last item made us snicker. We didn't come to Turkey to eat a hamburger.

We both ordered the grouper. Served with charred yellow peppers, juicy lemon halves, and rice pilaf cooked in fish broth with onions, butter, and salt, our meal was outstanding! The grouper was one of the best-grilled fish we had ever eaten anywhere.

Rivaling last night's splendid sunset, the morning sun washed the world around us in a pinkish, golden glow. Vince woke up first and kissed my forehead. "Morning Love, did you sleep well?"

Despite all the boats around us, Sarsala Bay was tranquil, and sleeping on board was surprisingly peaceful. "I slept like a rock," I replied, turning toward my husband for a long cuddle in his waiting arms. It was nice to lie together for a while, feeling fortunate, unhurried, and content. The rhythm of the waves slapping gently against the hull almost rocked us back to sleep.

Ultimately, we stumbled out of bed and climbed halfway up the companionway to peek through the open hatch. On top of the hill, we noticed a line of people forming at the outdoor grill. I wondered what they were doing. "Maybe they're waiting for the restaurant to open," I whispered.

Just then, Steve and Sue; the couple from Brittany returned to their boat, carrying an open-ended, white paper bag on its side.

"Morning," Vince called out to them, "what's going on up there?"

"Homemade bread…if you're a guest here, you can pick up a loaf of bread…on the house…one per boat," Steve answered. "See?" A look into the open bag revealed a beautiful, freshly baked, round loaf of yellow bread.

Quick as the wind, Vince and I threw on some clothes, slipped into our sandals, and nearly ran up the hill. The line moved quickly and when it was our turn, I asked one of the kind young chefs what type of bread it was. "*Misir Ekmegi*," he answered, "Turkish cornbread. Enjoy!"

"Thank you, we will," I shouted back. The warm bread smelled yummy and I couldn't wait to serve it for breakfast with melted butter, a little of the soft fresh cheese, fruit, and a sizable cup of coffee!

On this bright, sunny morning, everyone seemed to be having breakfast on board, and it felt kind of festive. Soon, Steve and Sue struck up a conversation with us. Taking a well-deserved vacation from their hectic Bed and Breakfast business in Brittany, they were on day six of a 10-day charter. So far, sailing along the Dalaman Coast and the Turkish Riviera far surpassed their expectations. While Sue and I talked about the B&B; a successful but stressful business, Steve and Vince talked about sailing.

"We're motoring to Wall Bay after breakfast," Vince said to Steve. "Have you been there?"

"Brilliant," Steve replied, "it's well worth a visit, and the Wall Bay Restaurant is outstanding." Steve's positive remarks confirmed our excitement to explore our next destination.

Before heading out, Sue and I exchanged contact information, hugged each other, and agreed that we should plan a visit to Brittany one day.

A mere thirty minutes after weighing anchor, we approached Wall Bay; so named for the Roman defensive wall, now in ruins on the southern end of the bay. Aiming for the empty dock alongside the restaurant, Vince turned our stern parallel to the dock before prompting me to jump off with the free end of the stern line in hand.

"Hon, use the cleat behind you, the breeze will push the bow toward the dock," he said, anticipating Mother Nature's helping hand. A few minutes later, *Juliette* was securely docked, Vince turned off the engine, and we set out to explore the area.

A horseshoe-shaped bay with pine trees sloping to a picturesque beach, Wall Bay was indeed (as Steve described) 'brilliant'. Nestled among the trees, the Wall Bay Restaurant and a few ramshackle wooden cabins emanated Turkish Riviera charm.

In a three-sided deckhouse, a makeshift open-air theater housed a large, flatscreen television with a handful of folding chairs arranged in a semicircle for viewing. One of the cabins appeared to be a souvenir shop and yet another sold handcrafted baskets and headscarves. A sign displayed the shops' hours of operation. I looked at my watch and secretly looked forward to browsing through the unique shops before dinner tonight.

When we returned to the boat, we noticed a 15-meter gulet anchored offshore, and a chartered sailboat tied up along the jetty behind us. "Rats!" I grumbled under my breath, "We are no longer alone," although I guessed that we wouldn't have been for long, anyway…

Vince held open the lifeline gate, gesturing for me to step on board. I intended to stretch out on one of the shady cockpit seats with a cold beer and maybe I would write in my journal for a while. Suddenly, several local food vendors in small motorized boats pulled up beside us.

"Would you like to buy something?" the first vendor asked politely. Holding on to one of our stanchions with one hand, he threw open a canvas cover to display his goods with the other.

"What are you selling?" Vince asked. He sold homemade pastries, the next vendor sold ice cream bars, and still another sold sandwiches and fruit. What fun! We loved supporting local businesses, bought several items from each vendor, and considered it lunch.

By mid-afternoon, the temperature was uncomfortably hot. "Grab your snorkel gear, and let's take a dinghy-ride to Cleopatra's Bath House across the bay," Vince suggested. "Here, take a look."

He handed me the Cruising Guide open to the page describing the magnificent bathhouse built for the thermal waters that flowed into the bay from a volcanic crater. Photos depicted the (alleged) bathhouse ruins submerged in crystal clear, translucent water. What a time for me not to have an underwater camera to capture the experience.

When we reached the site of the bathhouse, the water was calm and shallow. Effortlessly, Vince and I stepped out into ankle-deep water and walked to the rocky shore, pulling the dinghy behind us.

"We'd better put our fins and mask on in the shallows," Vince said, while he buried the small claw-style anchor under an exposed root of a pine tree. "We can glide into deeper water from there," he added, pointing to a sandy spot a few feet away. "And if you can help it, don't touch or stand on the ruins, they're very fragile and the stone will crumble."

Snorkeling along the ruins was mind-blowing! In between the fragmented arched windows and doorways, we held hands as we moved through the water in awe of the submerged bathhouse remnants. I imagined how beautiful this place must've been when Cleopatra and Marcos Anthony used to bathe here. Oh, I wished I had a camera!

My mask sealed well, I felt comfortable snorkeling, and when Vince said it was time to go, I didn't want to get out of the water.

"I'll snorkel back to the boat," I shouted, feeling empowered.

"OK, but it's four hundred feet or more," he warned with a tinge of concern in his voice. "Do you think you can make it?"

"Stay close by, and I'll let you know if I need to get in the dinghy."

"Go for it, sweetheart," Vince said, "I'll keep an eye on you."

When I reached *Juliette's* stern, I grabbed onto the swim ladder, removed my snorkel mask, and shouted, "I made it, I made it!"

Waving my free arm in the air so Vince could see me, I was overjoyed! I made it to the boat! No longer was I the apprehensive person in the BVI in

1987, afraid of the water, sailing, and my own shadow. Today, without assistance, I snorkeled from Cleopatra's Bath House back to the boat!

Proud as a peacock, I jotted the snorkel achievement in my journal and underlined the presumed distance. "I am proud of you," Vince said as he grabbed two cold bottles of beer from the fridge, opened them, handed one to me, and raised his bottle in my direction. "Hon, I am very impressed!" Vince knew how much his acknowledgment of my triumph meant to me. His words made my heart flutter.

With our beers in hand, we took our favorite positions on the foredeck, sitting down at the mast; Vince with his back against the structure, and I curled up in his arms with my back against his chest. I loved this time of day, just before twilight, just before Happy Hour.

When our beer bottles were empty, I slipped into the galley to assemble a quick charcuterie board with the Turkish cheeses we bought at the farmer's market in Göcek. *Mihaliç peyniri*; a hard, intensely salty cheese made from cow's milk, *Dil;* with a mozzarella-like texture, and *Kopanisiti Peynir;* a luscious cheese, creamy in texture, made from a combination of goat's and sheep's milk and unsalted butter.

The beautiful cheeses, a few dried apricot halves, briny green olives, and a crisp sliced apple, made an appetizing presentation. Vince opened a bottle of red wine, and by the time the sky became a spectrum of blue and violet, we were fully indulged in our Happy Hour ritual on deck.

Technically, today was the first full day of our Turkish Riviera sailing adventure, and as such, we decided that eating a home-cooked dinner on board was a luxury. With a few fresh tomatoes, diced onions, chopped black olives, a dried chili pepper, herbs, and a big healthy splash of olive oil, I created a fragrant, spicy sauce, while two chicken breasts marinated in freshly squeezed lemon juice, crushed garlic, salt and pepper.

Vince turned on the gas grill mounted on the stern railing, opened another bottle of wine, and filled a large pot with seawater to cook the pasta. I sliced more lemons to douse the chicken as it grilled, turned on our mast-star, inserted a mellow instrumental music CD in the nav station's CD player, and set the table in the cockpit. The pine-scented air and the murmur of muddled conversations from dinner guests at the restaurant and the other boats around us were somehow cozy and pleasant. Dinner was ready before the moon loomed large in the sky.

Preparing to share the meal we cooked together, Vince made a toast. To our adventure on the Dalaman Coast; the Turkish Riviera…may it be incredible."

The evening was romantic and our dinner was delicious. Maybe tomorrow, I will browse through the unique shops at the restaurant.

Karacaören Bay

Quick learners that we are, we were at the head of the line of hungry boaters waiting for the first batch of freshly baked, golden cornbread to come out of the oven this morning. Vince nearly salivated as he accepted the beautiful loaf of pastry perfection from the young chef. "Thanks for your hospitality, we had a wonderful time," I shouted to anyone who happened to listen.

Although we thoroughly enjoyed our time here, Vince was eager to set sail. Bound for Caracara Bay, he was determined to weigh anchor soon after breakfast.

Leaving Wall Bay was an easy endeavor, we quickly cleared the other boats in the bay and the lee of the land. Like clockwork, we worked in sync. When prompted, I held the boat head-to-wind, while Vince raised the mainsail and pulled out the jib. For the first time on our Turkish Riviera adventure, our sails were up and it pleased Vince immensely to be sailing!

Unfortunately, the wind would not cooperate. Even in the few puffs of wind, we were barely able to make six knots. Nevertheless, Vince was persistent and refused to take down the sails.

For hours, we stayed in windless water without moving forward, not even an inch! Ultimately, Vince gave in, lowered the mainsail, furled the jib, and turned on the engine. My heart went out to him, I sensed his disappointment. Attempting to lift his spirits, I grabbed a beer from the cooler in the cockpit, popped it open, and handed it to him. At that moment, I spotted sea life in the water. "Look, a giant green sea turtle," I shouted so loud I almost frightened the creature away, but Vince saw the turtle and it made him smile.

Another two hours later, we arrived at Karacaören Bay. Two docks jutted out from the restaurant; one shabby, wooden jetty, and one more stable and substantial. Several boats of various sizes were moored at the stable dock, but

Vince found room at the end and tied up. "We're here," he declared "I like being at the end of the dock."

I took a moment to stand on the bow and gaze at our new surroundings. The Cruising Guide described Karacaören Bay as a sheltered body of water, surrounded by a natural reef with fascinating, colorful fish, a white, sandy shoreline, and a pine-covered hillside, dotted with medieval ruins, and Lycian tombs dating back to 400BC. The bay was breathtaking, and it was not difficult to understand why this area was dubbed the "turquoise coast," the water was purely the color of its nickname.

The construction of the Karacaören Bar and Restaurant created a crescent-shaped cove with a handful of mooring buoys for boaters planning to dine at the restaurant. Minutes after our arrival, a man from the restaurant approached our boat.

"Welcome to Karacaören Bay," he said, waiving a paper flyer in his hand as he came closer, "we hope you'll join us for dinner…the owner is playing his violin tonight…here is a sample of our menu," he continued, handing us a handwritten list of tonight's culinary offerings. "You'll need to reserve a table, we're expecting a crowd," he added further, as he moved to another boat, waving another flyer in his hand.

"What do you think," Vince asked, "wanna give this restaurant a try?"

"Yes, and it might be fun to listen to a violin concert," I replied.

While Vince reserved a table for dinner, I assembled a platter with various no-fuss finger foods. Foregoing lunch this afternoon, and dinner still a few hours away, my internal time clock strongly signaled that it was time to nibble. Happy Hour on board with a glass of wine and some food, waiting for the sun to do its setting magic is always my happiest hour.

When the sun disappeared, we left for the restaurant, anticipating an authentic Turkish food experience. Upon entering the bohemian-style establishment, wonderful aromas coming from the kitchen made our mouths water.

The man who invited us to the restaurant this afternoon saw us coming and held the door open. "Welcome *Juliette*, we are happy to see you," he said. I always liked it when restaurants referred to us by our boat name.

He showed us to a nice table with a stunning view of the bay. The list of culinary dishes on the flyer was handwritten on a blackboard. "Tonight's menu is written on the board," he stated the obvious, "we serve typical Turkish cuisine, cooked in clay pots inside our stone ovens. Place your order at the counter, and I'll take your drink order when you return to the table."

The extensive menu included: sea bass, calamari, wild shrimp, lamb casserole, lamb meatballs, lamb chops, baked chicken, a vegetable casserole, lobster, dragonfish, grouper, amberjack, and red snapper. The side dishes consisted of seasonal fruit, bread, salad, and mixed vegetables. "Wow," I exclaimed, "that is quite a menu."

After pondering every item, I ordered the dragon fish and Vince ordered the lamb chops. Cooked to perfection, we enjoyed our meals tremendously, moreover, the wine selected by our waiter was an excellent complement to the food. We readily agreed that *this* was the best meal of our trip! Funny, it seemed to me that we had several *best meals of our trip.*

Before the music began, our waiter served a complimentary glass of Raki and a cup of bold Turkish coffee spiced with cardamom. When the owner began to tune his violin, Vince and I looked at each other with raised eyebrows and hoped that what we heard would sound better when the performance began. Gradually, the owner began his repertoire and lo-and-behold, his music made us downright laugh.

Honestly, he was the worst violinist we ever heard and it took every ounce of self-control not to roar out loud with laughter. It was hysterical…a truly unforgettable evening.

How I love waking up with the warmth of the sun filtering through a side hatch caressing my face. On this bright and sunny morning, I woke up feeling energized. Ever so gently, I slipped out of bed, trying not to disturb Vince. As I stood on the bow, gazing out at the boats at anchor in the bay, I felt that familiar sense of gratitude for this peaceful morning.

While Vince snoozed, I began preparing breakfast. In no hurry to leave soon, I was in the mood to cook. Just as the bacon began to sizzle and the coffee perked, I heard a happy "Morning, Beautiful." Vince snuck up behind me and kissed my neck.

"Morning, sweetheart, I felt like cooking this morning," I replied, as I flipped the eggs. With my over-easy fried eggs, crispy bacon, and toasted English muffins, I had the makings of an American breakfast, nonetheless, the addition of bright green Mediterranean olives marinated in spicy olive oil, a handful of dried apricots, and a dollop of the remaining *Kopanisti Peynir* Turkish cheese, transformed this breakfast into a feast any local would love.

Before the morning sun intensified, Vince was eager to explore the medieval ruins on a nearby island. So, while I cleared the breakfast dishes, Vince tossed a couple of bottles of water and two beach towels in the dinghy and primed the outboard motor. On the bay, a smokey mist arose from the surface of the translucent water and dissipated into the air, making this a magical-mystical, beautiful morning for an outing.

Suddenly, just as we were engaged in the experience and the solitude, the outboard motor sputtered and stalled. "What's going on!" Vince exclaimed. "Did we snag something?" However, a quick assessment of the situation determined that we ran out of gas!

Vince shrugged his shoulders. "There's only one option," he said, as he untied the oars from their position on the side of the dinghy and handed me one. "We'll have to paddle."

Ughhhh…I accepted the oar, placed the shaft in the oarlock, and planted myself firmly on the bench. I rowed on port while Vince rowed on starboard. Although we rowed in unison, it lasted only a few minutes before Vince took my oar and rowed with both oars faster and more sufficiently than we rowed together.

Fortunately, *Juliette* was at the end of the dock. When Vince brought us close enough to the quay, I stepped out with the free end of the dinghy line in my hand, pulling it to the stern. To hold the dinghy steady, Vince grabbed a pulpit. "I got it, Hon," he said, as I handed him the line to tie to a cleat.

Dismayed that we didn't see the ruins, we began to prepare for our departure from Karacaören Bay.

Cold Water Bay was only an hour away.

Cold Water Bay

Cold Water Bay, surrounded by olive trees, pine trees, and a lovely little beach, is aptly so named for the under-sea-level cold water spring that flows into the bay.

We arrived to find the few installed moorings already occupied, the bay was also crowded with boats at anchor and that did not appeal to us. Hoping to find a more secluded setting, Vince navigated to the west shore, where we turned a corner and came upon a beautiful area with only one boat disrupting the serenity we longed for.

In a 7-meter depth of water, Vince dropped anchor in an ideal sandy spot. As is routine, Vince snorkeled over the anchor to confirm that our hold would endure the night. Standing on the starboard beam, I could see him treading water. "Are we good?" I shouted.

"We may need a stern anchor too," Vince replied. "It'll keep the bow headed into the swells tonight, we'll be more stable."

"This will be interesting," I pondered to myself, I've been sailing with Vince for twenty-three years, and I have *never* seen him apply a bow-and-stern anchor before.

"How can I help?" Again, I shouted out, but this time I heard no response.

Lazar-focused, Vince climbed on board, and as if he searched for something specific, opened random hatches in the cockpit until he found a large bundle of rope that he tossed in the dinghy. Without saying a word, he rowed to the stern, tied one end of the rope to a port cleat, and left the rest of the bundle on the dinghy floor.

Still focused, he rowed approximately forty feet further toward the shore, tied the dinghy to a tree, and stepped on land with the bundled rope in hand. In awe, I watched the entire exhilarating process, when suddenly I heard the sound of an outboard motor heading our way. A local young couple in a wooden boat approached the shore where Vince was standing. The young man called out to him, they exchanged words, and then I watched him help Vince fasten our stern line to a large rock, achieving a fundamental bow-and-stern anchoring technique.

"Thank you," I heard Vince say while he sat in the dinghy and pulled himself along the tightly stretched rope back to the boat. "May I offer to pay for your help?"

"No, sir..., but maybe you can buy something from us," the charismatic young man replied. "This is Aysun; my wife, I am Hakan, and this is our floating produce market."

Shyly smiling, Aysun ceremoniously flung open a canvas cloth to reveal an impeccable selection of fruits, vegetables, bread, and a mini cooler filled with ice cream bars. Happily, we purchased several items, including two chocolate-covered ice cream bars. "Thank you, thank you," Hakan said, "in the morning, my wife makes homemade chocolate crescents. I can deliver them to your boat if you would like?"

"You're joking…yes…that would be fantastic," I replied emphatically before Vince had a chance to answer.

"OK, we will return before 8 o'clock tomorrow morning," Hakan waived, and drove off.

After Hakan and Aysun left, we remained sitting on the transom, dangling our feet in the water, eating our ice cream bars, and talking about the couple's kindness. Every Turkish person we've met on this trip has been admirably friendly and helpful.

This lazy, laid-back kind of day, with no plans to do anything special, was bliss. While Vince studied the Cruising Guide, I composed journal entries and wrote postcards that will probably be hand-delivered instead of mailed to our family and friends at home. In the late afternoon, we put on our fins and snorkel masks and searched for colorful fish, nevertheless, it was more fun to hang together, monkey-style, on the stern line until we felt the urge to take a nap.

Another local boat skippered by a slender, tall Turkish man pulled up on starboard. "*Merhaba, merhaba*…hello," he called out, "fresh crepes, we sell crepes. Would you like to buy a crepe?" An extremely heavy woman wearing a tan-colored smock, her hair wrapped in a white turban, held a stone crepe griddle on a charcoal burner between her extra-large legs. From a pan stationed next to her, she poured a ladle full of rich, velvety batter onto the sizzling, hot stone.

"Yes, two please," Vince said and walked to the stern, with me following quickly behind.

The woman flipped the batter and glazed the beautiful, slightly browned surface with a pat of butter, a sprinkling of powdered sugar, and a squeeze of lemon juice. Then she folded the crepe precisely into quarters and handed it to me on a paper plate. Wow, it was a masterpiece of deliciousness! Seconds later, she handed me another one, which Vince stood ready to devour. Each tasty crepe cost only $0.75!

Without wearing our snorkel gear or swimsuits, we spent the remainder of the day in the water. Indeed, this was a wonderful day in a true holiday paradise.

Our lackadaisical Happy Hour on deck, with a can of our favorite dehydrated potato chips, a sliced crisp apple, and a bottle of wine, drifted into a fuss-free dinner on board. In the time it took to cook rice, I sautéed chopped green onions, celery, and fresh tomatoes in butter until the butter browned.

Then, I added a drizzle of olive oil, the juice of fresh lime, and red pepper flakes, and stirred in the cooked rice to make a warm rice salad.

Sitting side by side at the table in the cockpit, we ate our 10-minute meal, shared more wine, and wondered what the rest of the world was doing at this moment in time.

In the evening, Mother Nature transformed our wonderful day into her best display of illumination; a starlit sky, enhanced by the glow of a silvery moon. "Look at the moonlight glistening on the bay," I said to Vince, "isn't it magical?"

"I'll show you magic, come with me," Vince replied, as he gestured for me to follow him to the bow. With just one other boat in the vicinity to distort the darkness, the larger-than-usual phosphorescence sparkled extra bright tonight. Vince jiggled the anchor chain, creating a million sparkles that bounced in the water. I will never tire of seeing this phenomenon of energy and light.

Kapi Creek

The sound of Vince's heavy footsteps on deck woke me up. "Hi Hon, Mornin," I shouted through the open hatch above my head without seeing him…"What's going on out there?"

"Morning Babe, I've been watching a couple of green sea turtles swimming around our boat. They just dove under…I'm waiting for them to come up again, I've been watching them for a while."

Feeling a bit bewildered, I slid out of our berth, made my way up to the third rung of the companionway, and poked my head out to find Vince standing midship. "Any sign of our chocolate crescents?"

Soon as I asked the question, I heard the familiar sound of an outboard motor approaching, but by the time I threw on a t-shirt and made it up on deck, Vince was holding a paper bag, and Hakan and Aysun were already in the distance.

The bag of buttery, chocolate crescents felt heavy and warm to the touch. I peeked inside and took a deep sniff. No other aroma compares to that of fresh-from-the-oven, chocolaty pastries and these were no exception. Quick as I could, I made a pot of coffee and peeled a banana and an orange for us to share. This morning's breakfast didn't require anything else. The crescents tasted as if an award-winning French chef had created them; they were divine decadence!

This morning we didn't linger after breakfast as we ordinarily did. With approximately twelve nautical miles ahead of us, Vince was eager to sail to Kapi Creek in the Skopea Limani area, with a planned stop at Gemiler Island to explore the Lycian ruins and the remains of Byzantine churches built before the 6th-century AD.

Unfortunately, exploring Gemiler Island was a disappointment. An undefined, way-marked footpath led us to the unmarked ruins. We did our best to speculate but without properly labeled descriptions, it was difficult to understand the significance of the ancient rubble. Consequently, we lost interest and continued on our course to Kapi Creek.

From the moment we arrived, I fell in love with this enchanting anchorage with its rickety, almost dilapidated, wooden jetties. Brimming with Turkish Mediterranean character, a quaint restaurant was the center focus of the inlet. Leaving enough room for only one boat on our port side, Vince aimed for a spot near the end of the dock to tie up for the night. End spots were always Vince's favorite, they are the farthest from the restaurant and less clamorous in the evenings.

Settled in our new destination, we watched other boats arrive, flying vessel flags from almost every European country. Feeling as if we were part of a worldly boating community was exciting.

Suddenly, someone on an advancing sailboat called Vince's name. "Hey Vince, great to see you guys…we're coming in next to you," a slightly familiar voice shouted in our direction. It was Steve from Brittany, he and Sue appeared to be guests on a friend's boat, preparing to dock next to us on starboard, just as they did in Sarsala Bay.

"Hang on…toss me your stern line," Vince shouted back as he jumped onto the jetty, and headed toward the targeted dock space.

Once their boat was situated and secured, I joined them on the dock to say hello. It was as if we were visiting with long-time friends. Steve and Sue introduced us to their boat-mates, we shared stories about where we had been since we saw each other and talked about other anchorages we still planned to see. We visited and drank beers together until someone mentioned lunch. While Steve, Sue, and friends headed for the restaurant, Vince and I soaked up the Turkish sunshine on deck and ate sandwiches on board.

After lunch, we took a walk along the beach and among the lushly vegetated shores thick with olive and pine trees. We climbed halfway up the hill for a most amazing view of Kapi Creek. When we returned to the boat, Steve and Sue were aboard their boat having a beer on deck. "How was lunch?" Vince asked.

"Outstanding!" Steve replied, "You guys outta try that restaurant tonight."

After hiking halfway up the hill, it was time for a swim. The water temperature was the warmest we ve encountered at any anchorage so far.

At first, we snorkeled in the vicinity of the boat, but the tropical fish seemed to be hiding and we saw nothing of interest. No matter…being in the water felt too good. We took off our snorkel equipment and stayed in unencumbered. While Sue stayed on board with their friends, Steve decided to join us, and until the sun began to cool and inch down toward the horizon, the three of us had a lovely chat as we floated back and forth between their mooring buoy and ours.

Kapi Creek was well known for the best sunsets on the Turkish Riviera, so breaking from our usual ritual, Vince thought it would be a nice change to have Happy Hour on shore this time. I dressed in my faded orange Cooper Island tank top and white capris, while Vince wore his favorite lightweight Bitter End shirt with a pair of khaki cargo shorts. Since the restaurant was likely to be crowded with early sunset worshippers, we wandered over ahead of time to snag a table on the water's edge.

Happy Hour on shore was indeed a nice change. I enjoyed being among European boating enthusiasts and hearing conversations spoken in foreign languages. The sunset was phenomenal; one of God s most magnificent masterpieces.

After the last flash of crimson sunlight was no longer visible, and the fireflies began to appear, Vince ordered a platter of fresh-caught, grilled anchovies with a simple salad made of thick sliced yellow and red tomatoes, and pitted black olives. Seasoned with black pepper and sea salt, and drizzled with olive oil, this light meal was a perfect ending to our day.

Tomb Bay

I was already awake and making coffee when Steve rattled our boat. "Hey, are you guys awake?" he called out.

"Mornin', mate," Vince shouted from the foredeck while he gathered our dried laundry from the lifelines and threw the load down the open cabin hatch where the clothes landed on our bed. "How about a cup of coffee?"

"That's why I came over, there are too many people on our boat," Steve grumbled, "it's chaos in the morning. The six of us stumble all over each other trying to grab the coffee pot."

While the two men chatted over coffee, I washed my face and folded the pile of clothes Vince tossed in our cabin. Then I heard both men leave and head for the restaurant, undoubtedly to pick up the highly coveted fresh round of cornbread. That was my cue to set the table, bring out the butter and orange marmalade, and slice the remaining *Mihalich* cheese.

With a sharp, slightly salty taste, this local cheese had become one of my favorites. At our hotel in Istanbul, we learned quickly that a Turkish breakfast is not complete without some form of cheese. Hoping that Steve and Sue might join us, I also boiled a few eggs and made a fresh pot of coffee.

When I appeared on deck to check on Vince and Steve's whereabouts, I noticed a boat tied up on our port side. They must've come in the dead of night because Vince and I were not disturbed by their arrival. By the Dutch flag on their stern, I assumed the crew was from Holland. "*Goeie morgen*, good morning," I greeted them in Dutch soon as the couple appeared on deck. "Goeie morgen," the man replied while the woman nodded back in response. I loved being able to communicate in my childhood s first language. Maybe later, we could strike up a conversation.

I watched Vince and Steve meander back, carrying the familiar bags of warm, wonderful cornbread, however, Steve only waived and said, Thanks for the coffee, happy sailing, we may see you in Tomb Bay," as he returned to his boat, leaving the two of us to enjoy breakfast alone.

Unfortunately, the Dutch couple was onshore when we weighed anchor. I would've liked to wish them smooth sailing in Dutch. Hopefully, we would see them again somewhere on the Turkish Riviera.

Leaving Kapi Creek was routine. When we reached open water, Vince asked me to hold the boat steady, head-to-wind, while he raised the mainsail. The weather had not been ideal so far, but today I hoped it would be windy enough for Vince to experience a few hours of excellent sailing.

At first, we flopped around with our sails up, not moving forward at a measurable speed, but eventually, Vince's tenacity paid off and he was able to enjoy a few hours of descent sailing. Finally, he was in his glory and I was thrilled for him!

When we approached Tomb Bay, I thought the harbor resembled an intimate version of Kapi Creek; it was equally charming, with a rustic flair, and those lovable rickety jetties. Now, fully experienced in deploying Med-ties, Vince pulled into a good dock space, stern to the quay, near the end of the jetty.

On shore, the inviting appeal of a grapevine-covered trellis shading rattan seating and a thrown-together wooden bar on the sand resonated with me. Next to the Nomad Bar and Restaurant, several makeshift stalls were available for taking hot showers on a first-come-first-serve basis, and for a nominal fee, a barber's shack offered massages, shaves, haircuts, and leg waxes. A luxury catamaran was the only other boat at the jetty, but again, Vince predicted that a fleet of boats would arrive before sunset.

While Vince busied himself with boat equipment, I cut two big pieces of the partial watermelon I kept stored in our icebox. Since it was difficult to keep such an unmanageable, oddly shaped package cold, I was happy to serve it for a mini-light lunch before going ashore for a cocktail, a more substantial bite to eat, and to do a bit of exploring.

It was almost noon when the Nomad Bar opened for business, and I couldn't contain my desire to check it out. "Honey, come on…the bar is open. Let's go ashore and have a drink," I pleaded impatiently.

"That's my baby," Vince replied, "the sun is over the yardarm somewhere."

I climbed up on a barstool and folded my arms on the counter. Vince stood next to me and ordered an Efes beer. I was in the mood to try something different and took a moment to ponder my choices. The bartender offered me a cocktail with a catchy name. "Try a *Turkish Hot Bunny,*" he said, "it is a lady's cocktail made with Raki, pomegranate juice, and pomegranate liquor, over ice, with a slice of lemon. I guarantee you will enjoy it."

The bartender was right, the eye-catching cocktail was tangy, sweet, refreshing, and delicious.

As we sipped our adult beverages and nibbled on grainy crackers, Vince gave me a quick history lesson about Tomb Bay, according to our trusty Cruising Guide. A prominent, archaeological Turkish Riviera sailing destination, Tomb Bay's hillsides are dotted with pigeon-hole and temple-style Lycian ruins from the 4th-century BC.

Always interested in seeing historical and archaeological sites, Vince told the bartender of our plans to hike up the hill today. The bartender promised that it would be well worth the effort. According to local folklore, a stone wall with an alleged hieroglyphic of a fish was also a must see.

Intrigued, we boarded the dinghy for the short trip to see the fish hieroglyphic, followed by exploring the ruins. However, when we arrived at the stone wall with the fish, we almost died of laughter. Nothing about it resembled an ancient *anything!*

"Oh my god, Vince, someone had a sense of humor!" I roared, "It looks like a cartoon drawing of a giant puffer fish…a kid could've etched that in the rock!" Although *R. Sarihan* signed the artwork, no one seemed to know who the artist was, or when the fish inscription occurred. Ultimately, we chalked it up as a modern-day tourist attraction and left.

"Let's explore the pigeon-holes," Vince remarked, referring to the tombs, "maybe they will be authentic."

Feeling disenchanted by the fish drawing exaggeration, I was more inclined to return to the boat, linger on deck, catch a few rays of the sun, and write in my journal. Vince agreed and navigated back to *Juliette.*

Positioned to grab our anchor chain, when we approached our bow, I heard someone's familiar voice.

"Fancy meeting you here," Steve said. To our pleasant surprise, Steve and Sue docked on starboard for the third time!

"We saw *Juliette* and decided to be neighbors again…hope you don't mind," Sue said.

We were pleased to see them. While Steve assisted Vince with our dinghy, I climbed on board and stowed our snorkel equipment. Vince brought out some beers and with Steve and Sue comfortably seated on their port beam and us on our starboard beam, we drank beer together and spent the rest of the afternoon engaged in good-humored conversation about everything from travel to politics to business.

Eventually, we switched from drinking beer to wine, and as Vince correctly predicted, Tomb Bay was a popular place to be. By late afternoon, yachts of various sizes occupied all the quay space on the jetty. Since it was too early to have dinner, everyone enjoyed being on deck with drinks and nibbles, waiting for the sun to set.

Sue brought out some cheese and crackers, Vince opened a can of mixed nuts and a bag of cheesy chips while I inserted a mixed CD of some good ole American hits from the '60s and '70s in the nav station's CD player. It was delightful listening to world-famous songs by Cat Stevens, Neil Diamond, and John Denver but when the mega-hit by Albert Hammond began to play, Sue asked me to turn up the music, and suddenly, everyone on every deck, on every boat around us sang in unison.

*Seems it never rains in Southern California, seems I've often heard that kinda talk before...*It was classic! It was a moment I will never forget! Here we were...a group of people of all nations...in the Turkish Riviera singing an American hit song! It was a wonderful, wonderful moment! The tune stayed with me all during dinner and for the rest of the evening.

As the cliché goes, I woke up the next morning with a song in my heart. Yes, there was *definitely* a song in my heart! I was still reeling from last night's amazing songfest and the best evening of our trip. *"It never rains in California, but girl, don't they warn you..."* Oh, I still felt so happy and my mood made me smile.

"Morning, beautiful," Vince said as he snuck up behind to give me my first kiss of the day. "Let's explore the ruins. If we go before breakfast, we can hike up the hill before the sun gets too hot. The views from the top should be spectacular this beautiful morning."

What a splendid idea! While Vince prepared the dingy for our excursion, I put on my tennis shoes and grabbed a large bottle of water, my camera, and a towel. Although I anticipated a strenuous hike to the top, I wasn't sure what to expect.

On shore, we quickly found the unmarked path leading to the ruins. Clearing the brush for me, Vince walked ahead, although I stopped at every clearing to take a picture. On this beautiful morning, the vast, panoramic view of Göcek Bay with its dramatic backdrop of brilliant blue water, forest-clad mountains, and picturesque islands was an absolute jaw-dropper! Once populated by pirates, and a stomping ground for Ottoman traders, it is easy to see why this has become the ultimate boater's paradise.

The climb up the hill was much steeper than I anticipated, and by the time we reached the top, I perspired like a leaky bucket. However, standing on the side of the mountain looking at the pigeon-hole caves, and countless temples with ornate facades carved into the rock-face cliffs nearly stunned us into silence. Temple entrances decorated with columns and intricate carvings were now weathered, crumbling relics but their succinct importance was undeniable.

These may have had large stones that rolled in front of the openings to close them off," Vince deduced. The Lycians buried their deceased in high places, believing that winged creatures carried them off to an afterlife. The older tombs were rugged grottos with raised stone platforms where the dead were laid to eternal rest. Archaeologists' excavations and soil samples revealed that the Lycian adorned the departed with pigmented soil and flowers, alluding to ancient funeral rites. As an archaeology and ancient history fanatic, this visit for Vince was a highlight.

We returned to the jetty just in time to share a cup of coffee with Steve and Sue before their departure. Excitedly we told them of our tombs exploration and insisted that a visit to this area would not be complete without seeing this important historical site. Consequently, they too decided to take a hike up the hill before sailing on.

Steve and Sue's charter ended in a few days, but ours ended tomorrow at noon, so saying our goodbyes this time was more definite. We made promises to visit each other in our respective countries or book a Mediterranean sailing charter together in the future, and although such plans seemed unlikely to transpire, no one knows what the future would hold.

Boynuzbuku 'Buku' Bay

By now, most of the boaters finished eating breakfast and were prepared to sail on. To position our boat for an easy passage to Marina Skopea in the morning, I sensed that Vince too felt eager to leave. We skipped standing in line for the freshly baked cornbread today, instead, I fixed a quick breakfast of fruit, cheese, and coffee. Vince hoped to reach Boynuzbuku Bay before noon. Also known as 'Mosquito Bay', by boating tourists and 'Buku Bay' by the locals, our next anchorage was touted to be the most splendid in the area; the perfect spot to spend our last evening onboard *Juliette.*

After breakfast, Vince wasted no time and started the engine. While I was still washing and stowing our dishes, Vince brought the leeward and windward stern lines in. With the boat in idle, he pulled up the anchor and, ever so slowly, steered us into clear water. Not once did he ask for my assistance.

After another short trip with the Iron Jenny and Auto doing all the work, we reached Buku Bay quickly. Standing on the bow looking for sea life, I wondered if we would ever return to the Turkish Riviera for another charter. Although it is truly a magnificent boaters' paradise, due to the light winds, Vince wasn't able to sail much, and I knew that was disappointing.

Lost in my thoughts, suddenly I spotted a large pod of dolphins ahead. Their fin-tips moved in and out of the water in a feeding frenzy. "Honey, look, a large pod of dolphins on our bow!"

Vince saw them too, slowed the boat down, and steered a wide turn around them. We delighted in seeing the dolphins jump acrobatically in the air as we left them behind.

On our approach to Buku Bay, an unfamiliar, sweet, somewhat spicy fragrance permeated the air. "What a beautiful scent," I said to Vince. "I wonder where it's coming from."

"The trees," Vince replied, "this area is overgrown with sweet gum and pine trees." I focused on the trees but didn't know what a sweet-gum tree looked like.

Anchoring spots in the bay appeared to be wide open. As we approached the T-jetty, I couldn't believe my eyes! An expansive, grassy lawn sparsely populated with majestic trees, bordered by a thick, old-growth pine forest extended from a sandy beach to the front of the Buku Bar and Restaurant. White chairs and tables covered with white tablecloths were attractively organized on the lawn. Paper lanterns and café lights strung between the trees, and colorful flower arrangements on each table created a festive place for a celebration or a party.

"Oh my goodness, it's beautiful here," I shouted from the bow to where Vince stood in the cockpit. "I think something special is happening here tonight!"

Soon as we docked, I scampered to shore to investigate. A man behind the bar glanced in my direction.

"Welcome to Buku Bay…where are you from?" he asked, looking up, while busily drying freshly washed bar glasses.

"California," I responded, "is there a party here tonight, or are these beautiful decorations for us?" I kidded.

"There was a wedding here last night, the bride and groom donated everything to the restaurant. Why don't you join us for dinner tonight? We have the best restaurant in the bay," he said with a wink of his eye, knowing full well that this was the *only* restaurant in the bay.

I darted back to the boat, urging Vince to come ashore to see the beach and the lovely decorations. He was also surprised. "That must've been some wedding party," he said to the man behind the bar, "were they Americans?"

"The couple was from Dalaman, we served over three hundred guests."

For the next hour or so, we sat at the bar, nursing *gin and tonics*, noshing on bar nuts and pretzels while we chatted with the man behind the bar. Born in Atatürk, he spent most of his adult life in Izmir before relocating here to care for his aging parents. He worked as a waiter-slash-bartender at the Buku Bar and Restaurant. Due to the interesting people he meets regularly, he thoroughly enjoys his job.

Suddenly, a small herd of goats wandered onto the lawn from the rocky hillside. The bartender told us they were wild and lived up in the higher hills. "The herd comes down every day to graze on the young grass and the nutrient-rich leaves that grow on the bushes near the beach," he said.

Tapping into the bartender's local knowledge, I inquired about the alluring sweet fragrance in the air. Although he confirmed that it came from the sweet gum trees growing on the lawn, he also pointed out a frankincense tree near the bar. Sap bled down the trunk where someone slashed into the bark. Allowing the aromatic sap to seep out and harden into a resin, it is collected and used in making perfumes, incense, and essential oils believed to reduce stress, anxiety, and balance moods.

When we returned to the boat, it was seriously time to take a swim. We spent the hottest part of the afternoon playing in the water near the boat, not realizing that it was our last time submerged in the crystal clear, kaleidoscope of blue, green, and turquoise Turkish Riviera.

Later, on deck, we bronzed our bodies in the sun, and when it was time for our last Happy Hour on board, I pulled out all the stops to assemble a beautiful appetizer tray with the cheese, nuts, and dried fruit remaining in the galley. Vince opened our last bottle of wine and prepared a seating area for us in the cockpit for optimum sunset viewing. We stayed out until the wine and appetizers disappeared with the setting sun.

Curious to try one of the shower stalls onshore before dinner, I wandered over with my bath towel and toiletry bag. The stall was surprisingly large inside, with a cement pad underneath the shower head, a bench, hooks for clothing and towels, and a round mirror attached to one of the wooden walls with a rusty nail. The water sputtered out of the faucet when I first turned it on but when the flow adjusted; the pressure was good. The warm water felt luxurious, and it was a pleasure to wash my hair with plenty of room to move around. Eventually, I finished my shower, wrapped my hair in a towel, and returned to the boat feeling as if I had just been at a lavish spa.

Despite the inviting ambiance, the restaurant was not overcrowded. I anticipated a quiet, romantic last dinner with my husband tonight. We sat at one of the beautiful tables adorned with a colorful flower arrangement and two tapered candles. With no fish on the menu, we ordered the lamb kabobs with couscous and herbs.

Unfortunately, dinner was a huge letdown, the first one of our entire Turkish vacation! The meat, full of fat and gristle, was difficult to chew and the couscous tasted horribly bland. However, we thoroughly enjoyed the lemon cake, mint tea, and Turkish coffee after the meal, and sitting among the sweet gum, pine, and frankincense trees was an opportunity we probably wouldn't have again anywhere else in the world.

Ughhh! Waking up on our final morning on board was bittersweet, nevertheless, our flight from the Dalaman Airport to New York was not until early evening, so it was nice not having to hurry.

"Let's have one last Turkish breakfast ashore," Vince said, holding the lifeline gate open for me to pass through.

"You always have the best ideas," I replied, gleefully clapping my hands and hoping that our breakfast experience would be better than dinner last night.

The same bartender was already behind the bar, spotted us, and waved. "We're open for breakfast, the coffee will be ready in a few minutes," he said, "or do you prefer black tea?" We both ordered coffee. *I will miss that earthy, nutty, Turkish coffee aroma*, I thought to myself.

When we reached the bar, the bartender shook our hands, "Good morning," he said cheerfully, "we have no menu, but we serve a traditional Turkish breakfast, so sit where you'd like, relax, and I'll bring it out for you." In the traditional way of serving Turkish coffee with foam floating on top, he filled two cups at our table and brought a basket of the usual freshly baked, yellow cornbread.

Breakfast rivaled the outstanding traditional Turkish breakfast we had at the Kitap Evi Hotel in Bursa. Many small plates of delicacies began to appear at our table; three types of cheese, warmed black and green olives, sliced cucumbers and tomatoes drizzled with peppery olive oil, jam, honey, and butter, a cured salami-style meat, dried figs, and apricot halves, hard-boiled eggs and two egg omelets filled with diced red and green peppers. Accompanied by clotted cream, sweet milk, and our choice of fresh fruit juices, the plentiful spread was fabulous and everything tasted fresh and delicious.

"Would you like Turkish tea?" the bartender asked. Stunned at the offering of an additional beverage, we both opted for another cup of coffee.

After we ate our fill and couldn't eat another bite, we thanked the bartender for breakfast, his warmth and hospitality, and the exchange of interesting conversations. Meeting him was a pleasure, but it wasn't until we were far from Buku Bay that I realized we had never introduced ourselves or asked him for his name. We just began talking. We had an instant connection.

Hours later, we arrived at Marina Skopea where our sailing adventure began eight days ago. While I packed our bags and prepared to leave *Juliette,* I reminisced about our time in Turkey.

From Istanbul to Ephesus to the Turkish Riviera on the Dalaman Coast, it had been extraordinary! We unlocked places typical tourists would not go. Sailing here exceeded our expectations in every sense. Tranquil bays with turquoise water, sheltered anchorages, magnificent scenery, ancient historical sites unlike we ve explored in other parts of the world, and the genuine, congenial, people we met made our time here unforgettable, and out-of-this-world, unique.

At the concierge's desk, Vince managed a smooth boat handover, signed the final documents, and then…all too quickly…we boarded the next ferry from Marina Skopea to Göcek where a shuttle service waited to whisk us to the Dalaman airport.

Afterword

On the flight from Dalaman to the Atatürk International Airport, on a sunny day with infinite visibility, I sat in a window seat next to Vince, holding my hand. As we flew over the area where we sailed only yesterday, we didn't speak a word. With my nose pressed up against the window, I watched bareboaters below, pulling their dinghies behind, and I was envious that they were still sailing while we were going home.

Exploring Turkey by land and by sea was unlike any other foreign destination we've visited. Everyone we met was genuinely friendly, hospitable and impressed us with their kindness.

I will always remember the woman in the Bursa who didn't speak English but offered to walk me to the Kitap Evi Hotel when we couldn't find our way there and the owners of the hotel who gave us a beautifully embroidered hand towel as a token of their appreciation for our business. I will remember the young man who came out on his scooter to escort us to the Urkmetz Hotel when we were lost, Oktay who invited Vince to have lunch with him and his father, and Hakan who helped us tie up bow-and-stern at Cold Water Bay. Literally, every Turkish local was the epitome of warm-heartedness.

And then there was the food! The local cuisine was unbelievably delicious and we became fans after our very first meal at the Ottoman Hotel Imperial in Istanbul. We will remember the elaborate breakfasts, the chicken wing soup garnished with crispy fried chicken skin that we ate at the gas station en route to Bursa, and the finesse with which Turkish black tea is poured. In the future, the puffy pillow of golden lavash bread is something I will search for on every Mediterranean restaurant menu.

From the mosques to the historical and archaeological sites on land, and from the beautiful sandy beaches to the immensely turquoise blue waters of the unspoiled Turkish Riviera, our adventure was more than we expected and better than we dreamed.

Chasing Dreams Log

Year	Destination
1987:	The British Virgin Islands
1988:	The British Virgin Islands
1992:	The British Virgin Islands
1993:	The British Virgin Islands
1995:	The British Virgin Islands
1997:	French Antilles; Guadalupe
2000:	French Polynesia; Society Islands
2001:	Tonga
2002:	Belize
2005:	Italy; Amalfi Coast
2006:	Spain; The Balearic Islands
2007:	French Polynesia; Society Islands
2007:	Italy; Amalfi Coast
2008:	Croatia
2009:	Italy; Aeolian Islands
2010:	Turkey; the Turkish Riviera
2012:	Italy; Amalfi Coast
2013:	Italy; Amalfi Coast
2015:	The British Virgin Islands
2017:	The British Virgin Islands